Uniquely You

A Faith-Driven Journey to Your True Identity and Water-Walking, Giant-Slaying, History-Making Destiny.

Jenny Williamson
Founder/CEO Courage Worldwide™, Inc.

A ten-week assessment based on the book
Do You Have the Courage to Be You?
By Jenny Williamson

PTLB
PRINCIPLES
TO LIVE BY
LIFE IS RELATIONSHIPS

Uniquely You
A Faith-Driven Journey to Your True Identity and Water-Walking, Giant-Slaying, History-Making Destiny.

Copyright ©2016 by Jenny Williamson

For more information on this book and the author,
visit www.jennytwilliamson.com.

ISBN: 978-0-9968855-3-9
RELIGION/Christian Life/Personal Growth

Published by Principles To Live By Publishing, Roseville, CA 95661
www.ptlb.com. All rights reserved.

Cover Design by John Chase, Rocklin, California
Copyedited by Jennifer Edwards, jedwardsediting.net
Book Design by Linné Garrett, 829 Design (829design.com)

Bible References marked NIV are from the *Holy Bible New International Version*, copyright 2011 by Biblica. Used by permission of Zondervan. All rights reserved.

Bible References marked AMP are from the *Holy Bible Amplified Bible Version*, copyright 2015 by Zondervan and The Lockman Foundation.
Used by permission of Zondervan. All rights reserved.

Bible References marked MSG are from the *Holy Bible, The Message: The Bible in Contemporary Language*, copyright 2002 by Eugene H. Peterson.
Used by permission of NavPress. All rights reserved.

No part of this publication may be reproduced, stored in a retrieval system, or transmitted in any form or by any means—electronic, mechanical, photocopy, recording, or any other—without the prior permission of the author.
When reproducing text from this book, include the following credit line:
"*Uniquely You*, by Jenny Williamson, published by
Principles To Live By Publishing. Used by permission."

Printed in the United States of America

Testimonials & Endorsements

"People who work with human trafficking victims, I call courageous – Jenny Williamson is one of those people. This book details her journey of purpose to helping young girls who have been rescued from sex trafficking. But it is more. This book is about you and me finding the courage to be and do all God created us to. Read it! You'll be encouraged and challenged." — **Jeremy Affeldt, Pitcher & World Series Champion, San Francisco Giants**

Jenny Williamson is a one-woman wrecking crew! She lives the message of this book and proves what you can do if you have the courage to be YOU!" — **Reggie McNeal, Best-selling author,** *Get Off Your Donkey! Help Somebody and Help Yourself*

"Life, as we all know, it can be hard and with that comes bitterness and pain. Often without even knowing it we can become jaded, disguising cynicism as maturity and some how down the line we forget how to dream. My hope is that this book will do the same for you as it has done for me. Stirring you on to shake of any doubt that you were made for incredible things. We get one shot to tell a great story and thanks to Jenny and this book I am re-inspired and re-ignited to write an incredible one with my life" — **Gospel Artist, Philip LaRue**

"The book, *Do You Have the Courage to Be You*, is the biographical statement of a water walker and giant slayer. Read this book and Jenny's story will become your story. Jenny knows that Identity precedes Destiny. This book will help you discover, define, and develop the future that you were made for from all eternity. God is on the move; participating with this book will help you join Him in your journey!" — **Dr. John Jackson is the President of William Jessup University and the author of six books on leadership, spiritual transformation, and communication.**

"Jenny Williamson is a trailblazer and exceptional leader. She has led ministries, companies, and non-profit organizations to new heights through her belief in each person's potential. God has uniquely equipped her to help unlock all of your potential. Spend the time and learn this way of discovering a new layer of your purpose and significance. She has packed into this workbook the tools you will need to uncover what God has designed you to do. Her unique perspective and exercises are extremely helpful. This material will thoroughly enrich you. I wholeheartedly endorse Jenny and her material. Enjoy; you will be significantly richer for having gone through it." — **Dr. Gil Stieglitz, Discipleship Pastor, Bayside Church, Founder & President of Principles To Live By (ptlb.com), and the author of twenty-five books.**

"*The Uniquely You* study is awesome. It helped me uncover my unique qualities and motivated me to move forward in life with courage, not settling for less than all that God has for me!" — **Celeste Reinhart, Uniquely You Conference Attendee**

"Jenny is a highly-effective communicator with a passion to help people find their purpose. Not only does she provide practical insights in an engaging way but she

embodies her message through the example of her own life. Her dedication to providing homes for girls who have been trafficked is unstoppable, and she motivates others to take action in ways that are changing our world. That is why we chose her and her organization, Courage Worldwide, to be featured in the documentary *In Plain Sight*."
— **David Trotter, Documentary Filmmaker, Author, Speaker, Executive Producer of "IN PLAIN SIGHT: Stories of Hope and Freedom"**

"Every human being has both a story and a journey. When God connects with us He wants us to understand how we are known in heaven. Identity is the catalyst for transformation because we can engage with a higher level of truth than the facts of our history. I really love Jenny's book *[Do You Have the Courage to Be You?]*. It is alive with kind intention, grace, powerful truth and life changing opportunities for us to step into a new story and take the road to a different destination." — **Graham Cooke, Speaker, Author, and Mentor**

"Many of us look at the atrocities of our world and say, 'How horrible,' but occasionally some brave soul says, 'How can I help bring an end to this?' Think of William Wilberforce, Martin Luther King, Jr., and Mother Teresa. Jenny Williamson is such a brave soul, and Courage Worldwide is a long-overdue answer to the problem of human trafficking. I am honored to be a friend and supporter of this tremendous ministry." — **Dr. Rick Stedman, Former Senior Pastor, Adventure Christian Church**

"As a fellow abolitionist, it is my privilege to join hands with Jenny and Courage Worldwide. Many people do not realize that sex trafficking is happening in the United States. I'm honored to help shine a spotlight on the problem and give people a chance to be a part of the solution."
— **Natalie Grant, singer/songwriter—a Grammy nominated, five time GMA, Dove Award winner for Female Vocalist of the Year and human trafficking abolitionist**

Jenny and her tireless team see the human being that has been brutally exploited, and set about to nourish her young soul back into health and possibility. They give a girl a chance to make the courageous choice to run away from her trafficker, because there will be a loving circle of arms to fall into." — **Mira Sorvino, Academy Award Winning Actress & United Nations Goodwill Ambassador to Combat Human Trafficking**

"In nearly thirty years of ministry, I have found that most people do not know their purpose or God-given destiny. I loved being able to be one of the first people to lead a group of nearly 100 women through the *Uniquely You* assessment by Jenny Williamson, following her powerful Courage Conference. Jenny's journey of courage and purpose is inspiring, to say the least, and she is able to make it very personal and engaging for the reader as they begin their own journey. It was beautiful to witness the personal growth and the "Aha!" moments each of the women had as they took their own journey of purpose… and even more beautiful is to see the lives that have been changed as a result of this study..women that now know their purpose and who are making a difference in this world."— **Stephanie Midthun, Community Relations and Resource Director, Courage Worldwide**

Dedication

To my first righteous girlfriends:
My small group from Fully Alive Community Church in the San Francisco Bay Area met together weekly for seven years (2000–2006). It was with you that I learned to have the courage to be me. This assessment was the journey I shared with you. Thank you for believing in me when I didn't believe in myself. To my friend Celeste Reinhart, who believes in this assessment as much as I do and who has encouraged me to finish it—for years! Thank you, Celeste, for persistent encouragement. I know you would have written it for me if you could have.

To Staff Sargent Heather Harris:
(who served our country during four tours of duty with the United States Army) You taught me that military strategy often mirrors spiritual strategy. You taught me the value of a tactical pause. Thank you for your sacrifice to our country, and for your friendship to my family and me.

To the women of Living Water and St. Peter's Church of Elk Grove, CA:
In 2009, many of you attended our Courage Conference and afterwards met weekly for eight weeks to go through this assessment. I sat up until the wee hours of the morning writing the words of the assessment giving it to you week by week in a three ring binder. It was full of typos, run on sentences, and my passion for you to be and do all you were created for.

To the women of Adventure Christian Church in Rocklin, CA:
You, too, received this assessment in a three ring binder after our Courage Conference. We met weekly for eight weeks, laughing and crying our way through this assessment, sharing our lives and weekly courageous acts of faith. After both of these conferences we had more women attend the small groups than the conference itself. To the first two hundred and fifty righteous girlfriends who completed this assessment in 2009, I pray each one of you is courageously changing the world, one individual at a time.

To my sons that I birthed:
It has always been my prayer that you would pursue your dreams and destiny much earlier in life than I ever did. I thank God I have lived to see that prayer answered! You are all so much more courageous than I ever was at your age. I pray the ceiling of my life will be your floor. I pray my life influenced you just a tiny bit to pursue your own crazy, big dreams that impact your world, one individual at a time. I pray you live lives worthy of your calling. You are mighty warriors and I love you madly.

To the sons & daughters I did not birth:
God used my dreams and destiny to lead me to you. I encourage you to trust Him for your true identity and water-walking, giant-slaying, and history-making destiny.

To my handsome husband:
I cannot be me without you. Thank you for believing in me, for pushing me to never settle for mediocrity, and for loving me so well. Madly.

Contents

Introduction 9
Assessment Format 11

Part One: Your Identity

Week 1: Identity Precedes Destiny 20
Week 2: Clues to Your True Identity 55
Week 3: Beloved. Belong. Believe 90
Week 4: What You Believe May Not Be True 119
Week 5: Body. Soul. Spirit. (Part 1) 150
Week 6: Body. Soul. Spirit. (Part 2) 205
Week 7: Welcome to Boot Camp! 241

Part Two: Your Destiny

Week 8: Just Be You 268
Week 9: Your Mission Is Impossible 288
Week 10: Clues! Passion, Fears, Anger & Broken Hearts 317
Go! Change the World! 354
Bibliography 357
About Jenny 358
Other Books by Jenny Williamson 360
Principles To Live By 362
Principles To Live By Resources 363

Introduction

"Every man and woman is born into the world to do something unique and something distinctive and if he or she does not do it, it will never be done."
— Dr. Benjamin Mays

Read this quote and let it sink deep into who you are—deep into the place where logic cannot interrupt what the essence of you already knows. From there, contemplate your own uniqueness. Let yourself become pregnant with the possibility there really is something *distinctive* that you and only you were created to do at this time, in this place.

Ponder this fact—if you don't dream it, create it, write it, tell it, sing it, or build it, "it" won't ever be done. Turn down the volume on the negative voices attempting to tell you another story. Dare to believe that you have a water-walking, giant-slaying, history- making destiny that will change you and change the world. I challenge you to intentionally choose *now* as the right time to begin your journey of purpose.

In my work, whether coaching individuals one-on-one, or speaking to live audiences, I have found that most human beings love to talk about the concept of uniqueness and purpose—in theory. Most people truly *want* to believe they were created on purpose for a purpose. That belief increases when they see evidence of other individuals living purposeful, meaningful lives. However, there seems to be a huge chasm, between the desire for purpose and the actual effort needed to discover it. Finding the answers to the age-old questions, "Who am I?" and "What am I supposed to be doing?" seems daunting, ambiguous, and unattainable. Already overwhelmed by the numerous demands placed upon our time and our lives—paying the bills, going to work, raising our kids, attending school, obeying the rules, and meeting everyone else's expectations—we quit the journey before we ever begin. Each of us offers an array of excuses that we believe are unique to us for why we have no time to contemplate our purpose. But I believe the real truth is that most of us just don't believe we have a purpose. We're scared that we just might discover that there really isn't more to this life, or even more frightening, more to us.

So we return to our routines, responsibilities, and lives filled with trivial things and mediocrity. It isn't so much a conscious choice as it is our defaulted reaction to the ambiguous discovery process. There just isn't much in the way of intentional resources pointing us in the direction of our destiny. NIKE, Inc., the international sportswear company, lends a bit of help by encouraging us to *"Just Do It!"* They make it sound so simple. But I, for one, needed much more in the way of direction when I began my own journey of purpose. I couldn't find much in the way of tangible resources to guide me, or any courses of this type taught in our high schools or colleges. The topic isn't one that is often given priority from the church's pulpit or in children's classrooms. I could find no one going into prisons, juvenile halls, or rehab centers declaring this message of purpose to the hopeless individuals confined there. Though many wonderful organizations exist to feed the poor around the world, I could not find many who devote their time and resources to proclaiming the life-changing message, *"You were created on purpose for a purpose."*

Sadly, in my own life I didn't know very many people who were living courageous, bold, purpose-filled lives. Still, I was determined to discover my own identity and destiny. I am thrilled to say that over time I have done just that, *but* I wasted a lot of time in the process because I just wasn't asking the right questions or consulting the correct sources.

I don't want you to go through the same frustration I did. That's why I created the *Uniqueness Assessment* to serve as a tool to accelerate the process I blindly went through when I embarked on my own journey of purpose in the year 2000. This assessment is designed to give a comprehensive and cohesive framework to the process of discovering who you were created to be and what you are supposed to be doing.

However, this assessment, this workbook, is just a tool. It was not designed or intended to replace the still, small voice inside of you directing and guiding you on the unique path created for you and you alone. Without the voice of God, without consulting your Creator, this assessment will be just another self-help book, eventually ending up on a shelf gathering dust with a host of others that have come before it. This assessment has no power or revelation in and of itself. The only true power comes from God's Spirit guiding you on this journey. However, I believe together they can launch you into the incredible adventure of discovering your true identity and your water-walking, giant-slaying, history-making destiny. It matters not where you are spiritually, how little or big your faith, or your belief is in God at this moment; I encourage you to just start by making an intentional decision to work through this assessment with an open mind. Like Nike said, *just do it!*

A personal message from Jenny: I will leave you little "bread crumbs" along the way to encourage you throughout your journey. Just scan the QR codes you find throughout this workbook with your cell phone or electronic device wherever you find them. If you don't have a QR Code scanner, you can download a free app on iTunes or Google Play. You can also visit our *Uniquely You* page on our website www.jennytwilliamson.com.

c2bu.com/vid1

Assessment Format

If you have read this far, you must have made a decision to move forward. Are you anxious to get started? I am so excited for you! Before we begin, I want to dedicate a few pages to the assessment format and processes so I can answer some common questions and set realistic expectations.

Can I do the assessment alone? Yes, this assessment can be done alone, but I have found it is best to go through the journey in a small group, with other people embarking on the same journey of purpose. I call these groups your **Righteous Girlfriend Groups (RGG)** for us girls, and for the guys, **Mighty Warrior Groups (MWG)**. If you do choose to do this assessment alone, call someone and share with them your intent to begin a journey of purpose and why you have decided to start now. If you don't feel comfortable sharing your story face-to-face, feel free to email me at jenny@c2bu.org. I would love to hear how you decided to begin this journey of purpose. Also, I will leave you little "bread crumbs" along the way to encourage you throughout your journey. Just scan the QR codes with your cell phone or electronic device wherever you find them and I'll be right there by your side. If you don't have a QR Code scanner, you can download a free app on iTunes or Google Play. You can also visit our *Uniquely You* page on our website www.jennytwilliamson.com.

What are Righteous Girlfriend Groups (RGG) and Mighty Warrior Groups (MWG)? I want to explain what a **RGG/MWG** is and what it is not.

- It is not a Bible study, but we do base our truth on the Bible.
- It is not a place to share only the circumstances of our lives, but to share both our lives and ourselves.
- It is not a prayer group, but we do pray.
- It is not a support group, but we do support each other.
- It is not a group based on everyone's belief *in* God, but we do believe God, for each other and ourselves in spite of our current circumstances.
- It is not a place to get or give advice, but instead encouragement is freely given and found in abundance.

What is a righteous girlfriend or mighty warrior's role in your life? Simple. To believe in you and for you when you can't believe in and for yourself. It is much easier for me to believe for you than my own circumstances, because my emotions aren't attached to your situation—but they are mine. Don't get tripped up by the word *righteous* ladies; it simply means, "right standing with God," which, per the Bible, is only achieved by **belief**—not behavior. On some days and in some ways we are going to need another person to believe in and with us when we just can't do it by ourselves. Make sense? The Bible says,

> "Confess to each other, pray for each other so you will be healed.
> "The prayer of the righteous *[girlfriend/warrior]* is powerful and effective."
> JAMES 5:16 (NIV) (Italics are mine)

Righteous Girlfriends and Mighty Warriors meet weekly come rain, shine, or holidays. If you are too busy to come to your group, then friend, you are too busy! You need to commit to meeting weekly with your RGG/MWG for ten weeks to work through the *Uniqueness Assessment* together. At the end of the ten weeks, if you would like to continue meeting, or if you would like to set up your own RGG or MWG, please contact us at info@c2bu.org and we will be happy to assist you in setting up a formal group and provide you resources so you can continue meeting together. I pray your Righteous Girlfriends and/or Mighty Warriors will come to be the lifeline mine have been to me.

Can men and women be in a group together? Mighty Warriors and Righteous Girlfriends CAN be in a group together, but I personally see great benefit in all male or female groups to promote a more intimate revealing of oneself. However, I have seen blended groups work. I have also had families tell me that they have formed a group with just members of their immediate family and what an impact it had upon them. What a great way for kids to learn their parent's story and to be a part of each other's journey of purpose.

How many people in a group? I suggest no more than eight people in a group. At one conference I led, we had over a hundred people come together weekly for the 30-minute overview and then break into small groups of eight. We spread out all over the building. There was another group of a hundred people wanting to do the assessment but didn't come together as a group to meet weekly. They met together separately in people's homes and coffee shops weekly until they finished the assessment. You can do what is best for you and your schedule. The important thing is committing to a specific time and place to meet together as a group once a week for two hours for the entire length of this assessment.

What do we do for two hours? The first thirty to forty minutes of each group session will begin with an overview of the following week's theme. A facilitator will lead this session. At the first meeting, choose a facilitator from the group. The facilitator is responsible for covering the **overview**, for being the first person to share their experience with the daily "homework," and then making sure every person in the group feels safe and comfortable enough to share their stories and insights.

What is the content like? The overview reads like a chapter from a book and sets up the **Daily Discovery Process (DDP)** for the upcoming week. There are ten overviews for the ten weeks of group sessions. In each overview, there are five days of DDP, allowing for a break two days a week. At the end of each week's DDP, there will be a **Pre-Group Form** you will be asked to complete and bring to the next group session to encourage group discussion.

There is also an interactive component in this workbook. Throughout the study, I'll be able to give you little reminders of things to think about and do, as well as some encouraging words for your journey of purpose. Whenever you see a scanning image, a QR Code, go ahead and scan it with your cell phone or electronic device and you can connect with a video of me recorded with you in mind. If you don't have a QR Code scanner, you can download a free app on iTunes or Google Play. You can also visit our *Uniquely You* page on our website www.jennytwilliamson.com/uniquely-you.

I also want to encourage you to join a dedicated Facebook Page www.facebook.com/JennyTWilliamsonAuthor for your journey. Just hit "Like" on the page and you'll be a part of a special group of fellow sojourners. This will be a place for you to connect with others as they travel on their journey of purpose, as well as an opportunity for you to encourage others by posting your experiences and "ah ha!" moments. You can also Tweet your experiences using these hashtags: #journeyofpurpose, #doyouhavethecouragetobeyou, #Iamuniquelymade, and #Iwascreatedforapurpose.

I'll follow along with you and promise to do my best to reply. I'm thrilled to be able to be a part of your journey and can't wait to see how it turns out for you! Isn't technology great?

What is the time commitment? Plan to invest one hour a day, five days a week, along with the two-hour group session weekly. Can you commit to this time to begin your journey of purpose? If you answered *no*, I would strongly advise postponing this assessment until you can. Instead, order a copy of my book *Do You Have the Courage to Be You* from Amazon and read at your leisure. The book may encourage you to carve out the time for this assessment.

Before you become overwhelmed by the amount of time required for the assessment and quit before you begin, I challenge you to keep a time journal for one week to truly determine if you are too busy. This exercise may reveal activities you could identify as time robbers. Record how much time you spend each week watching T.V., surfing the Internet, posting on social media, and/or answering emails. Those are my most common time robbers. If you discover your own pesky time robbers, you can then decide to use those hours intentionally and productively for your assessment. Most people are quite surprised when they see how much time actually gets wasted each day for lack of an intentional plan.

Before you decide to postpone a life-changing journey of purpose, make a conscious effort to discover places where you can find the time needed for this assessment. I believe you will not regret this investment. It is an investment in you.

Describe the written exercises. As I created this assessment, I tried to accommodate and incorporate all learning styles and personalities. However, this assessment wasn't designed to be fast and easy. The process is meant to stretch, enlarge, and expand your capacity to think, remember, dream, and believe. There are written exercises for five days each week during the ten-week assessment.

If you are a verbal processor, the written part of this assessment may seem tedious to you. Even if it is a struggle, I ask that you attempt to write something in each blank space provided. The written word is very powerful. Studies have proven over and over again that people who write down their ideas, goals, and dreams have a much higher success rate in realizing them. Dreams become goals when they are written down.

In the pages of biblical history, we find that each and every Israelite king had to write down for himself the Word of God—even though he had priests and prophets who read it out loud to him. If it was good enough for kings, then it is good enough for us. So write it down. Give yourself plenty of time and quiet to go through each day's assignment. If you do, I promise you will accelerate this process and receive so much more out of the group discussion time.

How much reading is there? For those of you who dislike reading, I'm sorry to say there are reading assignments each day, but they are much shorter than the writing exercises—except for the once a week overview. Keep in mind that you will be meeting weekly with your group to review your daily assignments and share your experiences. Skipping any reading or writing assignment may hinder your progress in discovering important pieces to your identity or destiny and take away from the group experience.

What do you mean by verbal exercises? If you are the type of person who benefits from writing your thoughts down and from processing information internally, you will actually enjoy going through this assessment page by page. However, the small group setting each week may be a bit uncomfortable for you. I ask you to take courage and, despite your comfort level, make an effort to share your notes and your heart each week at your **RGG** or **MWG**, even if you have to read them. This is a very important part of the process—coming together with others to share our journey. HEBREWS 10:25 (NIV) says, *"Let us not give up meeting together ... but encourage each other."* I promise you will receive so much more encouragement in your journey through this verbal participation and openness. The spoken word is also very powerful. It has been my experience that speaking a thought, an idea, or a dream out loud suddenly makes it tangible to yourself and others. It becomes your truth.

You must consult your Creator. The premise of this entire assessment and all the exercises is that God designed you. He created you for a destiny too big to imagine or carry out by yourself. That means He alone has all the answers to your questions about you and your purpose. The journey starts with Him—not an abstract, theoretical, cliché version of Him—but one that includes Him as an interactive participant in the process. *It has nothing to do with religion, but with relationship.*

Think of it this way. A newly purchased computer has an internal software program. It has two operating modes, default and design. The default mode creates actions that automatically happen in certain situations without the operator issuing a specific command. It is easy because it has been programmed. The design mode is much more complicated. To invoke all the complex applications of the software for the computer to do all it was created to do, the extensive operating manual or the actual creator of the program must be consulted.

Do you consult the manual when you buy a new computer to optimize performance? Not me. I like quick, easy, and automatic. Unfortunately, for many years, I lived my life that way and my default behaviors kept me from all I was designed to be. Yours may be, too.

We are not much different from a computer. We, too, have default and design modes. We are extremely complex with great potential, but at the same time have the ability to operate on autopilot, doing less than we were designed for. We have the ability to proceed throughout our day acting and reacting to stimuli and situations without much thought. We do this because our default mode is much simpler than our design mode. Our culture, family, and life experiences have programmed us. We have become comfortable with our familiar, predictable, and automatic behaviors even if we do not necessarily like them. We have convinced ourselves we are too busy to take the time required to evaluate our lives, beliefs, and defaulted behaviors in light of our created potential. If we are ever going to be and do all we were created for, we must consult our Creator, the one who designed us.

If this concept seems new or strange to you, I ask that you keep an open heart and mind during the process. I suggest talking to your Creator, as you would do with anyone you are in relationship with. You do not have to use fancy, formal words. You can be blunt and painfully honest about your doubts, and even be skeptical about the process, if that is how you feel. You do not even have to believe in God for Him to believe in you. What do you have to lose by entertaining the thought that there is a loving God, who created this universe, as well as you, for a grand purpose? I find it much more attractive, stimulating, and exciting to believe I am planned by God, rather than a cosmic accident of no consequence designed to turn to dust when I die.

However, I do admit that hearing His voice and even my own heart is often difficult in our noisy world. It seems easier for me to hear when I am outside in wide-open spaces far from noise, buildings, and people. You may prefer sitting still in a comfortable chair. Listening to music may help you contemplate your existence. There is no right or wrong way to communicate with God. Just talk. Then listen for His still, small voice and your own. Think of this process as the unwrapping of a gift each day and do it with the expectancy of receiving a great revelation about you.

Life coaching. In writing this assessment and planning the small group dynamics, I used a life-coaching model. When I coach one-on-one, I explain to my new client that the coaching relationship is a professional one, but one that also relates on a very personal basis. There are inherent expectations when entering such a relationship. I would like to spell out to the best of my ability what coaching is and what coaching isn't so that there are no unrealistic expectations of this assessment and the process.

1. Coaching (and thus this assessment) is not therapy, counseling, advice-giving, mental health care, or treatment for substance abuse. A life coach does not function as a licensed, mental health professional, nor did such a person write this assessment. Coaching is not intended as a replacement for counseling, psychiatric interventions, treatment for mental illness, recovery programs, or professional medical advice. A coach may actually recommend those services to a client. Beginning a journey of purpose can be done in tandem with the healing and recovery process. You do not have to wait for complete healing in all areas of your life before you begin an intentional journey of discovering who you are and what you are meant to be doing. All of us have those places in our lives that need healing. Healing is very often a process that does not have to be the sole focus of our lives.

Think of a cut or wound you have had on your body. Daily, the bandage should be removed and the wound cleaned and medicine applied. After that process is complete, you go about living your life. The wound does not consume you or dictate whether or not you live your life. Neither should a wound of the soul or spirit stop you from living your life. You can begin discovering who you are and what you are meant to be doing, while caring for the invisible wounds you desire healing for at the same time. In fact, beginning the journey of purpose very often serves as a motivation to face the things in life that do need healing.

The process in the following pages is for people who want to be all and do all they were created to be and do. In order to do that, intentional and significant changes in your life may be required. Your choices and decisions facilitate any change in your life. They are your responsibility and will not happen without you choosing to make them happen.

2. Coaching (and thus this assessment) is not a replacement for spiritual disciplines and guidance but is a supplement to them. I personally do not believe you can discover who you are and what you were created to do without a personal relationship with Jesus Christ. Being in a relationship with Jesus requires that you admit the need for a Savior and spend time alone talking to him and reading the Bible. Just as there are physical disciplines if we desire a healthy body, there are also spiritual disciplines that make us strong spiritually. Being alone, having a conversation with our Creator, and reading the truth from His Word are all ways to build our spiritual muscles. This assessment builds upon those disciplines and may even introduce you to your Creator. You will be asked to take specific questions to God, seeking Him as your Creator, finding your answers from Him as to your true identity and destiny. This could be your first act of faith on your journey to your water-walking, giant-slaying, history-making destiny.

3. Coaching (and thus this assessment) is designed to equip, encourage, and empower you to be and do all you were created for. It is designed to motivate you to action. Your small group can help. Oftentimes, other people can see things in you that you cannot see in yourself. It is you, however, who decides what is true and of value to you. You decide what you will and won't do; what you will keep and what you will throw out. A coach and your small group will hold you accountable for the changes you say you want to make in your life. Ultimately, you are responsible for your own process of discovery and change, but I have found having an accountability partner, or a group to serve as one, keeps me on track and moving forward.

4. For the coaching and group relationship to be effective, all parties have to be honest and open in their communication. If anyone in the group ever says anything that upsets you or that you totally disagree with, please bring it to the group's attention immediately. There may be instances where you, your behavior, or your habits will be challenged, but it is because of the desire you have expressed to live life differently than you have before. If you choose not to make the changes you agreed to, and instead, continue doing what you have always done, you *will* get the results you have always gotten.

5 Coaching relationships and the small group model are confidential relationships, thus all group members agree to keep all information discussed confidential, unless dictated by the law.

I am looking forward to our journey together through this assessment. For the duration, you can call me *Coach* if you like. I will be your biggest cheerleader on this journey. I believe that God has arranged for our paths to cross for such a time as this.

Things you will need. You will need this assessment, a Bible, access to a computer, a QR Code scanner (you can download a free app from iTunes if you have an iPhone, or GooglePlay if you have a Droid), a journal or legal pad, and a stack of 3x5 lined index cards. If you do not have your own Bible and cannot buy one, you can use www.biblegateway.com for multiple translations. My favorites are the New International Version (NIV), the Message (MSG), and The Amplified Bible (AMP), all of which are used throughout this assessment. If you do not have a computer or a Bible, you can get access to both at a local library. Many churches also have a stash of Bibles they would love to give you. Don't be afraid to ask.

Recording the process. Journaling is an important accompaniment to this assessment, because it allows you to record and see tangible evidence of your own unique journey and personal progress. Journaling is nothing more than writing down your thoughts, your feelings, your experiences, and even your prayers in that given moment. It serves as a reminder of where you have been and where you are going. Now, with that said, I have to tell you I am bad at journaling. I talk and think so much faster than I can write or type. It is hard for me to record my thoughts and feelings. However, I did it, and I continue to do it because of what it produces in my life. It is my journey. It is my life. It is proof of a process that led me to my Creator, my

purpose, and myself. My journals are some of my most valued possessions and ones I hope to share with my children and grandchildren one day to encourage them on their own journey.

Journal experiences you don't want to forget—memorable stories from your life, promises from God, and revelations you have received along the way that point toward your identity and destiny. My journals are real and raw observations, feelings, and experiences that are unfiltered and mine alone. It is evidence to me that God still uses ordinary people to do extraordinary things.

Finding the true *you* and what you were created to do is an amazing adventure. I encourage you to enjoy it and record it.

Let's get started. There are battles to be fought, giants to be slain, and treasures to uncover. This journey is one where logic is challenged, where the ordinary becomes extraordinary, and the impossible becomes possible. It is worth the effort required, because through you and your purpose, lives *will be* changed, history *will be* made, and prayers *will be* answered. It is what you were created for.

Is your heart racing? Mine is! Let's begin by inviting God into the process.

Dear God,

I'm really not sure about this process. I'm not even sure that You hold all my answers or even if there are any answers. But I am willing to keep an open mind. The Bible, which some say is Your divine conversation with man, indicates You created me, formed me, and knit me together in my mother's womb, and that I am fearfully and wonderfully made. I have to admit I don't feel that way on most days. In fact, I don't remember if I've ever felt fearfully and wonderfully made. Quite the opposite, actually! I'm not sure who I am, much less what in the world I am supposed to be doing.

I'm tired. I'm tired of trying to do everything everyone else wants me to, and be who everyone else wants me to be. I am ready to be just me—if I can figure out who that is. Will You show me who I am? I acknowledge that I have settled for less for so long that I don't even know how to dream for more. I need You to help me. I need You to reveal my destiny to me. Without Your help, I'm afraid I will never be and do all I long for.

Today, I choose to begin my own intentional journey of seeking You and I pray along the way I find myself. Who am I, God? Who did You create me to be? I'm listening—give me ears to hear and eyes to see.

Amen

Your Name _____ *Today's Date* _____

PART ONE

Your Identity

Identity Precedes Destiny

Before there was a moose or a mountaintop, an ocean or an otter, or a waterfall or walrus, before there were stars in the sky or lightning bugs in the dark, before there was a hippopotamus playing in the mud or a lion roaming the African plains, the Creator of the Universe imagined you. He planned you and deliberately designed you for a specific, incredible, unique purpose.

Yes, you!

Imagine your Creator as a painter standing before an enormous blank canvas. You are the canvas. With meticulous strokes, He carefully considers the unique plans He has designed for you as He chooses your eye color, your personality, your IQ, and everything else about you. The sound of your laughter, the size of your feet, your aptitudes and abilities, as well as your weakness and vulnerabilities, are all part of your design with your distinct purpose in mind. The date and location of your birth was strategically determined to optimize your arrival and success. During your creative process, dreams and desires were deposited deep inside of you that, when activated, will lead you to your purpose and destiny.

"Creation waits in eager expectation for the Sons of God to be revealed."
— ROMANS 8:19 (NIV)

All of creation is holding its breath in eager anticipation waiting for you to become you. The trees are having a conversation with the birds as the rocks are crying out to the mountains...

> *"Is today the day? We have been waiting for so long. Do you think today is the day she will embark on the journey of discovering her true identity? Is today the day he decides to do pursue his dream? Will they take courage? There is so much at stake."*

A hush falls over creation as you awake today. The whispered conversation continues as creation sends this question to the wind, *"Do you have the courage to be you?"*

These truths have transformed my life, and they still propel me out of bed every morning. They override my insecurities and fears. Although life altering and highly addictive, this journey of figuring out whom we are and why we are here is not an easy one. Quite honestly, it is incredibly difficult and very scary because it forces us to leave our well-crafted comfort zones for the unknown, the secure for the insecure, and the possible for the impossible. It requires courage to be and do all we were created to accomplish. For a long time I believed courage was a personality trait—one I was *not* born with! Thankfully, taking courage is something we can all do, an intentional decision all of us can make in spite of the fear we experience.

Choose courage.

I made my purpose discovery late in my life. Growing up in Jackson, Mississippi, I did not learn that we were meant for more. My family, who loved me, never encouraged me to embark on a path that would require courage. My teachers at school did not encourage risk. I did not hear it preached from the pulpit at the church I attended every Sunday of my life. I personally did not know anyone who was boldly pursuing a destiny that required a vast amount of courage. Everyone I knew was just trying to be good, pay their bills, keep their kids safe, go on a vacation once a year, and retire as early as possible.

Please hear my heart. There is only one thing wrong with that way of life—it is not what we were created for!

The messages I received for most of my life, whether covertly or overtly, were *do not take risks*, *stay safe*, and *be good*. Based on how often I heard go to college, get a job, get married, and have kids, I assumed that was my destiny. So at the ripe old age of forty, I was challenged with the question that would ultimately transform my life and the one I believe can transform yours:

"Do you have the courage to be you — the *YOU* I created?"

Week One  Uniquely You

For weeks and months, that provocative question seared my soul and tempted me to want more for my life. Daily, I heard those words whispered as I started my day. It created a restlessness inside of me that ruined me for the ordinary existence I had settled for. Though I was scared to death, an urgency and passion had been planted inside me to discover who I was and what I was supposed to be doing. I longed to know the *me* I was created to be. I wanted to discover if there really was something I was created to do that no one else could do. I longed to change the world.

I believe you long to do the same—to matter, to make a difference in this world.

However, I must warn you. Destinies of this kind…

    … are not safe.

    … will make you look crazy.

    … will require that you often say, "I don't know!"

    … will cause you to spend time alone.

    … will scare you to death.

It is a journey walked in wild abandon. Steps of faith are required, not self-reliance. You must take courage.

When we begin a journey of purpose, we generally want to know *what* we are supposed to be doing on this planet. It is the first question I asked. The problem with the question "What?" is that it never seems to produce any answers; at least it didn't for me. When I embarked on my own journey of purpose, it took me quite a while to realize I was asking the wrong question. The question I should have been asking starts with *who*, not *what*. This is the first question we will take to our Creator.

"Who am I?" or rather, "Who did you create me to be?"

*"Make a careful exploration of **who you are** and **the work you have been given**, and then **sink yourself into that**. Don't be impressed with yourself. Don't compare yourself with others. Each of you must take responsibility for doing the creative best you can with your own life."*
— GALATIANS 6:4–5 (MSG)

This verse provides the three steps to begin a journey of purpose. In the simplicity of the words, the life-changing message is very easy to miss ..

*You cannot uncover your destiny
until you discover your identity.*

You must figure out **who** you are before you will ever figure out **what** you are put on this planet to do.

- First, make a careful assessment of who you are,
- Then determine what you are supposed to be doing, and
- Finally, just do it!

One. Two. Three. Those are the steps we will take in this assessment. In Part One, we will spend time assessing who you are—***your identity***. Part Two will be dedicated to providing clues to what you are supposed to be doing—***your destiny***. Along the way, your small group will provide the encouragement you need to just do it—***action!***

Courage *will* be required. Do you have the courage to be you?

A personal message for you.
Scan this code — I'll see you soon!

c2bu.com/vid2

Do You Have the Courage to Be You?

Daily Discovery Process

In the year 2000, I looked back over the first forty years of my life to sadly discover there was no riveting synopsis. It seemed I had lived the first forty years in pure reaction to a whirlwind of circumstances, whipped around by whatever life or chance threw my way. There was nothing purposeful, intentional, or passionate about my life. Though I was extremely busy, I had not accumulated much in the way of meaningful accomplishments, passionate pursuits, or history-making exploits. This new awareness brought a desperate desire to have all three.

Though I had no road map or clue about how to start, with great intention and huge conviction I vowed to live the next forty years of my life vastly different from the first. Out of sheer desperation and with my birthday fast approaching, I made another intentional decision—I would seek God for my answers, not myself, or other people. After months of restlessness, He suddenly seemed to be the obvious source of enlightenment.

"What am I here for?" "Why am I on this planet?" "Do I have a purpose?" I now asked these questions to my Creator.

I heard no heavenly answers. I saw no burning bushes. The seas did not part. All I got was silence. Maybe I was wrong. My fortieth birthday came and went. I was frustrated and wondered if my search was in vain.

During this time of silence and frustration, I made another intentional decision. I began to read the stories in the Bible I had remembered from my childhood as part of my decision to seek God for my answers of purpose. I was desperate for answers and thought that maybe this was the way to break the silence and hear God's voice. I just assumed I knew all the stories and their endings. I doubted they would be relevant to my quest. But I was wrong. As I read the familiar stories, I was stunned but inspired by these woefully flawed, often dysfunctional, ordinary human beings that God had used to impact and change the world. As I read their stories, my doubts evaporated. God spoke to me through their stories. I realized He still wants to use ordinary, messed-up people like me to change the world. That is what I wanted to do—change the world. As I read those ancient stories, I wanted to walk on water. I wanted to slay giants with pebbles. I wanted to fly on the wings of eagles, change history, and the world I lived in. I wanted the scandalous grace and extravagant love I saw offered over and over again. The small flame of longing I had felt was now being stoked into an inferno.

Do you have the courage to be you?

The first time I heard the question whispered deep to my heart, my response was an emphatic "No!" Then I realized I had finally received an answer to my question, "What am I on this planet for?" It wasn't the answer I wanted, but nevertheless, it was an answer. I knew the question had come from God. My question had been answered..with a question. I waited for more whispered words, but none came. I was truly perplexed as to why it would take courage to be me. With the utterance of this question, my focus instantly changed from what I was created to do, to who I was created to be. There was a profound difference between the two. Evidently the me I was created to be was more important than what I was created to do. That was fascinating to me.

Having the courage to be me required a departure from the familiarity of my well-crafted mask and comfort zones into the unknown of the future God had planned for me. I discovered this journey is one that can only be taken by faith, not by sight, logic, or previous experience. That is why our journey requires courage. We are not in control of our destiny. The journey of purpose takes us down a path that is not created by our own will and personality. This path was created for us before time began but requires a leap of faith on our part. Congratulations! You are making that leap now, and it's your turn to answer a few questions.

Your Story
"Do you have the courage to be you—the you God created?"

Write down your immediate thoughts to this question. No filtering or editing please—just write. What does it mean to be you—the real you? Are you afraid of what that could mean? If so, explain.

_____
_____
_____
_____
_____
_____
_____
_____
_____
_____
_____
_____
_____
_____
_____
_____

Did you notice from my story that I had made two intentional decisions that changed the course of my life and propelled me into a quest to find my identity and destiny? Let me remind you. The first was to seek God for my answers instead of people, and the second was to begin reading my Bible. What intentional decisions are you willing to make as you begin this journey of purpose? The first could be to join a small group and/or complete this assessment. Give a few minutes to think through what you are committing to and list them below.

_____
_____
_____
_____
_____
_____

Uniquely You — Day One

In the space below, or even in a separate journal, write about how you arrived at this point in your life. List any specific people or events that helped bring you here. List anything you don't want to forget. What job do you have now? How old are you? Do you believe in God? Are you going through a transition or a change in your life? What are the desires of your heart right now? Are you afraid of leaving the known for the unknown? Why did you begin this journey of purpose here and now? What prompted it? Write it all down. It's time to tell your story so you will never forget this important crossroad in your life. Your story will inspire another. And Creation is so excited!

Discovering who you are and what you were created for is the grandest, most exciting adventure, but it is so much better when shared with another. If you are in a small group, you will be sharing your story with your group members. If you are doing the study alone, call a friend right now and share what you just wrote, or as I asked earlier, email me at jenny@c2bu.org. I would love to hear from you.

My prayer for you as you end this day is that you will have the courage to complete this assessment in full. This is your first day. That's a great start! Now vow to not quit until you discover your true identity and world-changing destiny. I'm right here with you every step of the way.

Understand the Source of Your Identity

Daily Discovery Process

As you embark on this very intentional journey of purpose, you must select to whom you will go for the source of your identity. Who will you allow to bestow your identity upon you? This entire assessment is built upon the precept that only God, your Creator, can tell you who you *really* are. My hope is that you will allow Him to do just that, even if this idea is new or unfamiliar to you. Through this discovery process, you will be trained to consult the one who made you for your true identity and the path to your destiny until it becomes a habit. You will never fulfill your true destiny and live out your ultimate purpose unless you believe that you are who God says you are.

Discovering your true identity makes it much easier to find and fulfill your destiny. If you don't know who you are, you won't believe you can accomplish your purpose, so you will never try. Your God-given purpose is so much bigger than you. In fact, it is utterly impossible for you to fathom what God has in mind for you, and it is not something you can do alone. If God revealed your purpose to you right now, you simply wouldn't believe it. You may be too shocked and shy away from it. He designed it that way. He intended that you would have to consult Him, your Creator, for the answers. You must come to a point in your life where you choose to believe that He specifically created your unique identity specifically so that you could succeed in fulfilling your destiny.

> *"If you don't know who you are, you'll just become someone else."*
> — Author unknown

How do we figure out who we were created to be? There are clues inside of us, but we must also look outside ourselves. We must consult our Creator. Most of us would have a very difficult time finding our identity within ourselves. I would go so far as to say that if you only consult yourself, you would not discover your true identity. Our identities are bestowed *upon* us. We innately look to someone to tell us who we are.

Doesn't that seem just a little unfair to be dependent upon someone else to tell us who we are? If God created this whole process, does He really want us to spend our entire lives running around asking everyone we meet, "Who am I?" No. That is exhausting and what I did for most of my life. For years I felt fragmented trying to keep up with all the identities others had bestowed upon me—both good and bad. The best place to start is with *the* source of creation—God himself.

My Story

I was called hyper, loud, talkative, bossy, and a know-it-all. I agreed to these identifiers because of the number of times I was told to be quiet, sit still, or let someone else go first. I also received the identity of "good girl" and "big sister." I embraced those titles too and tried very hard to be good and take care of others; I ended up being a people-pleaser. I could go on and on with my own examples. But know this. God never intended us to go to other people for our identities. Instead, He inspired a whole book describing whom we are and what we are to be doing with great love and passion He knows our potential for greatness and sets about putting us in circumstances and situations to draw us up to that place. He believes in us much more than we believe in ourselves. This quote describes what I'm talking about beautifully:

> *"Treat a man as he is, and he will remain as he is.*
> *Treat a man as he could be, and he will become what he should be."*
> —Ralph Waldo Emerson

That is what God does. He sees our potential, because He created our potential, and He believes in us more than we believe in ourselves.

I, too, see incredible potential in people. I always see more than what they see in themselves. I hate when the people I love settle for less than they were created for. Yes, I drive my spouse, children, family, and friends insane. I am often frustrated. I hate mediocrity. I am a "maximizer" wanting more for myself, for those I love, and for you. This is what drives me! If I feel this way, can you imagine what God feels when He looks upon us? How it must pain Him to see His creation that was made in His image settling for mediocrity, for so much less than He created us to be. Unlike me, however, He doesn't get frustrated and He doesn't give up on us; rather, He continues to speak to our potential, to the dreams and desires He planted deep within us, wooing us to be water walkers, giant slayers, and history makers. He longs to tell us who we are, to bestow our true identity upon us. Will you let Him?

Your Story

In this exercise, I want you to list any identifiers and identities that have been bestowed upon you by other people. Have you ever pondered where your identity came from? Think of any identities or labels you picked up from your childhood. Who did your parents, siblings, or friends say you were?

Do you agree or disagree with them? List your reasons.

As you got older, were there other identities or labels bestowed upon you? List them.

Now describe the identities you have for yourself, both the negative and positive. Try to answer the question—"Who am I?"

Was this exercise a little difficult for you? Were your responses along the lines of "I am a mother or father, sister, brother, wife or husband, stockbroker, teacher, doctor"? If you are like most people who contemplate this question for first time, you wrote down your titles or the roles you fill in life. Rarely do the majority of people actually write down "who" they are. Most people aren't even certain of the difference. If you had a difficult time articulating "who you are," if that one question seemed so daunting you just stared at the blank lines hoping answers would magically appear, don't worry—you are in the majority. Before our ten weeks are finished, you will be able to articulate your answer to the question, "Who am I?"

For our next exercise in discovering who you are, ask someone in your life—someone who knows you quite well—to answer this question about you. Select someone who will be honest and not flatter you. Words of flattery make us feel good for a moment, but they do not help us answer the question, "Who am I?" Explain to the person you select that you are on a journey of discovering your identity and fulfilling your purpose. Give them permission to be honest with you about you. Very often other people see things in us and about us that we do not see in ourselves. Again, ask them to describe who you are and not what you do. This is an important step. Do not proceed with the assignment until you either email or call someone to help you with this part of the assignment.

Who did you ask?

Describe your relationship.

Week One

Uniquely You

How did they describe you?

Do you agree or disagree with them? Why or why not?

Compare the words your friend or family member used with your own description of yourself. Did they describe you in a similar way? Were you nervous as you waited for their answers? Did it matter greatly to you what they said? Think through these questions and journal your thoughts and feelings. Reflect and journal about how you have perceived and received your identity. Have you counted on others your entire life to tell you who you are? Do you receive more positive or negative comments from other people? Are your descriptions of yourself more negative or positive?

My prayer for you today is that you are taking courage, doing the exercises, and consulting with others and your Creator to get a clear picture of your true identity. Rest assured that you are perfect for your destiny. You'll see!

Put Aside False Identities

Daily Discovery Process

This is a pivotal, monumental time in your life. You are beginning to assess who you are. I am so proud of you. I've asked you to answer the question, "Who am I?" You then asked a friend or family member to answer the question about you. Now let's consult God, your Creator, to see what He says about you. He is the only one who can tell you who you really are. Thank Heaven! The exercise we did before should have shown you how subjective this identity issue really is. After consulting my Creator about me, it was much easier to let God tell me who I am—who He created me to be. During the assessment, we are working from the belief and assumption that God created us, made us, shaped us, formed us, and His plans are unique for each of us. With that particular truth at the front of our minds, it makes sense to consult the One who knew us before time began and who knows us better than we know ourselves. He's the one to give us the answer to our very important questions, "Who am I?" and "Who did you create me to be?" instead of every human being we have ever been in a relationship with, most of who don't even know *their* true identity!

I want to introduce you to some ancient words that will begin to convince you of your uniqueness and significance. They are ones I literally stumbled across when I began my own journey of purpose. As I read them, they jumped off the page and seemed to penetrate my mind, my soul, and my spirit. They convinced me that before time began, I was created on purpose for a purpose. I am praying they have the same effect on you.

You'll want to grab your first 3x5 cards and write each of these verses on a card, inserting your name where there is a blank.

*"I know the plans I have for you, _____ says the LORD...
plans to give you, a hope and a future."*
— JEREMIAH 29:11 (NIV)

*"Before I shaped you in the womb _____, I knew all about you.
Before you saw the light of day, I had holy plans for you."*
— JEREMIAH 1:5 (MSG)

*"For you, _____ are God's workmanship [work of art] created in Jesus
to do good works which God prepared in advance for you, to do."*
— EPHESIANS 2:10 (NIV)

*"The things you have planned for me, no one can recount to you—were I to speak
and tell of them they would be too many to declare."*
— PSALM 40:5 (NIV)

*"You created me, in my inmost being, you knit me, _____ together in
my mother's womb. Your eyes saw my unformed body, all the days ordained for me,
were written in your book before they came to be."*
— PSALM 139:13–17 (NIV)

*"From one man he made every nation of men and he determined the times set for
_____ and the exact places where _____ should live."*
— ACTS 17:26 (NIV)

*"Before _____ was born the Lord called him/her, from birth,
he has made mention of his/her name. He said _____ you are
my servant, in you I will display my splendor."*
— ISAIAH 49:1–3 (NIV)

Week One — Uniquely You

"If you, _____ remain in me and my words remain in you, ask whatever you wish and it will be given to you, _____. This is to my Father's glory that you, _____ bear much fruit."
— John 15:7 (NIV)

"I tell you the truth, _____ if you who have faith in me, you will do what I have been doing. _____ will do even greater things than these."
— John 14:12 (NIV)

These words were written for you. Make them personal. Choose to believe they are for you. Now read them out loud with your name written in the blanks. If they are familiar to you, pretend this is the very first time you have heard these words. Let your Creator convince you of your value and grand purpose. Choose to let this be your new truth. Don't worry if you don't feel any different; that is normal. When these words become the truth you choose to believe, your feelings will catch up eventually.

Based on the words above, write down who your Creator says you are. Notice if it is similar or different from the description you gave yourself or from the person you asked.

_____
_____
_____
_____
_____
_____
_____
_____
_____
_____
_____
_____
_____

Everything in me longed to believe the identity God had bestowed upon me over my own ideas of who I was, and over the identities given to be my people who knew me. The problem for me was that I didn't have any identifiable talents that the world holds in high esteem. I didn't have a college degree. I had a job, but its only purpose was to help pay the light bill. I believed my dreams had been destroyed by the choices I had made long ago. But when I read the ancient words from the Bible, when I listened to the still, small voice inside of me, a spark ignited deep in my soul that soon consumed me with the belief that maybe, just maybe, there was something that I was designed to do that no one else could do. To hold on to that spark and new belief, I read these words with my name in the blanks over and over and over.

Your homework is to do the same. Keep these cards with you and read these transformative words out loud every day over the next ten weeks. Read them in the morning when you wake up and in the evening before you go to bed. They are your new truth, the truth that you were created exactly on purpose for a specific, unique purpose. These words will change the negative tape you have in your head or any lingering doubts you may have in your heart. Please don't skip this step. During this process you are literally crafting a new identity in which to live out of. My 3x5 cards, and the very words on them, became one of my most treasured possessions. They help solidify my identity and provide the courage I need when confronting obstacles to my destiny. They will do the same for you.

As you end this day of discovery, my prayer for you is for God to fan a flame of desire within you to be and do all you were created for, and for you to absolutely refuse to settle for anything less. I pray this day will be the day your life radically changes as you begin to entertain your significance, your purpose, and your water-walking, giant-slaying, history-making destiny. I celebrate you! You have taken courage!

You Were Created on Purpose for A Purpose

Daily Discovery Process

From the day you arrived in this world, I would bet there has been a never-ending supply of people telling you who you are—or rather, who they want you to be. Our society and the media also want a voice in bestowing our identity. They shout that we need to be rich, powerful, skinny, and gorgeous if we are to be happy. We must be wearing designer clothes and driving a sexy, expensive car to the hottest gathering place in town if we are ever to be noticed and called "significant." This false identity sells everything from iPhones to underwear. It is a lie we are all susceptible to believe.

These types of bogus media advertisements declare we are a society lacking identity. It is a plague on our world. No wonder so many people live lives of quiet desperation and lack of purpose. Who can measure up? Individually and collectively we have no sense of our unique identity or world-changing destiny. I am especially shocked with people who profess a belief in God, yet do not see themselves as valuable, cherished, planned, and loved. Their lack of identity is robbing them of their destiny, and it will rob you of yours, too.

Wasted lives. Unfilled purposes. There is nothing sadder and nothing further from God's plans for humanity—and from His plans for you.

Did you read your 3x5 cards today? If you have not had the time, get them out right now and read them out loud. In fact, go stand in front of a mirror and read them to yourself. Remember, I warned you that water-walking destinies could make you feel a little crazy.

Today we are going to continue consulting our Creator for the answer to our true identity. Let's begin with a prayer.

Father, I come to you for truth. I come to you for my true identity. Bestow it upon me and then help me believe it. Amen

Consult Your Creator
Grab your Bible or go to an online Bible site or app (www.biblegateway.com; YouVersion) and read Psalm 139:1–18. If you have access to more than one Bible version, then pick two or three different translations of this Psalm to read. Please read the verses out loud. Go back to the mirror and read them if you have easy access to one.

As you read and listen to these words written thousands of years ago, allow them to settle deep within you. Imagine they were written just for you and you alone. Let them affect you. If they are familiar, don't let the familiarity rob you of their profound, transformational truth. Ponder them as if reading them for the first time. Enjoy the poetry of them as you say the words slowly out loud. Introduce your heart to the concept that they are written for you, about you and you alone. Let the author's words become your words to your Creator as you entertain your identity as a unique creation, created on purpose for a purpose. Feel the author's wonder upon his discovery that he has never been alone, that his life, and your life, was planned before the beginning of time.

As you read, dare to imagine how your life would be altered if you truly believed these words; that you believed them for and about yourself. As you read, change the "you" to "I." Let these written words and your own voice become God's voice. Let Him speak these words over you and over your life. Try to personalize them by adding your name. As they sink deep within you past your own logic, let them touch the essence of you.

Take a deep breath when you are done, and as you exhale, ask God for the unique truth you need to know. Write down the words that resound within you. Paraphrase and personalize the author's words so that they become your own. Turn it into a conversation as your Creator expresses the wonder of you. I often journal this way to help me remember the truths that touched my heart, especially those I have a hard time believing.

 Uniquely You

I've copied a page from my own journal to demonstrate what I am asking you to do.

My Story

"Oh My God! I cannot believe your hand was on me before I was even born. You made me! You created and planned me before time began! Such knowledge is too big for me. You shaped me inside and out while I was in my mother's womb. I thank you for making me. You are amazing. I am amazing! I am a well thought-out, planned, and unique being. You planned me. That is so hard to believe, but I want to believe. Me? Breathtaking? Yes, body, soul, and spirit. You say I am marvelously made! Not only did you make me; you know me—inside and out. My secret desires are not hidden from you. You were there in the beginning of my life. I am never alone, no matter how dark my circumstances have seemed. You created me on purpose for a purpose exactly the way I am by design. Loud. Bossy. Hyper. All false-identities. You call me something different—a leader, full of energy, a communicator, nurturer, encourager. You sculpted me from nothing into something. I am an open book before you. Nothing is hidden and strangely that doesn't scare me. It frees me. You have watched me grow from conception, until birth, until now. All the stages of my life are spread out before you, even my mistakes, and yet you still delight in me! You still believe in me. You have prepared all the days of my life before I even lived one day. This knowledge is far too much for me to comprehend. But it changes everything. Thank you, Father. You are my Abba, my Dad. Thank you for creating me to be me. Show me who you created me to be and give me courage to be her! I want to be her! I am so sorry for settling for less for so long." —Jenny, January 2000

Your Story

Now it is your turn. Re-read Psalm 139:1–18. Listen with more than your mind and your logic. Pay attention to the words that particularly touch you. Tune out the negative thoughts that are coming at you. Try and internalize the words, make them your own, and then do like I did and write them in your own words—write God a note thanking Him for creating you and for your life. Be honest about your disbelief—God can take it. But also entertain the truth He wants you to know about yourself. He created you on purpose for a purpose. Yes, you! Let these words be your creed; let God tell you who you are.

_____

_____

_____

_____

_____

_____

_____

_____

Uniquely You Day Four

___

When I read those verses, I can't help but think about myself as a baby being formed in my mother's womb. I then think about the little girl I once was and the woman I have become. They were so very different at one point in my life. I wondered how that had happened. I needed to see that little girl so I looked for a photo of her—of me—when I was little just being me.

Now, please do the same. Find two photos of yourself—one of you as a child and a recent photo of yourself. Please don't say, "I hate photos," and skip this part. If at all possible I really want you to have a visual reminder of who you were as a child. If there are no photos of you as a child, then use one of yourself that you love at any age. Or ask a family member to help—there always seems to be somebody in the family who has all the old photos. If you don't have access to your family history, don't worry. We'll be asking God to bring that child to your memory later on in the assessment. If you don't have any photos of when you were a child, then perhaps draw yourself doing something you loved to do at a young age.

When you have the photos, place them in the designated spaces on the next page with the photo of you as a child in the first slot (or drawing) and your current photo in the second space provided.

Week One — Uniquely You

Write the name you were given at birth under this photo.

Write your full name as an adult under this photo.

Look into the eyes of the child you once were and the adult you have become and say out loud to both of them, "You were created on purpose for a purpose." Then write that sentence beside your photos.

Now get up and go to a mirror. Look at yourself. Really look at yourself. Avoid the temptation to critique yourself. Just look into your own eyes and say to your reflection, "You were created on purpose for a purpose." I know this can feel silly and awkward but please, please take the time to tell yourself that before time began, God imagined you, planned you, and created you on purpose for a purpose.

Write your name in the blank below. Read it out loud. This is a truth I want to cement into your soul!

"_____, you were created on purpose for a purpose."

Pause and give that sentence some thought. Can you wrap your brain around the fact that before time began God imagined you, planned you, loved you, and created you on purpose for a purpose? And not just any purpose, either. He has an amazing, thrilling, and rewarding purpose for you and you alone. It's mind boggling, isn't it? You bet. Life-changing, really. You were created by God to make a difference in this world. You were created to be the answer to someone's prayer. You were created to be God's solution to a problem. You were born "for such a time as this." You are necessary. You are needed. You matter.

Do you believe it? If you don't right now, that is okay. Just be honest with God and yourself. Take the time to contemplate why you have a hard time believing. Vow to choose to entertain the truth day-by-day or even hour-by-hour that you are uniquely created on purpose for a purpose. To end today's Daily Discovery Process, I would like to pray a blessing over you.

My prayer for you today is that you truly experience the implications of what it means to be "created on purpose for a purpose." You are fearfully and wonderfully made on purpose for a unique purpose. I pray you have the courage to believe it.

c2bu.com/vid3

The Child You Once Were

Daily Discovery Process

As we close out this week's discovery process, I want you to go back and look at your photos. Contemplate the little girl or little boy you once were and the person you have now become. Are they the same? Mine weren't. The little girl I once was easily believed she was created on purpose for a purpose, but the woman I had become never once even entertained the possibility.

My Story
When I began to make a careful assessment of who I was one of the first truths God revealed to me about myself was that the woman I had become bore no resemblance to the little girl I once was. That gave me great pause. I felt there was a deep chasm between the two and I couldn't remember how that came to be. This caused me to seek my Creator with a new sense of urgency. I recognized that there was a greater truth to unearth by remembering the child I once was. Was there ever! I truly felt God's delight in reminding me of the little girl I used to be. I am still amazed by the fact that the little girl I once was more closely resembled who God created me to be. I must have known it, or at least sensed it in me, because somewhere inside I often had an innate longing to be someone else. What was so incredibly freeing to learn was that the longing was not to be someone else, but to be *me*—the me God created me to be.

> ## *"There are two me's inside of me,*
> ## *the one I am and the one I long to be."*
> —Excerpt from the poem *"Do You Have the Courage to Be You?"*

I asked God to unveil me to me. He did exactly that by bringing to my mind memories of the little girl I once was so I could compare them to the woman I had become.

When I asked my Creator, "Who am I?" He unveiled *me* to me by reminding me of the child I once was. His answers were my memories. I had not thought about the child I was in many years. Now I was prompted to do just that. I could see her; I could even feel her. It seemed she held some of my answers.

I was a well-loved, extremely happy child. I had incredible confidence and was sure of my place in the world. I loved being first at anything and picked for everything. I treasured being the oldest and big sister to my siblings. I took that role very seriously as I did everything else. I cherished my family. I worked hard at being a good girl and tried to never hurt anyone's feelings.

I loved God and told everyone I met that He loved them too. It was easy to believe in a good God when you had good parents. Going to church was my favorite pastime. I was incredibly intuitive. Helping someone gave me great joy. I was caring and responsible. Though an extrovert, I was also comfortable being alone. I did not require much from other people. Someone said I was an old soul. Being with adults and listening to their conversations was much more fun than hanging out with kids my own age.

I loved to tell people what to do and how to do it. I never understood jokes but I laughed a lot. I loved those who no one else loved. I hated when someone felt left out. At the State Fair each year, my dad would win a stuffed animal for me at the basketball throw. After his victory, I was able to choose any prize I wanted. I always picked the ugliest, smallest stuffed animals, the ones I was certain no one else would choose. I took them home, bestowing upon them regal names and giving them prominent places on my bed. I slept with them all so no one would *feel* left out.

At school, I picked friends the same way I picked stuffed animals. I chose the ones never noticed or ever invited home to play. I picked the kids hurt by others with their hands or with their words. I became their protector and cheerleader. In fact, I was a cheerleader! I was extremely loud, active, and full of energy. I did not know how to whisper or sit still. In kindergarten, I got an "F" on my report card in *naptime* because I talked the entire time. I talked non-stop to anyone who would listen. I even talked to myself. When I talked, I assumed people would value what I had to say and agree with my opinions, even adults. I was always stunned when they asked me to be seen and not heard. I was shushed very often.

I was a tomboy who also loved baby dolls. My athletic abilities were well known in the neighborhood where I grew up. I loved competing with and beating boys in any sport. I threw footballs, hit baseballs, and shot basketballs. I was good at just about any and every sport I tried—gymnastics, diving, and softball, even the high jump. I liked to play on a team, and I loved to win. I was always the captain, and I always followed the rules.

I organized everyone and everything. I made decisions quickly and did not worry about outcomes or failures. I wrote poems, kept diaries, and told stories with great animation. I was a leader looking for someone to follow me. I was comfortable on stage and enjoyed having people watch me. I sang in the choir and danced whenever I could. I had no idea that I did not have talent for either. It never once occurred to me to question whether I was liked or accepted; I just assumed I was.

The memories brought a realization that felt like a ton of bricks falling on my head. Somewhere along my life's journey, I stopped being *me*. Sadly, I realized the woman I had become did not resemble the child I once was. *Why?* I screamed silently to my Maker. *When did I stop being me?*

Your Story
What about you? Are they the same—the child you once were and the adult you have become? You may not have thought about who you were as a child in a long time. Ask God to bring him or her to your mind.

But before you do that, before you begin to consult your Creator and write your story, I want to acknowledge that many of you have memories from your childhood that are extremely painful; ones that you have worked very hard at forgetting. Though I can never truly understand your pain or know what it is like to have gone through what you did, I do know there is value in remembering the child you once were. I'm not a therapist or counselor, though I highly recommend one if you have had trauma or pain from your past. What I'm asking you to do here is not remember your pain but to remember the child you once were. Very often the children we were lend clues to our destiny. I am asking if you are willing to let God reveal to you the little girl or little boy you once were. What were you like? Were you quiet? An introvert? Did you love to read, ride a bike, hit a baseball, or play with dolls? Were you always sure of your place in the world or did you always wonder where you fit? Can you remember what it felt like to be that little girl or little boy?

God may not reveal these memories all at once. My memories came slowly over time as I daily and intentionally sought God for my true identity and destiny. While I believe God loves to answer our questions, I also know He loves our companionship. He loves that you are seeking Him, learning to listen for Him. He loves that you just want to spend time with Him. Enjoy that time, the quiet, while you get to know Him and learn to trust Him for your identity and destiny.

God has many promises for those who seek Him. One of the first promises is that we find

Day Five

Him and He listens. This is often difficult for people to comprehend, that God listens and even talks back. This difficulty is often due to our relationship, or lack of one, with our parents. These relationships can often affect our ability to hear God or to have a relationship with Him. If you are having trouble trusting this process or trusting God, especially if you believe your memories can only bring pain, just tell God about them right now. If this is where you find yourself, journal your fears. Being honest is the beginning steps of a journey of purpose. No pretending allowed. If this is not difficult for you, skip to the next paragraph or journal how your relationship makes it easy to have a relationship with God as your Creator and Father.

_____
_____
_____
_____
_____
_____
_____
_____
_____
_____
_____
_____
_____
_____
_____

If you are ready to proceed and are comfortable with remembering who you were as a child, I'd like you to invite God into your memories and into this process. I would encourage you to talk to Him out loud. For me, talking to Him out loud helps me keep my focus and keeps me from being so easily distracted. You are also welcome to journal this prayer. Journaling also helps to minimize distractions.

> *"God, show me the little girl/little boy I once was.*
> *Help me to really see her/him, to remember her/him.*
> *Show me the keys this child holds to my identity and destiny.*
> *Thank you, Amen."*

Write down what comes to mind or what you see. Tune your thoughts only to describing that little girl or little boy. Who she or he was, not what happened to her or him. Describe your personality, what you loved to do, and whom you wanted to be when you grew up. Were you an extrovert or an introvert, talkative or quiet? Did you like to read, sing, or draw? Where, indoors or outdoors? Describe any crazy dreams you had. All of these questions can prompt memories that may be important to uncovering your identity and destiny.

If you are stuck, go back and re-read the description I wrote of myself. It may help you get moving.

_____
_____
_____
_____
_____
_____
_____
_____
_____
_____
_____
_____
_____
_____
_____
_____
_____
_____
_____
_____
_____

I know this exercise was difficult for some of you. I applaud your courage. As we end this day of discovery, I pray that remembering the child you once were made your grown-up heart tender. That child is still in you and is utterly delightful, whether you were told that or not by the family that birthed you. This is why it is extremely important for you to consult your Creator so He can tell you about that child.

Consult Your Creator

Has anyone ever called you delightful? Ladies, has anyone called you charming, enchanting, or adorable? Men, has anyone called you strong, brave, and responsible? Have you ever believed that you brought great pleasure to someone? Not me. I have absolutely no memory of anyone ever calling me any of those things—as a child or a woman. That's why I love going to God for my identity instead of others. God delights in me! He finds me utterly remarkable and He feels the same way about you. God delights in you! He delights in the little girl or little boy you once were *and* the person you have become. Doesn't that just send chill bumps up your arms and make you feel warm and fuzzy all over? God wants you to know this truth and I can prove it!

Read the verses out loud and personalize them by placing your name in each empty blank below. Imagine that God wrote these words to you and you alone. Imagine God as your Dad, your heavenly Daddy just delighting in you, speaking these words over you. I highly recommend putting them on your 3x5 card and referring to them often.

"_____, I brought you into a spacious place; I rescued you because I delight in you!" — PSALM 18:10, *paraphrased*

"_____, as you trust in me, I will rescue you and deliver you because I delight in you." — PSALM 22:9, *paraphrased*

"_____, I delight in you, fear me and put your hope in my unfailing love." — PSALM 147:11, *paraphrased*

"_____, I take great delight in you for you are mine, when you humble yourself I crown you with salvation." — PSALM 149:4, *paraphrased*

"_____ you are my servant whom I uphold, who I have chosen, the one in whom I delight; I will put my Spirit on you and you will bring justice to the nations." — ISAIAH 42:1; MATTHEW 12:18, *both paraphrased*

"_____, I am the LORD your God and I am with you. I am mighty to save. I take great delight in you, I will quiet you with my love and I rejoice over you with singing." — ZEPHANIAH 3:17, *paraphrased*

This is my prayer for you today. I pray that when tonight comes and you have ended your day of responsibilities and routines, you will go to sleep knowing, maybe for the very first time that God—the God of the Universe, delights in you, both the child you once were and the person you have become. Not only does He delight in you, but He also sings a lullaby over you and rejoices in who you are. He is so proud of you. He brags about you to all the saints and angels in Heaven. They are all cheering you on! I pray this truth settles deep within you and changes you. You are utterly delightful. Though your biological family members may not have ever called you that, God does.

End this day of discovery by repeating after me:

"I am delightful!
My creator delights in me."

Righteous Girlfriend/ Mighty Warrior

Your Identity Must Precede Your Destiny

– Day 1 –

Reflect back over the first day of homework. Share with your new righteous friends why you began this journey of purpose. What drew you to this point in your life?

– Day 2 –

Do you believe your life was planned? Share with your group how the concept of your life being planned affected you this week.

– Day 3 –

Share with your group any struggles you have had this week in answering the question, "Who am I?"

– Day 4 –

Show your righteous girlfriends or warriors the photo of the child you once were and the one of you now. As each person shows their photo, I'm asking for the entire group to affirm them out loud that both "were created on purpose for a purpose." After you have received your affirmation, read your little girl or boy description, then read your paraphrase of Psalm 139:1-18 to your group.

– Day 5 –

Looking back on your childhood memories, were you able to see how the little girl or little boy you once were differs from who you are now?

If time permits, share with your group what you feel when you hear the words "You were created on purpose for a purpose." No rules. Just respond straight from your heart. End each RG/MW Group with prayer requests and prayer. Write down your prayer request on a piece of paper and pass it to the person on your right.

Commit to praying each day for that particular righteous friend. Tuck their card into your Uniqueness Assessment so you will remember to pray each day. Believe God for this person as you learn to believe God for yourself.

Blessings, everyone!
I am personally praying for each Righteous Group.

Clues to Your True Identity

How was your sleep last night? Delightful? Are you starting to get a sense of who you were created to be? Are you remembering the little child you once were? Don't you wish you could give him or her a hug? I have a photo in my office that reminds me to do just that. The photo is of a woman I do not know. She is sitting in front of an old vanity table staring at her self in the mirror. She is an attractive woman. She looks satisfied. Fulfilled. From the deep lines on her face and the gray hair, it is evident that she is on the other side of seventy. The reflection she stares at in the mirror is not the woman she is now but of the little girl she once was. She's smiling at herself. That photo reminds me to do the same—to honor and remember the child I once was.

I want to continuing talking about the kids we once were and the individuals we have become. As I reflected and considered my own words describing the little girl I once was, I was struck by how different she and the woman I had become were from each other. As I got in the habit of seeking God for my identity, I found the courage to ask Him, "When did I stop being me?" He once again answered me with memories from my childhood.

My Story
I was ten years old when my teacher whispered in my ear, "The principal wants to see you in her office." Instantly, fear and dread washed over me. My palms started to sweat, and I felt sick to my stomach. Only bad kids went to the principal's office and I was a good kid— that was my identity. Walking to the principal's office in shame was not who I was.

As I inched down the long hallway, I felt my confidence slipping away. That was a new experience for me. My palms were wringing wet, and I kept wiping them on my pants. My mind searched for anything I might have said or done that could have warranted this summons. As I rounded the corner and peeked through the office window, the secretary caught my eye and waved me in. After what felt like an eternity, I heard my name called rather formally, "Jennifer." No one ever called me Jennifer. Now I was really scared. I did not correct the principal about my name. I just scooted off the chair and without looking up followed her into the room where all the bad kids went. She closed the door.

"Take a seat," she said.

I did, once more staring at the floor. I could not look her in the eye. I felt alone, vulnerable, and unprotected.

She wasted no time with pleasantries and attacked immediately. While I am prone to exaggeration, that is exactly what it was—an attack.

"Aren't you the young lady who wants to be a missionary and go around the world telling everyone that God loves them?"

Her words felt like an accusation. They were so different from the affirmations I was accustomed to receiving when I announced my career choice. I looked up for the first time. I was confused. She had just announced my dream, the not-so-secret desire of my heart. I passionately gave this answer to anyone who asked me what I wanted to be when I grew up. But something in the way she said it was wrong. At ten, I did not know it was her tone. Her words dripped with sarcasm.

The way she asked the question made the desire of my heart sound like a hideous aspiration for evil. Unfamiliar emotions began to pour into my young psyche —humiliation, shame, and embarrassment. I remember nodding, affirming her question. Though it was the truth, for the first time in my young life I was now embarrassed to admit it. My dream had never been ridiculed, only validated, and applauded. This fact caused me to look down and stare at my feet.

She broke the silence with another accusation.

"If you love God so much, how could you be so cruel to one of your classmates?"

I looked up again. Cruel? I had never been intentionally cruel to anyone in my life! I guess the confused look on my face caused her to continue. She explained how she had watched me being mean to Julia at recess during our softball game. Julia was my friend. We had spent many nights together at sleepovers. She did not have any other friends. Everyone laughed and made fun of her because of her weight, everyone except me.

She continued,

> *"You wouldn't let Julia play in the game. You excluded her."*

> *"No!"* I wanted to say. "That isn't true!"

However, I remained silent because I had been taught not to argue with an adult. I stayed silent remembering what had really happened at recess.

The game had already started and the teams chosen when Julia walked up. I would have welcomed her on my team, but she only wanted to bat and did not want to take a turn playing in the outfield. I told her she could not do that because it was against the rules. My dad taught me that. You must take a turn in the outfield if you want a turn at bat. Therefore Julia decided not to play.

However, I could not say any of this to my principal. I was taught it was disrespectful to talk back to an adult. I was taught to be good. I chose to be silent. That was not like me.

I wanted to run away from the disturbing emotions unleashed inside of me. I was in unfamiliar territory. This person in authority called my actions, my dreams, and me into question. She bestowed a new and foreign identity upon me—hypocritical, self-righteous, and unkind. Who was I to argue or question her authority? I was just a child. It must be my fault. I must have done something wrong.

My ten-year-old filter was inadequate and not yet equipped to reject the lies that were pouring into my mind and searing my soul. Lies such as,

> *It is wrong to be so passionate and vocal about my dreams.*

> *It is wrong to talk about God.*

> *It is wrong to be a leader.*

> *It is wrong to play by the rules.*

> *It is wrong to be me.*

In those very few minutes behind that closed door, I made a vow that I would never again do anything to make me feel what I had felt in that principal's office. I made a vow to stop being me. I did not realize I would keep that vow for almost thirty years.

I told no one about this incident; I was too embarrassed. I just quit. I quit having an opinion. I quit talking about God. I quit leading and started following. I quit writing and telling stories. I quit being on a stage. I did not want anyone to look at me anymore. I began to question who I was. I lost my confidence in being me because I no longer believed being me was a good thing. I morphed into a chameleon. I became an expert at discovering who and what people wanted or needed me to be. I assimilated and became like everyone else. I did not want to stand out anymore. I stopped trying new things. I stood for nothing. I never said "no," which got me in difficult situations, especially with boys, from which I was ill equipped to extract myself as a young girl and teenager. I was terrified of those hideous emotions called shame, embarrassment, and humiliation, and I stopped being me. I became someone else for a very *long* time.

As God pulled back the veil of my past, I saw the woman I had become was a direct result of the silent vow I'd made many years ago as a ten-year-old child. As I grew older, I grew more fearful of those hated emotions, so I continued to reshape myself. I had no idea I would completely lose me—the *me* I was created to be.

When I stopped being me, I stopped believing that my opinion was valuable, so I waited for others to offer theirs first. I still talked a lot, but only about things that did not matter and were not controversial. I joined whatever my peers were joining so I would be included and not stand out. I wore what everyone else wore, drank what everyone else drank, and carried on meaningless conversations. I compared myself to everyone and had become very judgmental of others and myself. I still went to church but I never shared my faith. I settled for mediocrity, comfort, and security. I traded in my dreams and desires, assuming this would protect me from ever being humiliated again. It did not work. I still felt embarrassed often. Embarrassed at being me. When I stopped being me, I had no idea I had traded in my destiny.

Now I finally grasped why I was afraid and could not answer the question,

"Do you have the courage to be you?"

I did not believe there was more for me. Even more profoundly, I did not believe there was more *to* me.

I finally realized why I was so scared, why I would need courage to be me. Deep in the recesses of my soul, where words are not necessary, settling for less was the only thing I knew how to do. I embraced the lifestyle of never believing in or expecting anything extraordinary. I did not know how to believe in me, much less *be me*, because I had embraced an identity that was not mine.

It was as if my Creator now pushed a pause button on my destiny. I was having an identity crisis that needed immediate attention. I was not being me. I had to remove the false, protective identity I had been wearing for years and accept the one that more resembled the bold, confident child I once was. Before I could ever walk on water, I knew that I must first learn to be me. I had to make a careful assessment of who I was before I could figure out what I was supposed to do.

This proved to be a long process. I had thirty years of mess to undo that I'd created. I called this time in my life *identity boot camp*. During the next few weeks, you'll be going through one of your own identity boot camps as you work through the pages of The Uniqueness Assessment. When I began my own journey of purpose, I started to hear these words inside of me.

*"There are two me's inside of me:
the one I am and the one I long to be."*

I remembered thinking to myself, "Is that a poem?" I got out a pen and a piece of paper and wrote the following poem in less than fifteen minutes. When I concluded it, I thought, "Isn't that strange? I have never written anything in my life!" Immediately after having that thought, I had a memory that contradicted what I believed was truth. I remembered being a little girl, climbing high up into a tree with pen and paper, positioning myself up high so that I could write poems and regard my thoughts. Wow! I once loved to write! And now I felt the desire to do that again. My little girl and the adult I had become were now becoming one.

You cannot settle for less than what you were created for. Safety and comfort are not what you were designed for. Rather, you were designed for a life lived fully alive so others can see that they, too, were created for a great destiny.

You being *you* really does matter!

BY JENNY WILLIAMSON

There are two me's inside of me.
The one I am. The one I long to be.

The one I am is familiar and true.
She expects so little of me, yet dreams of more, too.
She seems somewhat less, while wanting something more.
But comfort surrounds her soul, keeping her safe to the core.

Now that other ME, inside of me, is the opposite for sure?
She plots and plans her escape from the same.
She longs to do more, to see more, to be more,
All the while using my name!

The one me and the other was once the same child.
But as time hurried onward, I lost her somehow.
I gradually began wanting others to see,
Just a mirror, a reflection of themselves, instead of me.

I am not aware of when the thought first occurred.
Or when I recognized the truth,
But slowly I heard, "How did this happen or come to be?
When did you become less, so much less
Than I designed you to be?"

At first I grew sad, experienced a terrible ache.
I began to ponder all that was at stake.
Another thought surfaced, as scary as the last,
What if others needed me to be me?
Then I better become me, and fast!

A heavy sigh I let out, as I began to pray.
"Lord grant me the courage, (On this very day)
To cease to be more of the same.
But for me to become me and forever remain."

I then asked a question of my Father so true,
"What does she look like — this little girl I once knew?"
"Ah," he said, "In her I delight —
Let me tell you her secrets and how to give her life."

"She's as beautiful as a sunset, an original of mine.
Man's approval does not matter, as she completes her design.
She sings with the angels, dances only for My smile.
Laughs with abandon, knowing she is here for a short while."

"What are you afraid of?" My Father asked of me.
"Don't you know by now your purpose to be?
Lean close while I tell you what you are longing to know.
I created you only; only so —
That you would be the me I designed you to be."

Nothing more, my beloved one.
Settling for less cannot be done.
Take my hand and with courage soar
to the dreams and destiny I have in store.

Safety and comfort are not yours to be,
but a life lived fully alive so others can see
that they too were created for a great destiny."

When Did You Stop Being You?

Daily Discovery Process

Speaking of courage, you may need a little (or a lot) for today's discovery process. I shared my story with you about when I stopped being me during the overview, and now I am asking you to do the same. If, like me, you stopped being you, then you need to take the time to consult your Creator and ask Him, "When did I stop being me?" You may have no immediate memory of a particular incident that caused you to stop being you. For me, my memories came slowly, as I walked and talked with God, not while doing an assessment at the request of an author I had never met. Entertain the question.

Take time to talk with God about it. Go for a walk outside. Listen to the whispers of creation and the still, small voice inside of you. Ask the question out loud, "When did I stop being me?" Come back and write down anything you remember. If you don't remember anything, leave the space blank until you do.

Your Creator can give you insight into the connection between the child you once were and the person you have become. Typically there are clues and connections for your identity and destiny to be found in those memories. You may have made vows, much like mine, that are robbing you of your true identity and world-changing destiny. Until I asked God the question, "When did I stop being me?" I had no memory of that vow. Though my story wasn't one of physical or sexual abuse, it was a very emotional process for me. I still grieve for all the time I wasted. However, God reminds me over and over again that He is the Redeemer, which means He is the restorer of that which was lost. He restores honor, reputation, and years lost. I needed all three restored. He is my Redeemer. It is never too early or too late to discover whom you are and what you are supposed to be doing. Ask God to reveal your memory and your story to you when you are ready. If you already know the event, ask God to reveal to you any silent vows you made. Trust God to bring you truth. You do not need to fear it. It has the ability to set you free.

When did you stop being you?

_____

If you resemble the child you once were and have fulfilled all your dreams, I am so happy for you, even a little envious. This journey of purpose will go much quicker for you because you will have less to undo than the rest of us who, for some reason or another, decided that who we were was not such a good idea. If you never stopped being the you God created, then use the space below thanking God for this protection! I would speculate that you had amazing people praying for you, bathing you in prayer your entire life. Call them and thank them too! Most people I've met don't have a story like that, however that is my prayer and longing for my children and grandchildren's story. That is one of the reasons I am writing this assessment—so young girls and boys can begin early in their lives discovering and hanging on to their true identities. I want them to know who to receive their identities from, while encouraging them to pursue their destinies.

_____
_____
_____
_____
_____
_____
_____
_____
_____
_____
_____
_____
_____
_____
_____
_____
_____
_____
_____
_____

I cringe as I think back over the details of my own story. It seems so trite, even pitiful compared to the pain and abuse many individuals have suffered as children. When God first brought this memory to my mind I was embarrassed that an incident so small could affect my life so greatly. However as I began to consult my Creator, He began to show me that the enemy of our souls has a very strategic plan to steal our identities at a very early age. Our enemy knows better than we do that once we are completely confident in our true identities, we will be unstoppable in obtaining and fulfilling our destinies! Abuse, whether physical, mental, or verbal, does the exact same thing. It robs us of our identity and destiny. It is designed in the pits of hell to entice you to quit being you—the *you* God created! That is why this journey takes courage. That is why God asks, "Do you have the courage to be you—the *you* I created?" If I quit being me at ten years old over this small of an encounter, I cannot even imagine the courage it requires to begin this journey of purpose if you have suffered pain, abuse, or trauma from another human being, especially one who said they "loved" you. Please do not confuse that person(s) with God. Evil exists in this world. Some people find it difficult to believe in a good God when they have never met good people. But I promise you ... it is worth it. YOU are worth it!

The reason I vowed to stop being me was to avoid pain, to avoid feeling. It worked for a while. I felt that not being seen was somewhat safe. But very quickly I began to feel nothing. I felt dead, like an imposter who often wondered who I really was. I became exhausted from all the different and false identities I had allowed to be bestowed upon me. The truth I learned from God in my own journey of purpose is that if we build up walls to protect ourselves from pain, inevitably those same walls will keep us from feeling loved, valuable, and worthy. When you cut yourself off and make walls constructed with silent, yet impenetrable vows, you lose the ability to pick and choose what you will or won't let in. You end up shutting out all the good as well as all the bad. *This* is how we begin to settle for so much less than we were created for. This is how complacency and mediocrity slip into all areas of our life. It is still shocking to me how early in life this happens. That is why I am so passionate about teenagers and even younger children learning the truth, "You were created on purpose for a purpose." No matter your age, hold on to your true identity. Fight for your destiny.

Mediocrity, security, and complacency are so far from God's plans for us. Abundance. Adventure. The impossible. More than we dare ask or imagine. This is our destiny. God created us to be water walkers, giant slayers, and history makers. If we don't believe in our God-given identity, then we will *never* attempt to fulfill our destinies. Satan knows that. He knows our destinies far better than we do—he has been around a long time. Satan threw away his identity and traded in his glorious destiny for a counterfeit one. Now he is trying to steal ours. Please don't just skim over this "Satan" part. He is real. He is your enemy. Just as God has a plan for you, so does Satan. Ladies and gentlemen, there truly is a cosmic, supernatural, very real spiritual battle going on for your identity and destiny. That is why it takes courage to be you, the *you* God created.

As we end this day of discovery, my prayer for you is that you will have an awareness of any vows you made as a child that may be robbing you of your identity or destiny. I pray you will decide to fight for both.

What God Wants You to Know about Yourself

Daily Discovery Process

I know yesterday was a lot of work—a lot of remembering and writing. As we begin day two of this week, we'll consult our Creator to make sure our thoughts and feelings line up with truth. I believe this applies to our memories as well as our thoughts. God brought back memories of the little girl I once was so that I could extract the information I needed to assist me on my journey of becoming who He created me to be. Some of those memories were good and some were not. The negative memories were never meant to be the focus. The focus is where I am going, not where I have been. God used memories of the little girl I once was to give a reflection of the woman I had become. I found nuggets of truth I needed for my future nestled in my past. I pray the same is true for you. I do not want to cause you any unnecessary pain.

The sole purpose of processing your story and memories is to recognize any silent vows and negative agreements you made to protect your self. These vows do not protect, instead they hinder you from realizing your true identity and keep you from fulfilling your destiny. They keep you from becoming YOU—the *you* God created. Our Creator promises to lead you on the path He has chosen for you. *Trust His lead.* Trust He will reveal every truth you need to hear, each at exactly the right time. The most important thing you can do is to continue consulting your Creator, daily asking God to keep bestowing your true identity upon you so you can separate the lies from the truth. Take those negative thoughts and memories captive but don't ignore or deny them. God promises to bring healing to every piece of your mind, your soul, and your spirit.

Though this assessment is about moving forward into your identity and destiny, many people need healing from their past to be able to do just that, as I mentioned before. If you have painful episodes from your childhood or past that are still gaping wounds, my best advice as your life coach for the next ten weeks is for you to engage a professional Christian counselor to lovingly walk with you through the healing process. Even if you have to put this assessment on hold for a bit, that is fine. Do what you need to do to keep moving forward. I'll still be here when you return.

You have an inheritance promised to you by God. Don't give up. Keep searching. I promise it is worth it. Therefore, consult your Creator. Let His truth wash over you and clean the wounds of the past. You are delightful. You are chosen. You are unique. This is your identity!

Below are words I have taken from the Bible. They are words of truth. Words that declare who you are. Imagine God is shouting from the heavens declaring these truths about you to all who will listen. He is most possessive and protective of you. He longs for you to receive your identity and discover your destiny much more than you do. Open your hands and heart to receive His words deep inside of you. Put them on and wear them as you would a royal robe of a prince or princess with a crown or diamond-studded tiara on top of your head. As you write your name in the blanks provided, pause at any particular word or phrase that moves you. Circle it. Highlight it. Write it on your 3x5 cards, and then ask your Creator what truth He is trying to tell you.

I'm going to start this exercise by providing an example.

"Before time began, I knew you __Jenny__ and set you apart."
—JEREMIAH 1:5, paraphrase (NIV)

Based on this verse, what truth(s) do you think God wants you to know about yourself and your identity? (Here is what I wrote for myself.)

> *"That word, 'know' is so huge for me. I long to be known, truly known. But at the same time, I don't really reveal my heart or the 'real me' to many people. I always feel like I need to clean her up and make her more presentable. When I read these words, I feel like God wants me to know that He see me, knows me, the real me—everything I have done and everything I am afraid to do, and yet, He still has big plans for me. That truth changes me. It gives me rest. It gives me permission to just be me and to seek God for His plans for my life. It makes me feel I am worth it."*

Now it's your turn. Write your name in the blanks and ponder the questions before answering.

"Before time began, I knew you _____ — and set you apart."
— JEREMIAH 1:5, paraphrase (NIV)

Based on this verse, what truth(s) do you think God wants you to know about yourself and your identity?

_____
_____
_____
_____
_____
_____
_____
_____

*"But now, this is what the LORD says, I created you, _____ . I formed you.
Fear not _____ , for I have redeemed you for a purpose;
I have summoned you by name _____ ; you are mine."*
— ISAIAH 43:1 (NIV)

Based on this verse, what truth(s) do you think God wants you to know about yourself and your identity?

_____
_____
_____
_____
_____
_____

Uniquely You — Day Two

"_____ you are God's workmanship, created in Jesus to do good works which God prepared in advance of your birth to do."
— Ephesians 2:10 (NIV)

Based on this verse, what truth(s) do you think God wants you to know about yourself, your identity?

_____
_____
_____
_____
_____
_____
_____
_____

"God is the Father of Jesus and He wants to take us to the high places of blessing with Him. _____ , long before God laid down the earth's foundations, He had you in mind and settled on you as the focus of His love to be made whole and set apart by His love. Long, long ago God decided to adopt you, _____ , into His family, through Jesus.

What pleasure he took in planning this! He wanted you to enter into the celebration of His lavish gift giving by the hand of Jesus. _____ , because of this sacrifice of Jesus, His blood being poured out on the altar of the cross, you are free—free of penalties and punishment chalked up by our misdeeds. _____ , you are not barely free, you are abundantly free!

He thought of everything, provided for everything you could possibly need, letting you in on the plans He took such delight in making. He set it all out before you in Jesus, a long-range plan in which everything would be brought together and summed up in Him—everything in the deepest heaven and everything on earth.

So _____, it is only in Jesus that you will find out who you are and what you are living for! Long before you heard of God, He had His eye on you, had designs on you for glorious living, which is part of the overall purpose He is working in everything and everyone! _____, I [Paul] am asking God and Jesus to make you intelligent and discerning in knowing Him personally, so you can keep your eyes focused and clear so you can see exactly what He is calling you to do, grasp the immensity of this glorious way of life He has for us Christians — oh, the utter extravagance of His work in us who trust Him — endless energy, boundless strength!" — Various verses from Ephesians 1 (msg)

Based on these verses, what truth(s) do you think God wants you to know about yourself and your identity?

_____
_____
_____
_____
_____
_____

"Everything was created through Him [Jesus]; nothing—not one thing came into being without Him. _____, if you believe Jesus is who He claimed, He will make you to be your true self, a child of God with all the rights and inheritance that come from that identity." — John 1:12–13 (msg)

Based on these verses, what truth(s) do you think God wants you to know about yourself and your identity?

_____
_____
_____
_____
_____
_____

"If anyone knows Jesus personally, He is a new creation. The old has gone, the new has come. This is a gift from God, _____, just for you."
— 2 Corinthians 5:17, paraphrase (NIV)

Based on this verse, what truth(s) do you think God wants you to know about yourself and your identity?

_____
_____
_____
_____
_____
_____
_____

"_____, you have become the temple of the living God. He wants to live with you and walk among you. He wants to be your personal God. He will call you to come out of the world and be separated unto Him for his purposes. He will call you His daughter or son." — 2 Corinthians 6:16–18 (NIV)

Based on this verse, what truth(s) do you think God wants you to know about yourself and your identity?

_____
_____
_____
_____
_____
_____
_____

"_____, you were created to be light in the world. Do not hide that light. Do not hide who you are. Let your light shine before men so they may see your good deeds and know where they come from, so they will know to thank God."
— Matthew 5:14–16, paraphrase (NIV)

Based on these verses, what truth(s) do you think God wants you to know about yourself and your identity?

_____
_____
_____
_____
_____
_____
_____
_____

"_____, since you are the dearly loved child of God, live a life of love. Once you were in darkness, now you are light in the Lord. Live as a child of the light for the fruit of light consists of goodness, righteousness, and truth. Pursue this for this is who you are —light, goodness, righteousness, and truth for the rest of the world."
— EPHESIANS 5:1, 8 (NIV)

Based on these verses, what truth(s) do you think God wants you to know about yourself and your identity?

_____
_____
_____
_____
_____
_____
_____
_____

"_____, you are led by the Spirit of God, therefore you are the children of God. You did not receive a spirit that makes you a slave to fear but you received a spirit of family. That is why we cry "Abba, Father" or "Daddy." The spirit of God Himself testifies with our spirit that we are God's children.

Now if we are indeed God's children then we are heirs, joint heirs with Jesus — if indeed we share in His suffering we will surely share in His glory. Please consider any present suffering you have is worth nothing compared to the glory that is going to be revealed in you—God's glory. Creation waits in eager expectation for the children of God to be revealed."
— ROMANS 8:14–19, paraphrased (NIV)

(I just have to interject here! Do those words rock you? They do me! Creation is waiting for you to be you! The rocks hold their breath and the ocean asks, "Is today the day? Will they find the courage to be all God created them to be?" That is intoxicating stuff!)

Based on these verses, what truth(s) do you think God wants you to know about yourself and your identity?

_____
_____
_____
_____
_____
_____
_____

Last one for today.

"Do everything without complaining or arguing so that you may become blameless and pure, children of God without fault in a crooked and depraved generation in which you would shine like stars in the universe."
— PHILIPPIANS 2:14–14 (NIV)

Based on these verses, what truth(s) do you think God wants you to know about yourself and your identity? I think He wants us to stop playing small and apologizing for who we are! He wants us to be stars—stars that shine brightly! That's just what I think. What about you?

_____
_____

Reflect back over these truths God has given you about your identity. Direct your mind back to them throughout the week. Make a promise to yourself to re-read these identity verses before you go to bed tonight. Whisper them to yourself. Let your true, God-given identity be the last words you hear as you fall asleep tonight.

My prayer for you as this day of discovery ends is that your dreams will be filled with God's words as He bestows your true identity upon you. I pray you will truly contemplate who God says you are—who you were created to be. I pray you will not let anyone rob you of this truth. Hurry up, my friend! The trees are holding their breath for the real you to be unveiled!

You Were Planned

Daily Discovery Process

Just in case you are still reeling from the intensive last two days, I'm happy to say that today is going to be a short day. I don't want you to get discouraged with the workload and give up. Take your time to go back through the last two days if you need to finish your story and contemplate God's truths for you. We'll wait for you. It is worth taking the time to re-read the identity verses from yesterday. Continue only when you are caught up.

My Story
When I was twelve or thirteen years old, I discovered the Thornton Family Bible at my grandmother's house. (Thornton is my maiden name.) In that Bible were recorded all the births, deaths, and marriages of all my family members for generations and generations. Also recorded in that Bible was the date of my birth, as was the date of my parents' marriage. But the year of my parents' marriage was wrong—or so I thought. I showed the error to my grandmother. Being the strong matriarch of our family (with ten kids and fifty-three grandkids) and with great confidence in the Bible's recorded data (she was the only one allowed to write in it) she promptly guaranteed me that the date of my parents' marriage was correct. No argument. This was recorded truth. That meant that if the wedding date was true and my birthday was true, then something was very wrong! I began counting the months between those two dates. One, two, three, four, five, six, seven. Seven months—not nine—between my parents' wedding date and my birth! The realization slowly began to sink deep within me. My parents *had* to get married. My parents had to get married because of me! And then it occurred to me at that very young age—I was not planned..

I didn't tell my parents that I had learned their well-kept secret. Being the child I was, I didn't want to embarrass them, especially my mom. I instinctively knew that talking about the truth would do just that. Another reason I wasn't compelled to blurt out the truth was that I was a very well loved child. Upon contemplation, as only a twelve or thirteen year old can, the discovery of my parents' secret did not alter or undermine that truth. I may have not been planned, but I was loved—well loved!

Just recently, which was thirty-five years after I learned the secret of my conception, I blurted out the truth to my mom. "I know you had to get married because of me." Though I was a forty-seven-year-old woman, the voice coming out of me sounded like that of a small child. My mom was very quiet. Neither of us spoke. Finally, I heard her quietly whisper, "I thought you may have guessed." There was no discussion that followed. I could feel her embarrassment over the phone. I was sad we couldn't talk about it. A few days later, I was talking to my seventy-five-year-old aunt—my mom's sister—on the phone. I confessed what I had done. I truly hated causing my mom any pain or embarrassment.

My aunt, who has loved me madly since she first learned of my existence, had empathy for my mom, her sister's heart, and simply said to me, "She has guarded that secret for so long." Immediately after saying those words, she switched her focus from my mom to me and proclaimed the truth that traveled straight through the phone lines to my heart. "You know that you were no accident—you were planned by God on purpose for a purpose."

Warm waves of love flowed over me, on me, and through me. I caught my breath. Her words entered into the core of who I was. I knew she was right, and I felt her words in a place that I didn't know I needed to hear them. I didn't wrestle with it or examine it. I just received it and agreed with it. I knew deep within me, despite the details of my conception, that *it was truth*. My life was planned and for some reason I needed to hear that. Somewhere inside of me since I was twelve or thirteen, I was longing for someone to tell me, "Before time began, you were imagined, loved, planned, and created on purpose for a purpose."

May I be the first to tell you, "So are you!" *You* were created on purpose for a purpose. You and your life are no accident. To fulfill our destiny and uncover our identity we must know and believe this truth. Though my parents did not plan me, God did. This is powerful knowledge. God planned you even if your parents didn't. I was so blessed to have parents, and even though they didn't plan me, they chose to get married and love me! But even if they had not made that decision, I now know, and I long for you to know, that God planned us. He planned us, He sculpted us, and He imagined us. Now He has a destiny for us that involves changing the world, literally. You were planned.

Before we go forward, I long for you to receive, believe, and agree with this truth. It is yours to take and keep. It is my gift to you, but it really comes from God. Can you receive it by faith? Will you choose to believe it?

○ Yes ○ No

Day Three

Your Story

Record what you know about your conception. What is your birth order? Are you the independent, oldest child, the much-loved baby of the family, or the middle child who hates confrontation and just wants everyone to get along? Did you feel you were wanted, loved, and planned? Write what you know about your birth. Ask a trusted family member who loves you madly to shed light on your arrival into this world. As you remember and write, please keep in mind that even if your parents did not plan you, even if they put you up for adoption, even if you grew up hearing that you were unwanted and unloved, that it does not change the truth that God wants you to know today:

You Were Created On Purpose For A Purpose.

Consult your Creator as you work through this exercise. Recording the truth of your arrival into this world may be the vehicle God uses to shed some light on why you may feel rejection easily, why you have a sense of longing for something you can't articulate, or why you feel so confident in life. This entire assessment is designed to "make a careful assessment of who you are" so you can figure out "what you are to be doing"!

Record what you know about your conception and birth.

_____
_____
_____
_____
_____
_____
_____
_____
_____
_____
_____
_____
_____
_____
_____
_____

_____

_____

_____

_____

_____

_____

_____

Consult Your Creator

What is your first response when you hear these words, "I was planned." Is it easy for you to believe them? If like me you had loving parents, then yes, it is probably easy for you to accept and embrace this truth about yourself. However, if your parents abandoned or abused you, or never showed you tangible proof of their love, then these words may cause a terrible ache in your heart. If that is the case for you, I am so sorry. It is not my intention to cause you any heartache. This one area of identity boot camp may take incredible courage on your part. You may need a large dose of courage to believe a loving Creator planned you. I want to show you there is evidence of this fact.

In spite of the circumstances of your birth, you were planned. I say so, my aunt says so, and God says so. I have listed some verses below so you can take God at His word. He doesn't lie. Highlight any words that touch your heart and resound with your spirit. Circle words that speak specifically about how God planned, created, and knew you even before you were born. Write your name in the blanks and record them on your 3x5 cards. Yes, you must read them out loud.

"Before I shaped you in the womb _____, I knew you. Before you saw the light of day, I had perfect plans for you." — JEREMIAH 1:5 (MSG)

"Before I formed you in the womb _____, I knew [and] approved of you [as My chosen instrument], and before you were born I separated and set you apart, consecrating you; [and] I appointed you for a special purpose."
— JEREMIAH 1:5 (AMPC)

"For You did form my inward parts; You did knit me together in my mother's womb. I will confess and praise You for I am fearfully and wonderfully made. I praise you for the wonder of my birth! Wonderful are Your works, and my inner self knows

right well. My frame was not hidden from You when I was being formed in secret [and] intricately and curiously wrought [as if embroidered with various colors] in the depths of the earth [a region of darkness and mystery]. Your eyes saw my unformed substance, and in Your book all the days [of my life] were written before ever they took shape, when as yet there was none of them."
— Psalm 139:12–16 (AMPC)

"Many, O LORD my God, are the wonders you have done. The things you planned for me no one can recount to you; were I to speak and tell of them, they would be too many to declare." — Psalm 40:4–6 (NIV)

"I know the good plans I have for you _____ , plans to give you hope and a future, not to harm you, then you will seek me with all your heart."
— Jeremiah 29:9–11 (NIV)

"It's in Christ that you, once you heard the truth and believed it (this Message of your salvation), found yourselves home free—signed, sealed, and delivered by the Holy Spirit. This signet ring from God is the first installment on what's coming, a reminder that you _____ will get everything God has planned for you, a praising and glorious life." — Ephesians 1:13 (NIV)

"All this is proceeding along lines planned all along by God and then executed in Christ Jesus. When we trust in him, we're free to say whatever needs to be said, bold to go wherever we need to go." — Ephesians 3:11 (NIV)

"God had planned something better for us so that only together with us would they be made perfect." — Hebrews 11:40 (NIV)

My prayer for you as we end our day of discovery together is that you realize that before time began, you—the unique and original you—were created on purpose for a purpose by the God who created the Universe. I pray as He reveals your identity to you, you will begin to believe He has good plans for you, plans He created for you before time began. I pray that you will believe that you, my dear friend, were wanted and planned.

You can choose to believe it even if you don't feel it.

Your Name Has Meaning

Daily Discovery Process

We human beings have been bestowing names, using them to give significance to peoples' lives since the beginning of recorded history. If you have ever had children, you know the weighty responsibility that comes with bestowing a name upon another human being, a name they will carry throughout their life. It is a source of great conversation and even controversy during the long nine months of pregnancy. Almost immediately, the masses of family members begin asking, "What are you going to name the baby?" Everyone has an opinion, but no one gets a vote except the parents. Names, just like identities, are bestowed upon us and can provide clues to "who we are."

Southerners are especially fond of family names. We use our fathers' names as first names; we create double names from our grandfathers' names, and frequently use our mothers' or even grandmothers' maiden names in the mix. Just ask my sons. Some of us are named from books our parents loved or from the movies they watched. My dad named me Jenny after a movie he saw and loved while my mom was pregnant with me called *The Portrait of Jenny*. While I have never seen the movie, I always loved hearing how I got my name. It was a part of my unique story. My Aunt Dean thought Jenny sounded more like a nickname and bestowed the name Jennifer upon me and put it on my birth certificate. No one has ever called me Jennifer. That name never fit me. Since I was a tomboy, it sounded too girly and formal for me.

When I first discovered the meaning of Jennifer, it confirmed my suspicions that I was not one.

Jennifer means *fair one* or *white beauty*. I was neither fair, as in fair maiden, nor have I ever felt particularly beautiful. I was a Jenny. However, I hated the definitions I found. Jenny was either a *donkey* or a *washing machine*, a spinning Jenny. My middle name is Lee, inserted by my Mom. It was the middle name of my great-grandfather Benjamin. It gave my mom and me the same initials, J.L.T. Jenny Lee. Yikes. I have never loved my name; I thought it was ordinary and plain like me. It is interesting how my name and my self-concept became one and the same. I longed to be called Victoria or Alexandra. Those names sounded so daring and exciting to me, things I believed I was not. That is, until I took my journey of purpose.

I never contemplated how much weight a name carries from an identity and destiny perspective until a trip I took back to my home in the San Francisco Bay area just after having moved to Sacramento, California. I was going to be with the women who had served as my righteous girlfriends—women on similar journeys of purpose. I was their leader. We had met together once a week for seven years and I missed them. Unbeknownst to me, on that day the new leader of the group had been researching the names of each group member—mine included. When I arrived, these precious women surrounded me with love and bestowed a gift upon me I will never forget.

> *Jenny, your name means courageous, grace-filled, and straightforward. God wants you to know He sees you, that He has called you by name. Your name is the essence of your life's message.*

The words were like having living water and liquid peace poured over my soul. I was stunned. My name was not random after all. I found this new truth to be intoxicating, life changing, and transforming, especially on this day during a particularly difficult time in my life. It was one where I was fighting to keep my identity in tact and my dreams alive.

Sobbing ensued as these words went straight to my heart. Courageous. Me? I had been scared for most of my life, paralyzed by the fear of embarrassment. However, somewhere inside of me I remembered the active, courageous little girl I once was. In an instant, the past and present collided in my mind, giving me confirmation of who I was created to be. Hearing that description of my name on that day was as if a voice cheered me on telling me not to quit because I was created to be courageous. My name was a clue to my true identity and destiny.

Later, I pondered the other words *grace-filled* and *straightforward*. I wondered what they meant. Like the word courageous, graceful or grace-filled was not a description many would use to describe me. I tend to be more like a bull in a china shop. *Straightforward* was rather perplexing also. I had always been scared of hurting someone's feelings. Because of that fear, I would never come right out and say anything directly. Then I had a revelation, a whisper from my Maker.

"I created you to be a communicator, a courageous leader, whose words would be straightforward but filled with grace."

My heart almost burst. That is who I wanted to be! My soul recognized the truth and instantly I chose to believe. This was my identity. I was so excited over the revelation that my name produced that suddenly I wanted to *be* courageous, grace-filled, and direct. I loved this new identity and I chose to believe it. When I believed these new words about me, they produced feelings of confidence that were about to erupt into new positive behaviors in my life. I could not wait to be me, and now I want everyone I know to experience the same thing.

Consult Your Creator

Expect tangible, surprising evidence along your journey to help convince you that you have a grand purpose and destiny. Look for proof until you find it. Some clues to your identity and destiny are revealed as surprises just when you need them, but others you must go looking for. Have you considered your name for clues? I had not. Someone else did it for me. After my research, I am convinced that names offer important clues to our identities and destinies. It seems God and man have been bestowing names and using them to give identities since the beginning of time. As you read the words below, contemplate how important a name is.

"God spoke: 'Light!' And light appeared. God saw that light was good and separated light from dark. God named the light Day, he named the dark Night. It was evening, it was morning—Day One. God spoke: 'Sky! In the middle of the waters; separate water from water!' God made sky. He separated the water under sky from the water above sky. And there it was: he named sky the Heavens. It was evening, it was morning—Day Two. God spoke: 'Separate! Water-beneath-Heaven, gather into one place; Land, appear!' And there it was. God named the land Earth. He named the pooled water Ocean. God saw that it was good." — GENESIS 1:3, 4, 9 (MSG)

"God had formed out of the ground all the beasts of the field and all the birds of the air. He brought them to the man to see what he would name them; and whatever the man called each living creature, that was its name." — GENESIS 2:19 (MSG)

"The man called his wife's name Eve [life spring], because she was the mother of all the living." — GENESIS 3:20 (MSG)

"He created them male and female and blessed them. And when they were created, he named them [both] 'man.'" — GENESIS 5:2 (NIV)

"She gave this name to the LORD who spoke to her: 'You are the God who sees me,' for she said, 'I have now seen the One who sees me.'" — GENESIS 16:13 (NIV)

Your Story

Have you ever searched the meaning of your name? Are you intrigued? Many books and websites give the origin and definition of names. However, be diligent and dig for the root meaning of your entire name. Some of us receive immediate revelation about our names and identities. I've met others for whom the correlation was not so obvious. Do not be discouraged if this is the case when you search for the meaning of your name. Consult your Creator to determine if your name can give you clues to your unique identity and world-changing destiny. I once met a woman whose name was Melanie. When she looked up the meaning of her name said told me it meant "dark." She asked me, "How can this be a clue to my identity or destiny. Am I dark?" I could see the hurt on her face. I paused as I looked into her eyes and revelation filled my spirit. "Maybe your name means you are to bring light into the darkness." We both smiled.

Researching your name is only the beginning of the process. When you find the true meaning of your name, then you must consult your Creator to ask Him how it applies to your identity and destiny, or even IF it does.

When you find a good "name" website, research your first name, then your middle, and then your last. Scan the words to see which ones resonate with you. Ask God for the relevance of your name. Do you know who named you? Do you know the story of why that name was chosen for you? If so, write it down. Search for the hidden meaning and significance of your name like you would a diamond in the rough. Don't be discouraged if the information doesn't immediately come to you, or if you don't like your name or its meaning. I was forty-six before I was given the gift and significance of my name. Neither God, nor the mountains easily gives up its treasures. You must hunt for it. Ask a family member to help you on your journey. Sometimes a grandparent, aunt, uncle, or cousin has information about our lives that even our parents don't have or aren't comfortable sharing with us. Think about someone in your family that you are particularly close to—maybe they have your treasure. Even if they don't, know *you* are the treasure!

_____
_____
_____
_____
_____
_____
_____
_____
_____

Week Two

Uniquely You

My prayer for you today is that your name search and assessment has given you clues to your true identity and destiny. I pray perseverance and patience for you this week as you continue to seek your Creator for them.

Family Names Can Be Clues, Too

Daily Discovery Process

If you are disappointed or less than excited about your name, don't worry; there are exciting things to come. I received my entire identity *without* the name piece. The name piece for me came later in my journey on the very day I needed a reminder of my identity and destiny. Your situation may be the very same. Be patient. Consult your Creator and listen as He whispers your name. Admit it—you love hearing your name lovingly called.

"Fear not for I have redeemed you [restored your honor, your worth, your reputation, your name, and recovered all that was lost]. I have summoned you by <u>name</u>, you are mine." — Isaiah 43:1 (AMPC)

When your name is called, hear the hidden whisper of your Maker claiming you as His own child. Your name is important.

"May your heavenly father's name be echoed and perpetuated in your life. May your name and his be joined." —Author Unknown

Having God call you by name, imagining He even divinely inspired your parents to give you your name, is something that fills me with wonder. It all says to me, "You are mine, you belong and you are known."

Being Known. That is what our hearts long for; that is our identity as a unique child of God and what we need to hear to be able to do the great things planned for us before time began. I pray you are beginning to understand the depth of God's love for you as His child and that you are beginning to catch a glimpse of how carefully God imagined, planned, and uniquely created you. I pray you are starting to feel God's delight in you and that you are beginning to know you were created on purpose for a purpose. It is your inheritance. It is your identity. You must believe. God not only has plans for you but for your entire family.

My Story

I became curious about the names of the people in my life I loved. Revelation continued as I researched my families and friends' names. I was shocked at how the definitions of their names represented many facets of their personalities.

I found my father's name incredibly appropriate: Charles, a mighty warrior. He is a mighty warrior, but I had married one as well. My husband is Charles Michael. Per the Bible, Michael is a fierce, warrior angel. Both men have a strong, fighting spirit that will not allow them to ever quit, turn tail, or run. They have infused, inspired, and encouraged me to be me with their love, courage, and tenacious spirits.

I was amused, but not surprised, that all my sons, Steven Austin, Michael Dean, and Benjamin Kemp, also have champion, victorious, or warrior descriptions attributed to one of their names. They are each strong young men who do not give up easily. The other name held meanings that were unique to them alone and very appropriate. One is a peace-filled green valley, another is called beloved, and the other is royal or regal. I was fascinated by how accurately their names described aspects of their personalities. I was fascinated because I did not research the meanings of their names prior to naming each one.

My middle name, Lee, is translated as "a green valley or a place of rest," which is my favorite color and my favorite place in the world. It is also the same meaning as the names of my beloved great-grandfather, grandfather, aunt, and middle son—*Dean*. Being in the presence of each one of them is like walking beside still waters near a green valley. Janey, my mom's and niece's name, means "God is gracious." It is true. My mom is one of the most gracious human beings on this planet. Her middle name is Lucy, meaning "bringer of light." Everyone in my family would agree that my mom is a gracious light bearer in each of our lives. Again, I was wowed by the meanings of our names and the part they had played in our individual identity, but also our collective family identity. From my name search and by studying our family history, I learned we have a collective identity of fighters, warriors in a battle who are to be a voice for those who have no voice.

Day Five

Your Story

Look up your family names. Last names, middle names, as well as your children's names. In these family names, you may come to see a common identity thread like I did in my family. Write your discoveries below. Did they provide any clues to your individual or family identity?

_____
_____
_____
_____
_____
_____
_____
_____
_____
_____
_____
_____
_____
_____
_____
_____
_____
_____
_____
_____
_____
_____
_____
_____
_____
_____

My prayer for you as you end this day of discovery is that you'll hear your heavenly Father whispering these words to you, *"I am pleased with you and I know you by name,"* (EXODUS 33:17, NIV). I pray that today has you contemplating, not only your identity and destiny, but also that of your entire family.

Righteous Girlfriend/ Mighty Warrior

Identity Boot Camp

– Day 1 –

Reflect back over the first day of the DDP. Share any "ah ha!" moments you had during day one of the DDP, such as silent vows, negative words, or any one event when you quit being you.

– Day 2 –

What truth(s) do you think God wants you to know about yourself? Share 1-2 things you learned.

– Day 3 –

Do you believe your life was planned? Share with your group where are you in the journey of discovering your identity and destiny and how this issue of your life being planned has affected you.

– Day 4 –

What does your name mean? Discuss whether it gives you any clues to your identity or destiny.

– Day 5 –

Did you make any discoveries or common identity threads as you looked up your family names as to a collective family identity or destiny? Ask your group for their input or thoughts.

Remember to ask for prayer requests and pray at the end of each session. If time allows, write down your prayer request on a piece of paper and pass it to the person on your right. Commit to praying each day for that particular righteous friend. Tuck their card into your Uniqueness Assessment so you will remember to pray for them each day.

Believe God for this person as you learn to believe God for yourself.

Beloved.
Belong.
Believe.

Beloved. Belong. Believe. I love these words. They resound deep within me, providing a much-needed melody to my soul. They soothe and encourage me. I want to be called *beloved* by another. I need to have a place to *belong*, where I am a part of something bigger than myself. I long to *believe* that the world, or at least someone, needs me to be me. Beloved. Belong. Believe. These words reveal the secret desires of our hearts, planted there by our Creator, used to draw us to Him.

To live and make choices out of our true identity, we need to hear these affirming words. None of us are immune to their powerful, transforming work. They are essential ingredients of water-walking, giant-slaying, history-making destinies. When we know we are *loved* and have a place to *belong*, it becomes much easier to *believe* that we have a world-changing destiny. Belief allows the impossible to become possible and the ordinary to become extraordinary. Subsequently, when this belief saturates our entire being, our behaviors that don't line up with our true identity and keep us from our destiny will begin changing to align with how we think and feel about ourselves. It seems even Jesus needed these words of affirmation from His Father (MATTHEW 3:17; 17:5).

Beloved

In Henri Nouwen's book *Parting Words*, he talks about the identity of *beloved*.

> *I very much believe the core moment of Jesus' public life was the baptism in the Jordan, when Jesus heard the affirmation, "You are my beloved on whom my favor rests." That is the core experience of Jesus. He is reminded in a deep, deep way of* **who he is**. *The temptations in the desert are temptations to move him away from that spiritual identity. He was tempted to believe he was someone else: You are the one who can turn stone into bread. You are the one who can jump from the temple. You are the one who can make others bow to your power. Jesus said, "No, no, no. I am the Beloved from God." I think his whole life is continually claiming that identity in the midst of everything ... Prayer, then, is listening to that voice—to the One who calls YOU beloved. It is to constantly go back to the truth of who we are and claim it for ourselves. I'm not what I do. I'm not what people say about me. I'm not what I have. Although there is nothing wrong with success, there is nothing wrong with popularity, there is nothing wrong with being powerful, finally my spiritual identity is not rooted in the world, or the things the world gives me. My life is rooted in my spiritual identity. Whatever we do, we have to go back regularly to that place of core identity.*

Being called *beloved*, knowing we are loved, is essential to believing we matter and have a grand purpose in this world. Other people may or may not have called you beloved. It seems human love is fickle at best and very often is dependent upon our behavior, performance, or ability to meet the needs of another. *Loving ourselves well is our responsibility* and a directive from God. Matthew, Mark, Paul, and James all highlighted it in the books they authored in the Bible. Look up the following these verses. I used the Message translation. What is the common message in each passage? Summarize them in your own words and compare what they are telling you.

MATTHEW 22:37–40

MARK 12:29–31

MARK 12:32–33

Romans 13:8–10

Galatians 5:13–15

Philippians 2:1–4

James 2:8–11

If you didn't already come up with it on your own, the common message is: **"Love others as well as you love yourself."** It is very difficult to love someone who does not love him or her self. In this effort of discovering our identity and fulfilling our destiny, loving ourselves, even liking ourselves, is paramount to the journey. To love yourself, you must make a careful assessment of who you are and who you are not. It is very interesting how other people will love you to the degree that you love yourself. However, God longs to love you as you are, all the while wooing you to be the person He created you to be so you can fill your mission on this planet.

God unveils His intentions for you through the lens of His extravagant love. He sees who you are supposed to be, who He created you to be. He does not see what you lack. He sees your potential. He doesn't focus on your weaknesses but reveals your strengths. He uses His love to transform you into a water-walking, giant-slaying, history-making individual. It will absolutely take courage to be and do all you were created for, but it will also require that you choose to see yourself as God sees you and hear Him whisper *beloved*.

You are called beloved. You can choose to embrace this as part of your identity. It may be the most courageous decision you ever make. Embarking on an exciting journey of purpose without loving yourself is extremely difficult. If you do not love yourself well, you will never believe you have what it takes to step out of your familiar boat or situation and walk on water. Loving yourself may take practice if the concept is new to you. Having a place to belong helps.

Belong

Before time began, you were intentionally created on purpose for a purpose. God wants to display His splendor in you. Your identity and destiny is to convince the world there is a God. You were designed to bring His presence and power into every situation you enter. You are a beloved child, planned and picked to be in a family. You were meant to "wow" the world.

"For you did not receive a spirit that makes you a slave again to fear, but you received the Spirit of sonship (adoption/being chosen). And to him we cry, Abba (Daddy), Father. The Spirit himself testifies with our spirit that we are God's children. Now if we are children, we are heirs – heirs of God and co-heirs with Christ if indeed we share in his sufferings in order that we may also share his glory. I consider our present sufferings are not worth comparing with the glory that will be revealed in us. Creation waits in eager expectation for the sons of God to be revealed." — Romans 8:15–19

"But when the time had fully come, God sent his Son, born of a woman, born under law to redeem those under law, that we might receive the full rights of sons. Because you are sons, God sent the Spirit of his Son into our hearts, the Spirit who calls out, Abba Father. So you are no longer a slave, but a son and since you are a son, God has also made you an heir." — Galatians 4:5–7

Excerpt taken from the footnotes in the NIV:
"Under roman law, an adopted child was guaranteed all legal rights to his father's property, even if he was formerly a slave. He was not a second-class son; he was equal to all other sons, biological or adopted, in his father's family. As adopted children of God, we share with Jesus all rights to God's resources. As God's heirs, we can claim what he has provided for us – our full identity as his children."

"He foreordained us (destined us, planned in love for us) to be adopted (revealed) as His own children through Jesus Christ, in accordance with the purpose of His will (because it pleased Him and was His kind intent)." — Ephesians 1:5 (AMPC)

You are a child of God. Let that sink in. You have been adopted into His family. If you were raised going to church your entire life, that sentence may not wow you or seem the least bit significant to your identity and destiny. Often, mere repetition of a phrase can remove its designed impact and implication. If you have never heard or entertained the thought, it may seem like religious jargon and not carry much weight for you either. However, I promise you this: Your entire world-changing destiny hinges on you believing and accepting this divine identity.

Believe
This is the real identity secret. This is the key that unlocks your destiny. Belief. It is a choice, not a feeling. You are a beloved child of God adopted into a loving family much larger than your biological one. It is an unmovable, never-changing, irrevocable identity. If you do not realize, internalize, and personalize this identity, then you will never believe you can walk on water, slay giants with stones, or change the course of history for all eternity. Without believing in this identity and claiming it as your own, you will never step into your destiny.

This identity guarantees that you are loved, planned, and have a place to belong. Your identity does not depend upon the family you were born into, or the labels bestowed upon you by yourself or others. This identity is truth. Low self-esteem, co-dependent, addict, overweight, orphan, or any other label you struggle under is simply that—a label. It is not who you are; it is not your identity. Chosen, cherished, and valued now describe you. This identity guarantees you success in your destiny. However, it requires belief.

This week we will go deeper into the concepts of being beloved and having a place to belong. During week four we will concentrate on the choice of belief. Before the two weeks are up you will be chanting with me—beloved, belong, believe.

c2bu.com/vid4

You Are Royalty

Daily Discovery Process

My grandmother's father died when she was still in the womb. Her mom was twenty-one years old, pregnant with my grandmother, her fifth child. She was far away from her family and home when he died. She was scared, alone, and pregnant with four other small children. She had to get back home. I cannot imagine how scared she must have been. There is no detailed account or family stories of how my grandmother Maude traveled with her small family back to her home in Memphis, Tennessee. However, we do know that during this journey she gave birth to my grandmother and buried her oldest daughter, Clara, who died of scarlet fever. I do not know how she kept going. Courage? A sense of purpose? Faith in God? I have no idea.

However, I do know when Maude arrived in Memphis, she sought the help of family members. Sadly, no one's financial or living situation was such that they could provide for an additional family. She found no one who would or could take them in. Therefore, Maude did the only thing she could do—she gave her children away.

It was easier finding homes for the boys. Boys could milk cows, chop wood, and pick cotton. So when various family members offered to take the boys, Maude agreed. What choice did she have? To save them, she had to let them go. The girls proved more difficult to place. My grandmother, the youngest, was placed in an orphanage and put up for adoption.

Meet Eleanor and Benjamin
In another small Tennessee town there lived a loving couple. Though they had everything money could buy, the one and only thing their hearts truly desired—children—was denied

to them. While they hoped and prayed for little ones to hold, Benjamin Lee Thomas and Eleanor Glass Thomas lived a generous life, helping those in need in their community. Though physically barren, they remained pregnant with the possibility of having a child.

Somehow, during the course of their ordinary days, Benjamin and Eleanor heard about Maude's situation and how my grandmother was put in an orphanage. They left their hometown in Milan, Tennessee, and booked a train ride to Memphis to meet Maude. I wonder, did they know it was a journey to their destiny, to their long-awaited daughter, to my grandmother and eventually to me, their great-granddaughter?

After many visits and many hours of sharing their hearts, the Thomas's offered to adopt my grandmother. They wanted to give her a new home, a new family, and a new life. They offered Maude dignity by asking her permission, and they offered my grandmother a new name and identity.

The day Benjamin and Eleanor took my grandmother to their home, they adopted her into their hearts. She was their long-awaited daughter. They called her family, giving her their name and a new one of her own, "Elizabeth," which means, "God's promise." She was to them a promise fulfilled.

My grandmother loved her new name. She believed it reflected her identity and solidified her destiny. With adoption, her life changed. She was now a beloved daughter, not an abandoned child left in an orphanage. She had a place where she belonged, and no one could take that away from her. She not only believed she had the same rights and privileges of a biological child, but she saw evidence of it daily. Her identity became one of chosen, redeemed, and loved. Because of that new identity, my grandmother came to believe she could change the world!

I love this story of my grandmother's, my Mimi's, adoption. It mirrors our own. It does not matter how or as whom we started this life. It matters not what circumstances we have been through—pain, death, infertility, poverty, or even abuse. They are no matches for the extravagant love and good plans our Creator, our Heavenly Father has for us, His adopted children. We are His and He loves us madly. We cannot change our past, but adoption into God's family can certainly change our future.

Consult Your Creator

As you consult your Creator for your identity, choose to embrace your royal heritage. Ask your Heavenly Father to pour His truth on any lies you have believed. Thank God for adopting you into His family. Ask Him if He truly delights in you. The following are fabulous identity verses to write on your 3x5 cards. Write your name in the blanks below.

Uniquely You

Day One

"The spirit himself testifies (bears witness) with our spirit that you _____, are God's child. Now if you _____, are God's child then you are an heir of God and co-heir with Jesus. Your present sufferings are not worth comparing with the glory that will be revealed in you. The creation waits in eager expectation for you _____, the child of God to be revealed." — ROMANS 8:16–19 (NIV)

Doesn't that last sentence of that verse make your heart sing? Creation—the trees, the flowers, the creeks, and rivers are eagerly waiting in great expectation for you to be you—the *you* God created!

"But when the time arrived, set by God the Father, He sent His son, born among us of a woman, born under the conditions of the law so that he might redeem us who have been kidnapped by the law. Thus we have been set free to experience our rightful heritage. You _____, can tell for sure that you are now fully adopted as his own children, because God sent the Spirit of His Son into our lives to cry out Papa! Father! Doesn't that privilege of intimate conversation with God make it plain that you _____, are not a slave to anything but a child? And if you _____, are His child, you are also an heir with complete access to the inheritance." — GALATIANS 4:4 (MSG)

Your Story

You, my friend, are the child of the King. You are royalty. You have rights and an inheritance that no one can ever take away from you.

Before you can be and do all you were created for, this issue of identity is one that must be settled in your heart and in your mind. You cannot seek your identity from other human beings, even those who say they love you. Their love is flawed and imperfect, and they probably struggle with their own identity issues. Only your Creator, your Abba Father, can tell you who you are and who He created you to be. Take a long walk and listen for His voice, His confirmation of whom you are—His child, His beloved.

Take a moment to journal your thoughts about the implications of this new identity, your adoption. Does your relationship with your earthy parents affect this concept? What type of relationship did you have with your earthly Dad and/or Mom? Did someone delight in you?

Did you have a sense of belonging? Did you grow up with both parents in your home or were you a part of a blended family? Who were you the closest to? What is your first reaction to the words *Mom* or *Dad*? Exploring these relationships may help you embrace your identity as a child of God.

Many times our earthly relationships greatly impact our relationship with our Heavenly Father and our ability to believe His truth about our identity as His children. If your father or mother was a strict disciplinarian, distant, cold, or even absent, you may believe your Heavenly Father is the same way. Write and reflect on your relationships. Ask God to free you from any unhealthy emotional ties to them. Reflect upon the fact that despite your biological relationships, you have been adopted into a new family and bestowed a new name—you are the daughter or son of the King. You are royalty. You have an inheritance. You are now free to receive both. God is bigger than the circumstances into which you were born. God is bigger than the parenting you did or did not receive. Can you forgive your parents for not being all you wanted or needed them to be? Ask God to help you.

_____
_____
_____
_____
_____
_____
_____
_____
_____
_____
_____
_____
_____
_____

If you grew up with loving parents in an emotionally healthy home, thank God for that relationship and for that firm foundation in your life. Then write your parent(s) thanking them for loving you well. Reflect on how that relationship impacts the one you have or don't have with God.

_____
_____

My desire and prayer for you is to experience the freedom that comes from knowing your true identity as a child of God. Your inheritance is a world-changing destiny that will change you and others. It is birthed out of this identity. This identity is one you can be secure in and courageously act out of, even if it takes a while for all the implications to sink in. It certainly did for me.

As we end this day of discovery, let me impart a blessing on you that I quoted earlier in this assessment:

> *"May your heavenly father's name be echoed and perpetuated in your life.*
> *May your name and his be joined."*

I pray you are beginning to believe God really loves you and that you are letting that love seep into the secret places of your heart. I pray you are beginning to catch a glimpse of how carefully God imagined, planned, and uniquely created you. I pray you are starting to feel God's delight in you! I pray as you end your day today you will go to sleep hearing your Father call your name and whisper these words to your soul: *"You are my beloved, in whom I am well pleased."* I pray you let that affirmation change you. I pray it softens your heart and tears down the walls you have erected for protection. I pray you are beginning to awaken to the inheritance you have as a child of the King. I pray you are beginning to know you were created on purpose for a purpose. Blessings dear one.

You Are Adopted

Daily Discovery Process

I love my grandmother's story on so many levels, not just because it is my family history, but because of the message it bears about God of how He holds our lives in His hands. God continues to bestow our identity upon us as He leads us into our destiny in spite of the worst of circumstances—pain, death, infertility, and poverty. None of these are a match for the love God has for His adopted children. The choices Maude, Eleanor, and Benjamin made are still rippling down to me, my brothers and sisters, and our children. Though adopted into that family, we are their heirs and the recipients of their legacy. It is our inheritance—our spiritual inheritance.

You are no different. We all have been chosen and adopted. Before time began God bestowed upon us His name and title of "beloved daughter" or "beloved son." You, my friend, are quite simply the child of the king. A royal prince or princess! Your spirit already knows it—it just may be that your mind and soul haven't caught on yet. You may need to go get a tiara or crown to place upon your head and parade around your house! If that doesn't work, maybe this story will.

My Story

When I first tried to truly understand and embrace what it meant to be a child of God, I asked God for a picture. I am a visual learner so I thought a picture might help. One day as I was journaling the verses I had you write your name in yesterday, I saw in my mind's eye a picture of a corporate boardroom high in the heavens with large ornate, wooden double doors.

In this vision..
> *I was a small child approaching those huge doors. I slowly walked up to those doors and reached up for the handles. I had to stand on my tippy toes just to grasp them. It*

took both my little hands and the weight of my entire body to twist and push the door open. When I did, I literally spilled into the room. From my position on the floor, I looked up. There was an enormous room, surrounded on all sides by glass. I could see clouds floating by the windows as if I was high in the sky on an airplane but we weren't moving, only the clouds were. Beyond the clouds, I could see earth in the distance. In the center of the room, an enormous conference table dominated and took up most of the space. I surveyed my surroundings further and noticed large, plush chairs with very high backs surrounding the table that almost looked like thrones.

There were some very serious people sitting in them, some dressed in silk robes, some wore crowns filled with jewels, and some wore business suits with ties. However, each of them wore a confidence that instantly made me know they were very important people and that I was interrupting a very important meeting. The expressions on their faces were one of disdain and disapproval both for my surprise entrance and for me. Before I could collect myself or catch my breath, I felt the old, unwelcome emotions of embarrassment and humiliation begin to cloak and choke me. I was frozen to the spot on the floor, incapable of moving. Tears began to slide down my cheeks as I dropped my gaze. I was filled with shame. Then all of a sudden, I heard a chair quickly being pushed back across the magnificent hard wood floors and a voice called out my name. "Jenny?" I immediately recognized the voice and looked up. It was my Heavenly Father, looking more regal and confident than anyone in the room. He began to run toward me and scooped me up in his arms. As he did he proudly announced to the entire room, "This is my daughter!" There were murmurs followed by laughter and clapping. In a deep, rich voice my Heavenly Father cleared the room. He told all these very important people to leave because his daughter needed him. Immediately, everyone obeyed.

It was obvious my Dad was in charge and the most important person in the room. He tucked me under his chin and walked me back to his chair that sat at the head of the table. He sat me in his lap, comforted me, and stroked my hair until the ugly emotions of embarrassment and humiliation left, just like all the important people had. I was surrounded by the clouds and by an intimate cocoon of love. I whispered, "I'm sorry I bothered you and interrupted your important meeting." My Dad took my chin and lifted it until we were almost nose-to-nose. He found my gaze, looked deep into my eyes, and whispered to me, "Jenny, you are the most important thing in my life. I am here for you whenever you need me. You delight me. All you have to do is ask." Liquid love entered the core of my being whispering to my spirit and confirming my identity as His beloved child. I belonged here. It was my rightful place.

With that new confidence, I began to pour out all my hurts and disappointments of the day. Someone was mean to me. Someone didn't include me. Someone betrayed me. I was hungry and sad and tired. He listened to me intently. He asked me questions. He

validated my feelings. When I had exhausted all my words, He asked me if I needed anything else. I shook my head yes. "I need a hug." He honored that request, enveloped me in his arms once again, and then kissed me on the top of my head. With that, I jumped from his lap and ran back through the large double doors. "Bye Dad!" I called.

A few days later, I was at church. The pastor was speaking on God's love. During her sermon, she showed an old black and white photo of President John F. Kennedy. He was at the White House in the Oval Office. In the photo there was an enormous desk. It filled the room and the photo. President Kennedy was dressed formally, deserving of the office and room. He was in a suit and tie. He sat in the overstuffed, leather presidential chair. To a child, it could look like a small throne. Windows surrounded the room, along with paintings of important looking people. The American flag was to his left. It took me a minute to notice that in the front of the desk there was a cut out, a secret door that a little boy was peeking out of. He could not have been more than three or four years old. It was John John, his son. He was playing in the Oval Office, literally inside the President's desk, as if it was a fort.

What person would have been allowed that type of access to arguably the most important, influential person in the world? Only the man's son or daughter could have access like that. Though the President of the United States, John John called him "Daddy," and he was just as important to him as ruling and governing the nation and influencing the world.

This is the picture God wants to paint on your soul. You matter to Him. He calls you "child" and that title gives you complete access to Him—anytime. Though He rules the Universe, He is not too busy to hear your heart, your hurts, and kiss your bumps and bruises. He desires your presence. He delights in you. He wants you to live out of that identity as "dearly loved child."

Your Story

In the spaces below, reflect and journal your thoughts, feelings, as well as any doubts or questions regarding the concept of you being adopted and called "child" by the one who made the stars in the sky, the planets in orbit, the sun and moon, as well as all the creatures on this planet, including you. Start by saying out loud, "I am the child of the King. Loved and beloved, I belong."

_____
_____
_____
_____
_____

My prayer for you as we end this day is that you will be free to experience your rightful heritage as an adopted daughter or son of the King. I pray this knowledge will give you confidence in whom you are and that you will begin to call God your Abba Father. Your heavenly Daddy longs to tell you whom you are—all you have to do is ask. I keep a tiara beside my bed as a reminder of who I am. A princess! You might want to get one, too.

You Are Beloved

Daily Discovery Process

My husband owns his own business; he is a natural gas consultant. We have worked together since the year 2000. At one particular time in our business life, our natural gas supplier informed us that we would have to obtain letters of credit from all of our clients or else we would no longer be able to purchase our natural gas. This simple revelation meant we would have no business, thus no jobs or income. Let's just say this proclamation produced a tad bit of stress in our home.

Prior to our supplier's phone call, I had begun to live out my new identity. I had even made strides in discovering my water-walking destiny. For the first time in thirty years, I was being me and loving it! That is until my husband declared that obtaining the letters of credit was *my* new job responsibility. I did not even know what a letter of credit was much less how to obtain one. My boss (i.e., my husband) offered no advice except *figure it out or we lose the business*. No pressure whatsoever.

The first thing I felt was the old, yet familiar fear: I am about to be embarrassed, humiliated, and ashamed. It seemed imminent or so I convinced myself. For days, I did nothing. Fear paralyzed me. I felt like I was ten years old again walking to the principal's office. Suddenly, I had no ability to access my new identity.

Then the phone rang. It was a dear woman and my spiritual mentor, Terri Fenwick. She asked,

> *"What are you doing?"*

Without taking a breath or uttering any pleasantries, I blurted out my predicament. I was blatantly hoping to receive sympathy from her for the incredible burden and responsibility my husband had saddled me with. She and her husband owned their own business so I thought she would commiserate with me. Much to my surprise, I got neither from Miss Terri. Instead, she confronted me.

> *"How many phone calls have you made to the bankers?"*

> *"None,"* I whispered in my most pitiful voice.

> *"Why?"*

> *"I have no idea what to say, what I need, or what I am asking for,"* I whined. *"I feel like an idiot."*

> *"What are you wearing?"* she asked.

What am I wearing? I could not figure out what that had to do with my situation.

> *"Uh, my workout clothes from the gym?"*

With a very firm and forceful voice, she said to me something that I have never forgotten.

> *"Go take a shower right now, then put on your very best clothes and do your make-up and hair. After that, I want you to make ten phone calls to banks this afternoon, expecting with each one that you will receive exactly what you ask for. Jenny, you are the daughter of God, and His favor rests upon you. Act like it."*

Then she hung up. I felt like someone had dumped cold water on my head.

Terri's words empowered my heart and seemed to add steel to my backbone. She was right. I was a child of God. As that realization once again settled in my mind, I no longer felt like an embarrassed ten-year-old, frightened child. I was no longer afraid of being humiliated. I was nervous, but I was no longer paralyzed. I did what Terri said. I took a shower, and I took courage. Then I made those calls. With each one made, I gained more and more confidence, even though I received many very polite no's. However, they did not matter and could not alter my conviction of who I was. *I was beloved.*

I made a choice. I chose to act out of my new identity. It did not matter what I felt. I could choose. The old fears and negative feelings no longer held me hostage. My true identity was now securely in place. I continued to make those calls with complete confidence, expecting great favor. Finally, through a series of truly miraculous events, we received the letters of credit we needed to continue our business all because I had the courage to be me.

Consult Your Creator

We must stop seeking our identity and sense of self-worth from others, the past, what we do, whom we date, the title before or after our name, or how we perform. None of them matter. We must consult our Creator. He wants us to live out of our new identity.

"... therefore as dearly loved children, life a life of love ..."
— EPHESIANS 5:1

"For you are all sons [and daughters] of light and children of the day; we do not belong either to the night or to darkness but to the light."
— 1 THESSALONIANS 5:5

"For you were once in darkness but now you are light in the Lord. Live as children of light (for the fruit of light consists in all goodness, righteousness and truth. Find out what pleases the Lord (your Father). Have nothing to do with the fruitless deeds of darkness but rather expose them." — EPHESIANS 5:8–11

How do well-loved children act? What are the characteristics of a child who has been loved and called "beloved"?

_____
_____
_____
_____

They smile a lot, don't they? They have complete confidence in themselves and in those that love them. They trust easily. They aren't afraid. They are affectionate, prone to giggles and laughter. They easily believe in things they cannot see. They also believe they can do anything. That is how your Creator, your Abba Father, wants you to live.

Your Story

What would it mean for you to live out of this new identity? The identity of one who is delighted in, of one who is called "beloved child." How would that change things for you? Would you try new things? Apply for a new job? Quit an old one? Would you ask a girl out on a date? Would you be able to trust your spouse with your heart? Would you begin to believe you just might have a water-walking, giant-slaying, history-making destiny? Reflect for a moment and think about some tangible changes you could make if you believed and embraced this concept of being someone who is well loved.

_____
_____
_____
_____
_____
_____
_____
_____
_____
_____
_____
_____
_____
_____
_____
_____
_____
_____
_____
_____
_____
_____

I want to encourage those of you who did not receive the love, blessings, and affirmation from a biological father or mother when you were growing up. I recognize it can be very difficult to have a positive connotation of a Heavenly Father or adopted family if your experience with an earthly one was abusive, distant, or neglectful. It is hard to believe in others, much less yourself, when others have bestowed a false or negative identity on you. If this has been your experience, I am so sorry. How I wish I could change that reality for you.

However, I have good news! While the past cannot be changed, you can change how you think about it and what you believe about it. Old labels and identities can be replaced with new ones that reflect your true self. You are now called "beloved." You have a place where you belong. You are planned, unique, and an original. You have a destiny. That is your true identity. Believing that will change everything. Journal your thoughts and feelings in the space below about the concepts discussed today.

_____
_____
_____
_____
_____
_____
_____
_____
_____
_____
_____
_____
_____
_____
_____
_____

My heart's desire is for you to know you are the beloved child of God and to claim that identity and the inheritance that comes with it. I want you to experience the freedom that comes from only going to your Abba Father (which means "daddy" in Hebrew) for your identity instead of to another human being, whose love is flawed and imperfect. In most cases, he or she has no idea of *their* true identity.

My prayer is that you will soon have the courage to be you—the *you* God created before time began. To truly know these truths is to know freedom—the freedom to be you! Claim it! Declare it daily! Walk in it! Believe it! You are the *beloved* child of God. Don't you just want to get up and dance? Go ahead! Put on some great music and dance your heart out before the Lord! I dare you to just be you—the *you* God created. If you are reading this with your righteous girlfriends or warriors, get up and dance together! God declared that we were to have celebrations and festivals. So celebrate! Celebrate you! You are called beloved and God's favor rests on you.

You Belong

Daily Discovery Process

We have been consulting our Creator, asking Him to bestow our true identity upon us. I pray you found, maybe for the first time, that the Bible is full of life giving words; ancient words filled with unfathomable mystery and absolute truth. I pray you are now beginning to experience how God personally and uniquely uses those words to speak to you today, right where you are. Have you started making your 3x5 cards of truth? I want you to have tangible proof with you at all times that you are *created on purpose for a purpose.*

It seems we human beings have an insatiable desire to belong to something bigger than ourselves. As soon as we are weaned from our mother's breast or the bottle, the desire to attach our independent selves to another person or group begins. Both little girls and boys alike seem to announce their pick of a best friend as soon as they launch into their first social situation. Play dates and birthday parties then ensue.

Today's definition of good parenting demands that parents sign their child up to as many organized groups as early as possible. Girl and Boy Scouts, dance troupes, choirs, martial arts, drama, and every sport imaginable, all offer a child a place to belong. As we get older, neither the desire, nor the groups diminish. Book clubs, supper clubs, bars, and country clubs are on the menu to meet this need in us as adults. We are so desperate to belong that we are even willing to pay money for the privilege to add our names to a group's exclusive roster. We long to belong, to attach our names to another.

In the very beginning of the Bible, God addressed this longing, a longing that I believe He created. Almost immediately after He created and named Adam, God issued a profound statement we still recognize and still hold as truth today: "It is not good that man should be alone," (Genesis 2:18, niv). Amen! Loneliness can be incredibly painful and very far from God's design for mankind. Being alone or being left out breeds a host of emotions that are lethal to your newly uncovered identity.

The Bible is very clear that before time began there was companionship, community, and oneness. It existed between God the Father, God the Son, and God the Holy Spirit—what we call the Holy Trinity, which, when literally translated, means "the perfect three." While I do not even pretend to understand this most amazing and complex relationship, I feel I must mention it because I believe it helps explain the basis of our longing to belong. Because we belong to God, He longs for us to experience the perfection of the Holy Trinity—separate identities coming together and then becoming one. We can see the greater sum does not diminish the uniqueness of each part but only serves to enhance it. God wants us to experience this mysterious completeness that alone we never will. Thus we should not be surprised by our strong need to belong and our aversion to being alone. We started life literally attached to our mother. We were then birthed into a group, a family.

I am Jenny, the oldest daughter of four children, a single entity. However, I *belong* to a family, a family that numbers hundreds of aunts, uncles, cousins, and grandparents. When we are all together, I truly feel a part of something that is bigger than myself. Being a part of a family provides me with a shared name and identity. Though now married, I was born a *Thornton*. That one word meant that we were resilient, independent, confident, loud, athletic, and hard working. We even had a family motto, a collective identity: *We bend, but we do not break.* I can see glimpses of myself in the generations before and after me. It feels good to be connected to this group. When we are together, the longing to belong is appeased, at least for a time. However, being in one place at the same time is very difficult because we are all now scattered across the United States.

The movies we love also often highlight this longing to belong. Do you remember the classic line from the movie *Jerry Maguire?* To this day, it is one of my favorites. Tom Cruise's character whispers to Renee Zellweger's character, *"You complete me."* Every woman, who heard those words at the movie theater, gasped as her secret desire was broadcast on the screen so simply and clearly from an actor's lips straight to our own hearts.

Romantic love, belonging to another, is something we all believe will complete us. Marriage was designed to give us that sense of belonging. It was to be a place where two separate, unique individuals come together to become one, and from that oneness each entity was to be enhanced, a new life formed, and a family created. In my own marriage, I have been so fortunate to experience just that. However, I have also been divorced. I know how difficult it can be when separation occurs. It is a pain-filled process for everyone.

Friendship is another profound way I personally have experienced unity that creates a sense of belonging. Many have said that friends are the family you get to choose. I totally agree.

There are people in my life upon which I have bestowed the identity of *my friend*, but that title woefully lacks the ability to describe what they mean to my heart. One of the kids in our clan coined the phrase *God-family* to describe friends who become family. Time and distance cannot diminish the bond and the oneness we share. These friendships are divine and I believe also *created on purpose for a purpose*. We belong to each other. We regularly share our hearts and holidays, burdens and bread, joys and sorrows. We generously serve, love, and give to each other. We share every aspect of our lives. These relationships help me not to feel like I am alone in this world. These people encourage me to be and do all I was created for. They believe in me. I belong .. until one of us moves away, gets divorced, or the relationship becomes broken. Then I feel alone again.

When we are healthy, all of these attachments and relationships *can* provide us with a much-needed sense of belonging and an identity intertwined with others. However, they only seem to meet our need to belong on a temporary basis. It does not matter how many groups we belong to or identify with, each of us will find ourselves, at one time or another, alone or lonely, divorced or estranged, left or abandoned. This is incredibly painful and can breed a host of emotions that can prove lethal to our newly discovered identity.

That is why God adopted us into His family and provides an irrevocable place for us to belong. This place is not based on efforts or performance. He loved us first. He chooses us and offers a mysterious completeness that other human beings and groups can never provide. I learned this the hard way, and you will probably have to as well. People will never complete me. Your relationships will never complete you. People, and our relationships with them, are imperfect, just as we are.

People alone will never meet our need to belong. When we grasp this truth, it takes the pressure off our relationships and we can just enjoy them. We stop the frantic search to belong.

A bride and groom. Families. Friendships. All of these relationships were to be glimpses, imperfect copies, of the original design God intended for us to experience in relationship with Him. He wants to give you a permanent place to belong so you are no longer sifting through the rubble of earthly relationships looking to a mere human being to provide what only He can. As I learned this lesson, my relationships with people got stronger because I no longer depended on them to validate me. I know I have a place where I belong. I know that I am never alone. I know my identity and that I have a world-changing destiny. Do you?

You must look to your Creator to solidify this truth within you. You, too, are called beloved. You, too, have a place to belong.

Journal today about a particular relationship or group you have belonged to that made you feel a part of something bigger than your self. Attempt to articulate your longing and desire to be a part of a greater whole. Ask God to reveal the divine glimpses He has orchestrated for you on this earth to see what cannot be seen but only experienced with another. Do you have a relationship that can be called "a strand of three"? If not, ask your Abba Father for one. Do you struggle with loneliness and isolation? I pray you will be open to the righteous girlfriends or warriors in your group. I believe your heavenly Daddy has brought them into your life "for such a time as this," (ESTHER 4:14). I pray you can be open to the others who love Him and love you.

However, remember that these earthly relationships were meant to only be a taste of what you were created for and only God can provide that perfect oneness and intimacy. Only He can complete you. Only in Him will you find the place you belong.

_____
_____
_____
_____
_____
_____
_____
_____
_____
_____
_____
_____
_____
_____
_____

My prayer for you as we end today is that you are thinking about yourself differently; that you are contemplating what it means to love yourself well. I pray that you are embracing your rightful identity as a child of God and also contemplating what it means to live out of that identity. I pray the negative voices and labels you have embraced for years are being silenced and changed by the truth we have learned from our Creator.

Believe!

We Belong

Daily Discovery Process

Relationships are an important part of our identity and critical to carrying out our destiny. When relationships are coupled with a love for God, it is truly a strand of three that is nearly impossible to break. These types of friendships are divine and created by God "on purpose for a purpose." They help us feel a sense of belonging. When these relationships are coupled with a common purpose or goal, we literally can change our world. Creativity, energy, and power are increased when we come together. This is no accident.

> *"For where two or three come together in my name, there am I with them."*
> — MATTHEW 18:20

When God is in the middle of our relationships, powerful, life changing, history-making things happen! Authentic relationships divinely meet our need to belong to something bigger than ourselves and keep us from feeling so alone in this world. The people in my life, whom I call friends, my righteous girlfriends, my chosen family, are my church! In many ways, we behave like the participants of the first church written about in Acts—we regularly confess to each other, bear each others burdens, serve each other, love each other, encourage each other, give to each other, and point each other to God. It is extremely difficult for me to describe with words this experience of belonging when I am with them. Together, we truly believe we can change the world one individual at a time. I found evidence of these types of relationships in my Bible.

David and Jonathan. I love their story. I think it is one of my favorite friendship stories because it involves two men. Most men I know and have known—I have three sons, two brothers, a husband, a father, and male dogs, so I have extensive experience observing men—have such a difficult time sharing their hearts with me and with each other. They easily hit, wrestle, and joke around. Playing sports and watching sports together seems to create and solidify the male bonding experience and they are always suspicious when I want to join in with them. But in stories I have read and in movies I have watched, nothing bonds men together more than fighting together—fighting an enemy, side by side. This was also true for David and Jonathan.

Jonathan was a prince—literally. Saul, his father, was the king of Israel, which made Jonathan the rightful heir to the throne. But because of Saul's blatant disobedience to God, his throne and his title were taken away and bestowed upon another, David. In what should have been a very volatile and competitive relationship, a bond and a friendship were forged between the two unlikely friends instead. They fought, talked, and dreamed of a united kingdom together. Because of their mutual love for God, they formed a strand of three not easily broken. Other relationships in their lives were severely broken, but not theirs. Today, we might call this a soul tie. David said his sense of belonging and companionship with Jonathan was greater than any he had shared with a woman. That is pretty powerful since David shared his bed with so many of them! This statement gave me great pause. David shared physical intimacy with many women but I don't find a single biblical reference where he ever shared his heart with one. That is the essence of our longing to belong—a place where we can share our hearts. That is intimacy! That is what we were created for. Intimacy with God, and our friendships are supposed to reflect that.

Mary and Elizabeth. Theirs is another friendship I truly love. Their friendship mirrors exactly what most of us as women crave—another woman to run to and share the details of our lives and hearts with. Both are desperately needed. My righteous girlfriends, this small group of intimate friends, have been a reservoir of encouragement, hope, and laughter during my journey to uncover my identity and destiny. They believe in me and in God for me on those days when I just can't for myself. In them, as well as in my marriage and my family, all of which I equally treasure, I get glimpses of the completeness and belonging only God can provide. Slowly and sometimes painfully, I have learned to never look to them for more than that. They are just a glimpse, though, for they are an imperfect copy of the original design God intended for us to experience with Him. The sense of belonging we are looking for is an eternal one. It is imperative we grasp this truth so we can stop putting undue pressure on the people and relationships in our lives and stop frantically searching for the one person we believe can. The proverbial "they" were never meant to "complete us," but were designed to direct us to the only One who can. Our Creator.

Friendships. A bride and groom. A parent and child. All were used in the Bible and in our lives as illustrations to give us an understandable picture of what God wants with and for us.

 Uniquely You — Day Five

God wants to give you a permanent place to belong so you are no longer sifting through the rubble of earthly relationships looking for a mere human to complete you. As I consulted my Creator more and more for my identity and destiny, I found I began to depend less and less on the people in my life to validate me and give me an identity. Instead, I began to long for the relational descriptions I found in the Bible that God gave to a few. One such identity was bestowed upon Moses—He was called a friend of God. Another one was King David, a man after God's own heart. With these labels and identities it was obvious—they knew to whom they belonged and who could complete them. This knowledge is paramount to discover your destiny. You belong.

Consult Your Creator
No fill in the blanks today. Grab some more 3x5 cards and let's write. The words below are so important to your purpose. I don't ever want you to look to another person to complete you or ever feel you are alone and don't belong. Let these ancient words be your truth. Write the verses below on your cards, personalize them with your name, and title these: "*I am a child by God and I belong in His family.*"

"Everyone who confesses openly his faith in Jesus Christ — the Son of God, who came as an actual flesh-and-blood person—comes from God and belongs to God. So you my dear children, come from God and belong to God. You have already won a big victory over anyone telling you different, for the Spirit in you is far stronger than anything in the world ... We come from God and belong to God. Anyone who knows God understands us and listens. The person who has nothing to do with God will, of course, not listen to us." — 1 JOHN 4:2–4 (MSG)

"But you are a chosen people, a royal priesthood, a holy nation, a people belonging to God, that you may declare the praises of him who called you out of darkness into his wonderful light." — 1 PETER 2:8 (NIV)

"But you belong. The Holy One anointed you, and you all know it. I haven't been writing this to tell you something you don't know, but to confirm the truth you do know, and to remind you that the truth doesn't breed lies." — 1 JOHN 2:20 (NIV)

"Therefore you are no longer outsiders (exiles, migrants, and aliens, excluded from the rights of citizens), but you now share citizenship with the saints (God's own people, consecrated and set apart for Himself); and you belong to God's [own] household." — EPHESIANS 2:19 (AMP)

Week Three  Uniquely You

"That's plain enough, isn't it? You're no longer wandering exiles. This kingdom of faith is now your home country. You're no longer strangers or outsiders. You belong here, with as much right to the name Christian as anyone. God is building a home. He's using us all—irrespective of how we got here—in what he is building. He used the apostles and prophets for the foundation. Now he's using you, fitting you in brick by brick, stone by stone, with Christ Jesus as the cornerstone that holds all the parts together. We see it taking shape day after day—a holy temple built by God, all of us built into it, a temple in which God is quite at home." — EPHESIANS 2:19 (MSG)

"It is through Him that we have received grace [God's unmerited favor] and this includes you, called of Jesus Christ and invited [as you are] to belong to Him."
— ROMANS 1:5–7 (NIV)

"Just as each of us has one body with many members, and these members do not all have the same function, so in Christ we who are many form one body, and each member belongs to all the others." — ROMANS 12:4–6 (NIV)

"If we live, we live to the Lord, and if we die, we die to the Lord. So then, whether we live or we die, we belong to the Lord." — ROMANS 14:8 (NIV)

"He who belongs to God hears what God says." — JOHN 8:47 (NIV)

"If you belonged to the world, the world would treat you with affection and would love you as its own. But because you are not of the world [no longer one with it], but I have chosen [selected] you out of the world, the world hates [detests] you."
— JOHN 15:18–2

These words are the evidence I present to you that only your Creator can complete you. With His extravagant love, you can begin to love yourself well. THEN you will begin to feel a sense of belonging that will allow you to love others well. Keep these verses close this week. Read them out loud. Let them become your truth. This truth will set you free and give you the courage you need to be and do all you were created for.

I pray as we end this day, this week, you know deep within your spirit that you are a beloved child of God and belong to his family. Now as Miss Terri said, act like it!

Righteous Girlfriend/ Mighty Warrior

Beloved. Belong. Believe

– Day 1 –

There are no matches for the extravagant love and good plans our Creator, our Heavenly Father has for us, His adopted children. We are His and He loves us madly. We cannot change our past, but adoption into God's family can certainly change our future. What are some of the implications of this new identity in your life?

– Day 2 –

What were your thoughts, feelings, as well as any doubts or questions regarding the concept of you being adopted and called "child" by the One who made the stars in the sky, the planets in orbit, the sun and moon, as well as all the creatures on this planet, including you?

– Day 3 –

What would it mean for you to live out of this new identity? Reflect for a moment and think about some tangible changes you could make if you believed and embraced this concept of being someone who is well loved. Share your answers with your group.

– Day 4 –

Discuss a particular relationship or group you have belonged to that made you feel a part of something bigger than yourself. Do you have a relationship that can be called "a strand of three?"

– Day 5 –

As you wrote down and read the verses from this day, which verse helped you to know that you are a beloved child of God and that you belong to His family? What was it about the verses that spoke to you and why? Do you still struggle with this concept? Discuss your thoughts about this with your group.

Pray for each other. Write down your prayer request on a piece of paper and pass it to the person on your right. Tuck their card into your Uniqueness Assessment so you will remember to pray each day. Believe God for this person as you learn to believe God for yourself. Blessings, everyone! I am personally praying for each of you.

You are going to change the world.

What You Believe May Not be True

Did you know that what you believe could have nothing to do with truth? Your behaviors, choices, and actions could all be based upon a lie or multiple lies that you have internalized as truth. Psychologists call these erroneous beliefs negative core narratives. Established early in our childhood, they result from a negative or traumatic experience that greatly affected and shaped our choices and behaviors. Inevitably, these beliefs become deeply rooted within us, providing a lens for how we view others, our Creator, the world, and ourselves. They become the unconscious programming in our brain from where our behavior originates.

Our positive beliefs and *core narratives* do not pose many problems for us. However, the negative or false beliefs we obtained from past experiences can distort truth, limit our behaviors, and entice us to settle for so much less than we were created for. Left unexamined, they become our engrained, default behaviors and habits, which rarely align with truth.

The Psychology of Belief

I have read numerous books written by professional counselors, therapists, and psychologists who specialize in human behavior and trauma. What I found greatly influenced my own life.

You must change the way you think before you can change the way you feel, which ultimately changes how you choose to act.

In other words,

If I want to change your life, you have to change your thoughts.

Your mind is the battlefield over which your emotions, actions, and reactions are produced. Your thoughts produce your emotions, which produce your choices, behaviors, and actions. It is so very simple. We act upon that which we believe, even if it's not true.

I remember helping my boys with their fourth grade world history homework years ago. We laughed at the *truths* believed by the majority of people during Columbus' day, truths which influenced all their choices and behaviors. What they called truth, we now call silly—even to fourth grade boys. The people's fears, we quickly determined, were based on unproven truth. We examined their beliefs, and in light of what we know to be true today, judged them to be lies.

1. The world was flat, and if you tried to sail to the edge, you would fall off the edge.

2. If you sailed near the equator, your skin would turn black.

3. There was a great sea monster that would eat you alive if you sailed a certain distance from home.

We all laugh at those beliefs, now. They seem ridiculous. However, long ago many people believed and based their choices on these commonly held truths, despite the fact that they were completely false. Their beliefs produced an emotion—fear, which caused them to make the choice to stay very close to home. Their false beliefs produced self-limiting behaviors that kept them from exploring the world and from their destiny. That is, until a man came along and courageously and publicly challenged the widely held "truth" of the day. He changed the world. And you can do exactly the same thing if you begin to examine, evaluate, and challenge your own truths.

Earlier, I told you my story of the day I stopped being me. As a ten year old, I had an experience that impacted me in a negative way. When I was subjected to the principal's ridicule of my dreams and values, I felt I had done something terribly wrong, and for the first time in my life, I felt embarrassed and humiliated. In that moment, I made a silent vow *never* to attempt anything that would cause me to *feel* those emotions again. That negative experience caused me to make an incorrect assumption. I was the embarrassment. There was something wrong with *me*. It was always *my* fault. Those emotions were so strong that I agreed with the assessment.

Did you catch that? *I agreed.* I had an experience that produced a thought or an assumption about the situation. Strong, negative emotions were produced that helped persuade me to come into agreement with that assumption. That agreement produced such a strong belief that whenever I thought about it, it produced those very same negative emotions that swayed my choices and behaviors.

All this happened with lightning speed in my brain. My thoughts produced my emotions that ultimately influenced my will, my choices, and my behaviors. When I agreed with the assessment, it became a belief that produced the very emotions I was running from: embarrassment and humiliation. I was embarrassed to be me. Unconsciously, I began a systematic reprogramming of myself. Those negative emotions influenced and produced self-limiting behaviors for most of my life because the belief was buried in my little girl's heart. It went unexamined for over thirty years. However, my behaviors betrayed the belief I had about myself. Soon, I had predictable and default behaviors ready to erupt during any potentially embarrassing situation. The lies and subsequent behaviors robbed me of my destiny for years—and if left unexamined, yours will, too.

Default Behaviors

Let's break down the process that I have described. At the center is an experience. That experience produces an assumption telling us whether the experience was good or bad. In our minds, we then come into agreement with that thought. At that moment, the agreement produces a belief that has nothing to do with truth. From that point on, whenever we think about that experience or belief, an emotion is produced that is in line with our belief.

Therefore, what we think and then how we feel will produce a behavior in line with those beliefs and feelings. This process repeats year after year, faster and faster, until that behavior becomes a default one—a behavior to which you give no thought. It has become a knee-jerk, yet predictable action that occurs in common situations. You may not even remember why.

Here is a visual to help you connect the dots.

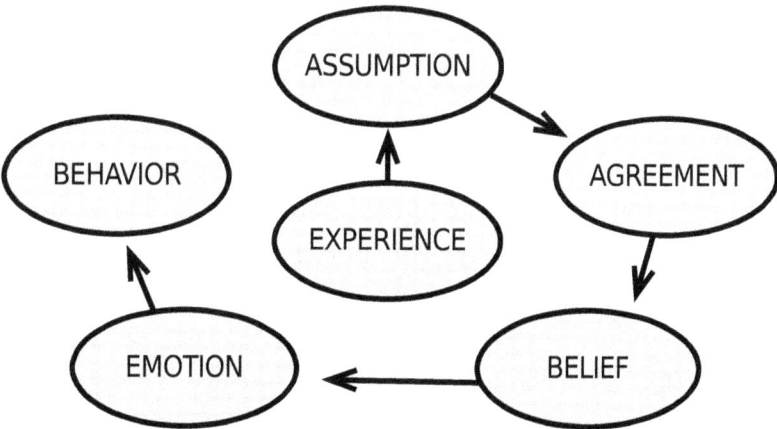

Now, let us break the sequence down into smaller components.

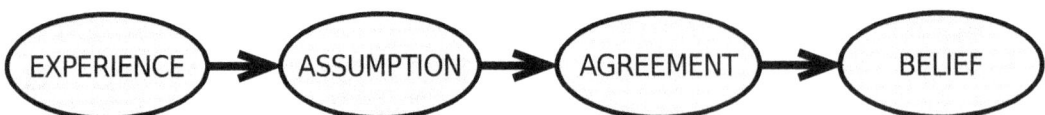

We have an experience where an assumption is formed. We then either agree or disagree with that assumption. Based on that decision, a belief is formed. Where and when was truth examined in this scenario? Nowhere. Truth has not been introduced at all.

Now consider the following:

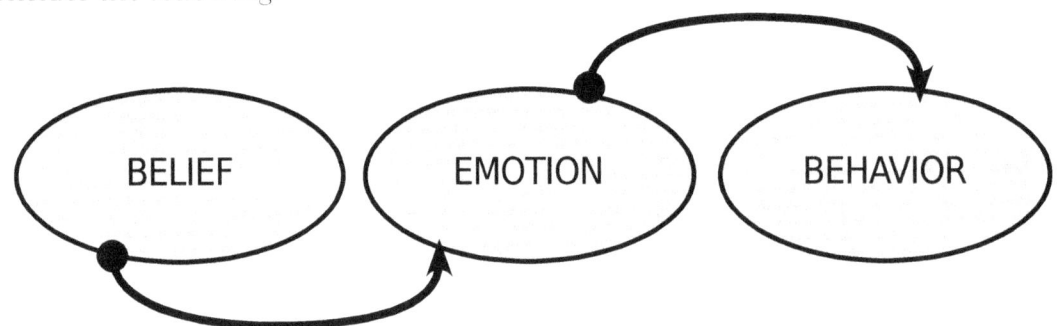

Belief produces an emotion that constructs our behaviors. We do not even have to think about them. Our brains just keep speeding up the process until those behaviors become default, knee-jerk reactions when we sense the emotion.

We act as if we have no control of them. But that is not true. That is a lie. We can literally take every thought captive before it becomes a freight train wreaking havoc in our lives. Our default mode is what keeps us from our destiny. It is crazy to keep doing the same things over and over again while expecting a different outcome. Yet we do.

Again, the positive reactions and behaviors are not the problem. The negative core beliefs or narratives are what will keep us from being and doing all we were created for. We must get off autopilot. We must examine our programming. We must dig deep. We all have behaviors we want to change, and when we muster up the courage to try to change those behaviors, we fail because we have not challenged the belief that is producing the emotions that helped construct the default behavior. We get frustrated and quit because we do not see the results we long for. We come into agreement with the lie that we are failures. We hate the emotions that belief produces, so we vow to live with our unwanted, self-limiting behaviors. Around and around we go on this merry-go-round of defeat, never being and doing what we were created to be and do.

As humans, we focus and spend so much time and money on trying to change our behaviors. We try to lose weight, quit smoking, stop drinking, and more, but so many of our behaviors are typical symptoms of deep-rooted emotions that spring from false beliefs or lies implanted in us, typically during our childhood. I found when I began to examine my negative, unwanted behaviors, I could trace them all back to a lie or a label that someone bestowed upon me, or a lie I had bestowed upon myself. However, I discovered if I wanted to change a behavior, I first had to identity the feelings and negative beliefs associated with it. Then the behavior became easy to change by replacing the lie with the truth.

We must ask why. We must be authentically self-aware. We must be mindful of the stored experiences and the beliefs they produced that may not be true. The why of the belief is the key to change. It is the bull's-eye we must hit. My behaviors and emotions were easy to identify, but they cloaked the belief. To determine whether my beliefs were true or not, I had to consult my Creator. I made the decision that I was tired of living out of my default mode; I wanted to operate from design. It was a rigorous process that yielded great results in my life—results that can be replicated in yours.

"Become what you believe." — Jesus, MATTHEW 9:29 (MSG)

I find this statement by Jesus recorded by his disciple fascinating, because it confirms what psychologists are telling us. We will become what we believe.

But what is even more fascinating to me is that we can choose what to believe. We can believe a lie or we can believe truth. Either will produce emotions that will alter and/or affect our behavior. We have got to examine our beliefs and determine if they are truth or lies. This week's discovery process will help us do just that. First, let's make a vow. Let's commit from whom we will receive our truth. If you are ready, read the following aloud, then initial and date it.

"Starting today, I am going to seek and believe only my Creator for the truth about me. For too long I have listened to the negative voices inside of me, and the ones from other people telling me who I am. God's words sound so much better. They are truly life giving. I am going to choose to believe them for my truth. I am a child of His and I will act like it. I will live and act out of that identity He has bestowed upon me."

_____ Your Initials _____ Date

We Become What We Believe

Daily Discovery Process

Behaviors betray our beliefs. They are simply a symptom of our deep-rooted beliefs. If the belief is positive, healthy behaviors result and become our default mode. But an unexamined, false belief produces negative emotions that produce what can be, life-long negative or even harmful behaviors. We become so discouraged when we focus on a behavior we want to change. Often it feels impossible after we fail repeatedly.

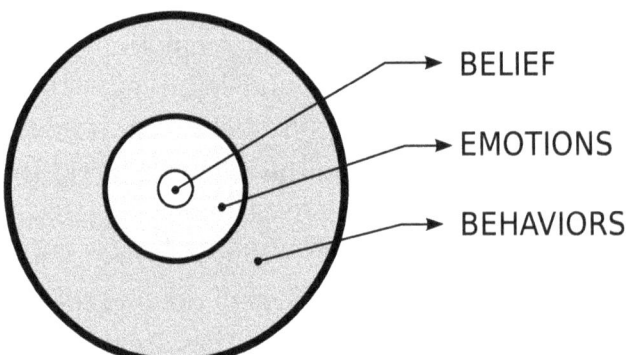

If we are to have success in changing an unwanted behavior, in living like the beloved children that we are, we must confront our beliefs. We must consult our Creator about the lies we may have come in agreement with and believed. I have said it over and over in this assessment, but it bears repeating: *You must choose from where and whom you will get your truth, but then you must take it one step further and choose to believe it.*

Beloved. Belong. Believe. Done in that order, unwanted behaviors will change.

My Story

When I was challenged with the ancient words we read last week, *live as children of the light, live as well-loved children,* I started with the things that were keeping me from my destiny. I identified any unwanted, default behaviors that did not line up with my identity as a well loved, beloved child. I had a strong desire to behave like the child of the King and Creator of the Universe. To begin with, I examined my avoidance of anything that had the potential to produce the feelings of embarrassment or humiliation, which can be just about anything except breathing. If you would have asked me ten years ago to go on a stage, make a presentation, or speak to a group of more than four people, all of which I now frequently do, I would have run screaming for the hills. I literally became physically ill at the thought. I paid attention to this gross overreaction. For the first time, instead of avoiding the activity, I examined my behaviors, my emotions, and beliefs about speaking in front of people. I remembered as a child I loved to be on a stage. I took courage and faced the truth.

When I began this journey of uncovering my identity and discovering my destiny, I realized I avoided many things that I once loved as a child. Things like athletic competitions, having an opinion, speaking up, and being on stage. Deep in my brain, I believed it would be embarrassing to lose, have a different opinion, or, God forbid, have everyone look at me and freeze with nothing to say. Irrationally, I argued with anyone about anything because I believed it was embarrassing to be wrong. These scenes were all too risky for one as frightened of embarrassment as me, so I either avoided them or I went on attack mode. All of these behaviors were by default; they required no thought on my part. They happened automatically in my brain if I sensed potential embarrassment or humiliation. These emotions, which were producing my behavior, stemmed from the erroneous belief that I was an embarrassment. I constantly felt unsettled in my soul because any activity or conversation had potential to stir up the feared feelings. My behavior betrayed my belief about myself.

I became so tired of overreacting to the insignificant. I hated my reactions in certain situations and could not understand the why behind them. I hated being afraid of things that I once loved. I finally became so weary of settling for less than I was created for that I was now willing to take the time necessary to examine my negative core narratives and expose them to truth. I knew I could not trust myself or another person for the truth, so I consulted my Creator. I began to ask these questions:

- What are the lies?
- When did they start?
- What is really true about me?

I asked the questions and journaled the process. It was truly life changing. I remembered the false identities and negative labels bestowed upon me by others and myself. *Too* loud, *too* bossy, and *too* embarrassing. The message I received and the lie I believed was clear—I was *too much*. During this process, I began to see the ways I had intentionally dumbed myself down and limited my own potential with my negative beliefs.

You are too much, or the other lie, *you are not enough*, seem to be two very common negative core narratives bestowed upon people—narratives that greatly limit their behavior. Neither is true! We must stop this merry-go-round of negative thoughts, beliefs, feelings, and behaviors if we are going to be and do all we were created for.

My heart's desire is for you to experience what I have. Freedom. Freedom to just be you. That is what your Creator wants for you also. So take courage. Let's figure out what is keeping you from being you.

Your Story

What are your negative, default behaviors that may be keeping you from being you? In just a few minutes I am going to ask you to write them down. To identify them, begin to pay close attention to your intense emotional reactions to seemingly benign situations, situations where you react or overreact without cause. Anger, rage, sweaty palms, racing heart, and abject fear are all clues to situations that do not warrant those reactions. Do not gloss over the behavior with rationalizations; instead, begin to ask why of your Maker. It is imperative for you to examine these negative narratives to determine if they are clouding your identity and limiting your destiny. Ignoring them does not work.

Think about any sentences you use about yourself that begin with *I am*. A core narrative always begins with I am—negative or positive. For this exercise, we are focusing on the negative, self-limiting ones. Here are a few examples to get you to thinking about the negative tape running in your own head.

- *I am an embarrassment.*
- *I am unplanned.*
- *I am of no value.*
- *I am unattractive.*
- *I am unworthy.*
- *I am unintelligent.*
- *I am ugly.*
- *I am an accident.*
- *I am unlovable.*

- *I am insignificant.*
- *I am the problem.*
- *I am a failure.*

Do you see how any of these statements could bestow a false identity upon us *if* we come in agreement with them? When we come in agreement with a negative narrative, they become a belief. These negative and untrue beliefs produce strong emotions and feelings that we act out of by default.

Your behaviors will always betray your beliefs.

If you believe you are unlovable, you will feel unlovable and eventually act unlovable. If you believe you are unintelligent, you feel stupid and will act that way. If you believe you are ugly, you will feel ugly and begin to display ugly behaviors. If you believe you have no value, you will feel insignificant and invisible and begin to make choices that reflect that belief and those feelings. After a while, all those behaviors become second nature to you. They become your default mode. Are light bulbs going off? Any flashes of lightning? Is the haze clearing?

Your behaviors stem from who you *believe* you are. What is extremely frightening is the fact that these beliefs may or may not be true. You must examine them. Ask your Creator to reveal to you any default behaviors you have that are based on an erroneous belief. Sit still for just a moment, take a deep breath, and ask God's spirit to testify to you about who you are. Quiet your mind and ask your Abba Father to reveal any agreements you have made with a lie. Think about any negative descriptions you use that begin with "I am .." Pay attention to statements you make that begin with *always, no one,* and *never.* "*No one will ever love me. I will always be overweight. I have never had a friend.*" Sentences containing those words can provide clues to negative programming. If you are stuck staring at the blanks, consult anyone you are in a close relationship with to help you identity any negative or irrational behaviors. Those very behaviors may be hurting your relationships, and those who love you will cheer you on when they discover you want to include them in your journey of purpose. When they give you truth about yourself, especially if they give you that truth with love, guard your heart and don't make them your enemy. You are not looking for flattery. You need truth.

"What has happened to your joy? I can testify that at one time you would have torn your eyes out and given them to me if I needed them. How have I now become your enemy by telling you the truth?" — GALATIANS 4:15–16

Let truth be your friend, not your enemy. Truth that is poured over lies and untrue beliefs has the power to change your negative core narratives, irrational emotions, and the adverse behaviors they produce. I am willing to bet those very same behaviors are linked to lies about your identity that are keeping you from discovering and fulfilling your world-changing destiny. Pursue truth.

___

Tomorrow we are going to dig through these negative core narratives, these unwanted or default behaviors, to try and determine when they started and what emotions they produce in you. But for now, end the day journaling your heart, the unvarnished thoughts and feelings you are having right now at this point in our journey together. Ponder the thought with your Creator that your beliefs about yourself may not be true.

Uniquely You — Day One

My prayer for you as we end this day of discovery is that you will have the courage to examine your beliefs and that God will use His truth to set you free to be and do all He created you for.

Week Four  Uniquely You

Emotions Produce Behaviors

Daily Discovery Process

You did great yesterday listing your unwanted behaviors and default reactions. As we continue today, feel free to keep adding to your list. Our goal today is to identify and associate the emotions that produced those negative behaviors. Your feelings are the link between your behavior and beliefs, which may or may not be true. Our end game is to expose the lie you came in agreement with and the situation that produced this entire cycle.

Read over your list from yesterday, and then read my examples below. We are going to be taking your unwanted behaviors and determine what emotion produces the behavior.

UNWANTED BEHAVIOR	EMOTION PRODUCED
*I always **walk out** when I feel angry.*	**Anger** produced the unwanted behavior
*I always **quit** if I feel embarrassed*	The feeling of **embarrassment** caused the quitting.
*I always **lie** if I feel worried.*	Feeling **worried** preempted the lying.
*I **steal** when I feel inadequate or do not measure up to others.*	Feeling **inadequate** rationalized the criminal behavior.
*I **cheat** on tests when I feel stupid.*	Feeling **stupid** caused the unethical behavior.
*I **sleep around** when I feel undesirable.*	Feeling **ugly** produced an unhealthy choice.
*I always **eat too much** when I feel sad.*	Feeling **sad** caused the overeating.
*I always **drink excessively** when I feel stressed financially.*	**Stress** produces the excess.

Look back over the list you made yesterday. Take the behaviors you identified and put them in the blanks below in the left hand column that begin with I always. After you do that, ask yourself what you feel. Work through all the blanks.

UNWANTED BEHAVIOR	EMOTION PRODUCED
I always _____ when I feel _____ .	_____ produced the unwanted behavior
I always _____ when I feel _____ .	The feeling of _____ caused the _____ .
I always _____ if I feel worried.	Feeling worried preempted _____ .
I _____ when I feel inadequate or do not measure up to others.	Feeling inadequate caused me to do what? _____
I _____ when I feel _____ .	The feeling caused what unwanted behavior? _____
I _____ when I feel rejected.	Name the emotion that produced the undesirable behavior _____ .
I always eat too much when I feel _____ .	Feeling _____ caused the overeating.
I always drink too much when I feel _____ .	_____ caused the excessive drinking.

Did you have any "ah ha" moments? List them below. Consult your Creator as you list these revelations asking for any more He may want to provide.

_____
_____
_____
_____
_____

My prayer for you today is that you will not run from truth, but that truth will be your friend instead. I pray you will tire of unwanted behaviors and that you're ready to confront the lies that have produced emotions and those behaviors. I pray you will courageously allow your Creator to wash those memories in His loving grace.

Are Your Beliefs True?

Daily Discovery Process

Today is going to be fun. We are going to take the behaviors and emotions you have listed over the last two days and determine the belief behind them. Revelation and connections may not come to you all at once. Be patient with yourself. I have listed some examples from real individuals and my own life; see if any of them sound familiar to you. In this exercise, again, pay attention to the words *always* and *never*. We will start the sentence with *I believe* and then use the word *so* to link the belief with the emotion, then the behavior.

I believe I will always hit someone if I get angry; I feel afraid so I walk out during any confrontation or argument.

I believe I will always be laughed at if I try something new; I feel embarrassed so I quit, or worse, I never try.

I believe I will always hurt someone's feelings if I speak the truth; I fear rejection so I flatter them or lie to them.

I believe no one will like me for myself; I feel inadequate so I steal things to make myself seem cooler.

I believe I will never go to college; I feel dumb so I cheat on all my tests.

I believe I am not attractive and will never marry; I feel undesirable so I sleep with anyone who shows interest in me.

I believe I will never be happy; I feel sad so I eat to try and make the feeling go away.

I believe I will never have enough money to pay my bills; I feel overwhelmed so I drink to forget.

When you read these examples, do they seem silly or ridiculous to you? Remember the people of Columbus' day? We laugh at their beliefs now, but those beliefs, though they were faulty, caused them to remain in the very small, comfortable world they lived in. Their erroneous beliefs seem ridiculous, but at the time they held them captive and caused them to settle for less. Do yours?

Do you see how any of the erroneous beliefs from above can produce negative feelings and subsequent behaviors that could keep someone from being and doing all they were created to be and do?

Flip back to yesterday's homework and the answers you put in the blanks provided. Take those answers and place them in the second and third blanks below. After you have done that, consider the first statement that begins with *"I believe"* and the subsequent blank, the first blank provided. What is the belief that produced the emotions that produced the behavior you wrote in the second and third blanks? Please do not worry if you cannot make all the connections right now. Some of my own discoveries and connections took a great deal of time to uncover as I reflected, journaled, and consulted my Creator.

Use this graphic to guide you:

BELIEF → EMOTION → BEHAVIOR

I believe I will never be _____, that makes me feel _____ so I _____.

I believe I will never be _____, that makes me feel _____ so I _____.

I believe I will never be _____, that makes me feel _____ so I _____.

I believe I will never be _____, that makes me feel _____ so I _____.

I believe I will never be _____, that makes me feel _____ so I _____.

I believe I will never be _____, that makes me feel _____ so I _____.

I believe I will never be _____, that makes me feel _____ so I _____.

I believe I will never be _____, that makes me feel _____ so I _____.

I believe I will never be _____, that makes me feel _____ so I _____.

I believe I will never be _____, that makes me feel _____ so I _____.

Now, read the complete sentences out loud. Does seeing and saying them cause any revelations or "ah ha's"? Do any of them sound or seem absurd or even ludicrous? Journal your thoughts and reflections here. I am so excited for you! This is a huge day of discovery. Keep pushing to understand you. I promise it will be worth it. Consult your Creator as you record your discoveries.

_____
_____
_____
_____
_____
_____
_____
_____
_____
_____
_____

As I mentioned in the introduction of this assessment, my goal is to provide you tangible steps to take in order to expedite your timeline of uncovering your true identity and fulfilling your destiny. However, your Creator provides the ultimate connections and timing. For now, it is okay to have some gaps and blanks. Trust the One who made you. He will provide all your answers at just the right time.

My prayer for you as we end this day of discovery is that you are beginning to see that what you believe about yourself or your circumstances may have nothing to do with truth. I pray that you have begun to be aware of the untrue beliefs that have produced negative emotions and behaviors. Being self-aware and making a careful assessment of you is critical in this journey of purpose. New truth is coming for you to apply, and when you do, new emotions and new behaviors will be produced—and that will be a wonderful day.

Identify the Source

Daily Discovery Process

There is one last step in this process. You need to see if you can remember what incident or experience produced the *always* and *never* belief(s) as well as any subsequent agreements or vows you made.

My Story
When I was younger, I had multiple negative experiences and disappointments. We all do. However, the trip to my principal's office, the one where I made a vow that caused me to stop being me, caused a great deal of my negative core narratives. When my dreams and identity were challenged, even ridiculed, I came to believe I was an embarrassment, and I vowed to never be humiliated again. In my ten-year-old mind, the obvious way to do that was to stop being me. That vow followed me into adulthood. A friend of mine just recently pointed out a habit of mine that was a direct result of this childhood experience.
Ask people who know and love you to describe you in a paragraph. This is always a fun and interesting exercise for people. This exercise is not meant to encourage you to run to others for your identity. Rather, it is a way to prove how very often the negative narrative can cloud your own self-perception, which for most of us, began in childhood. I am hyper-vigilant in examining my default behaviors. It is an area of intrigue in my own self-assessment. The emotionally healthy people in our lives can often help us spot a negative core narrative that is buried deep in our soul. They are able to hold up a mirror so we can truly see ourselves.

I have never really struggled with low self-esteem or lack of confidence but I am always surprised when someone compliments me or describes me in a positive or flattering manner. For some reason, I feel bad instead of good. I *feel* I need to immediately list all my faults and flaws. I feel like my disclosures would allow them to see that I do not deserve a compliment.

I *believe* I do not deserve a compliment. Notice how my feelings were associated with what I believed and they had nothing to do with truth.

One of my friends pointed out this habit of mine and challenged me as to why compliments made me uncomfortable. Instead of ignoring my feelings, I examined them; they were the bridge that led me back to a belief that had become a core narrative. Unbeknownst to me, I discovered my brain was rewinding the tape of my life back to when I was ten years old as I walked down the hall to the principal's office. Though it was a default reaction with no conscious or intentional thought on my part, I still felt the emotions associated with the belief that I had done something wrong, which produces the assumption that I do not deserve compliments. I do not even realize that my brain is looking for every failure, fault, and bad decision I have ever made as evidence. Embarrassment is the feeling that produces the conclusion that I am not special but flawed, thus unworthy of a compliment or praise.

The culprit of this behavior was the situation in the principal's office and the vow I made to never feel embarrassed again. The core narrative—the lie I came in agreement with— was that I was an embarrassment. Fundamentally, I was wrong or flawed. I now see this as a lie, but for over thirty years, it was what I believed, thus what I felt and drew my behaviors from. I wasted so much time.

Your Story

You may also just have one incident or even multiple ones that produced an erroneous belief you came in agreement with. That is what we want to discover today. Keep in mind that you are unique and there is no exact formula that applies to us universally in this process. That is why it is imperative to consult your Creator. Ask Him to bring to mind any experience or experiences where you made a vow that has had an impact on your identity and could right now be robbing you of your destiny. It may very well be a forgotten memory from childhood. Review your lists from the previous days to jog your memory. I have also provided some examples below. I highlighted the incident that caused the belief, which produced the feelings that prompted the behavior.

Past Experiences

When I was in the fifth grade I got so angry during dodge ball that **I hit another child with my fist.**

When I was in junior high, I tried out for the basketball team. The **entire school laughed at me when I shot the ball at the wrong basket.**

When I was younger, **I told my sister she was a bad dancer, which was true. She cried and said I hurt her feelings** *and that she would not play with me anymore.*

When I was little, **I did not have many friends,** *so I watched a lot of television. On the*

shows I watched, kids who had a lot of cool toys seemed to always have a lot of friends. **I vowed to do the same.**

When I was in first grade, **I was diagnosed with a learning problem. I had to go to special classes.** *I thought I was stupid.*

My brother told me **I was ugly and that no one would ever want to marry me.** *I believed him and started doing anything for boys to notice me.*

My teacher told me I had a critical personality and that I would never be happy. I told my mom and she baked cookies. **I ate them all and felt better.**

When I was little, my dad always yelled about not having enough money. He said it was my mom's fault. **She always drank when he said that.**

Now, put this assessment aside. Sit still for a moment. Close your eyes, breathe deep, and ask your Creator for a memory of an incident that may have caused you to believe you were too much or not enough—a memory where you made a vow to *never* or *always*. This might be the incident that caused you to stop being you. Don't worry about making any connections. Just remember all that you can. What you were wearing. How old you were. Any smells or sounds. Record them all. Write your story. You may have another memory since we talked about this earlier. That is pretty common. Many times you do not have an answer right away. That is fine. Write whatever comes to your mind.

_____
_____
_____
_____
_____
_____
_____
_____
_____
_____
_____
_____
_____
_____

_____
_____
_____
_____
_____
_____
_____
_____

Any incident you wrote about, if it happened in your childhood, may have produced very real, negative core narratives that would have induced vows or assumptions that produced beliefs and feelings that influenced a lifetime of negative behaviors. Though I could not have articulated it at the time, the one I internalized from my little girl experience was this:

I am embarrassing and I am wrong, so I will stop being me and be someone else.

It was a powerful, life-changing statement internalized as a ten year old. It became my negative core narrative. Though it was a lie, it became my truth because I believed it and came in agreement with it. It produced negative emotions that produced behaviors that kept me from my true identity and destiny for years.

The core narratives and lies always start with **I am**. The vow or subsequent assumption that comes afterward always begins with the word **so**. Do you see the connections above in my example? Can you deduce any from the story you remembered from your childhood or the negative behaviors or emotions you have examined this week? Here are some examples of negative core values to get you thinking:

*I am violent, **so** I will never be in a relationship.*

*I am hurtful, **so** I will only tell people what they want to hear even if it is a lie.*

*I am alone, **so** I will use things even if I have to steal them to buy me friends.*

*I am stupid, **so** I will never try hard. Then I cannot fail.*

*I am ugly and have no value, **so** I will let others use my body.*

*I am unhappy, **so** I will eat to numb my pain.*

*I am inadequate, **so** I will drink to numb the pain.*

Your Story

You may think my lie or the examples above seem simplistic or preposterous. However, silly as they may seem, when they are yours, they are very real and greatly influence our lives. I am certain there is something your Creator wants to reveal to you about you that will jumpstart your journey of purpose and catapult you into discovery so you can fulfill your water-walking, giant-slaying, history-making destiny. But first, you must believe the truth about you—the truth your Creator gives you—not the lies you have internalized. Reread your list from yesterday. Think about the situation, the emotions, and unwanted behaviors. Write any negative narratives that come to mind in the spaces below. See if you can determine the lie you came in agreement with, the lie that became your belief.

"I am _____ (followed by)

so I _____."

"I am _____ (followed by)

so I _____."

"I am _____ (followed by)

so I _____."

"I am _____ (followed by)

so I _____."

If you haven't connected all the dots, please be patient and remain open to the process. Keep coming to your Creator asking questions. Examine any of your behaviors or habits that you would like to change and see if you can determine the incident that produced a false belief and negative emotion. Determine if you made a vow that you believed would protect you, but instead hindered you from being you. Keep letting truth be your friend. I promise ... no, your Creator promises, that you will receive your answers if you keep seeking Him.

c2bu.com/vid5

That is my prayer for you as we end this day of discovery, that when you go in search of Him, you will find you; that when you go in search of truth, all the lies will be exposed.

Choose Your Truth

Daily Discovery Process

Your beliefs may have nothing to do with truth. As I said at the beginning of this week, that statement scared me to death and caused me to go in search of the truth about me. My Creator whispered to me that He had created me on purpose for a purpose. But I realized the little girl I once was more closely resembled the true me than the woman I had become. I realized I could choose what I believed—the truth. I could change my beliefs, which would change my emotions, which would then change my behaviors.

Your Creator has all of your answers and can provide you with all the courage you need to make these changes. He has your truth. He knows your design mode because He created it. Just as with our computer analogy, you are much more complex, created for so much more than your default, destiny limiting behaviors.

My Story

After all the memories, revelations, and realizations, I finally had the courage to ask God (my Creator), *"Who did you create me to be?"* How sweet and intimate was this process my Heavenly Father took me through. Instead of the familiar, negative core values, His sweet voice whispered different words to me, words I longed to believe about me.

Instead of *"I am an embarrassment,"* and *"I am too loud,"* I heard *"You are vivacious and full of energy."* Instead of *"I talk too much,"* I heard *"You are a good communicator."* *"I am bossy,"* was replaced with *"You are a strong leader."* *"It is all my fault,"* became *"You are victorious."* On and on the transformation went until I had a new vocabulary whispered to my spirit by my Creator. Every negative thought and subsequent lie I believed about me was exposed, examined, and then replaced with truth by the One who made me. These were words I wanted to believe about me for me. These words were the ones I now came in agreement with. It took much discipline to change my thoughts, which changed my feelings and my behaviors. I wrote these positive affirmations down on my 3x5 cards and read them out loud three times a day for months before they silenced the lies I had believed for years.

- *I am a good communicator.*
- *I am a strong leader.*
- *I am not an embarrassment.*
- *I am victorious.*
- *I am vivacious. (I love that word!)*
- *I am a child of God created on purpose for a purpose.*
- *I have a destiny.*
- *I am beloved.*
- *I belong.*
- *I am planned.*
- *I am an encourager.*
- *I am a water walker, giant slayer, and history maker.*
- *I am created on purpose for a purpose.*
- *I am courageous, straightforward, and grace-filled.*

This is my new identity. My job now is simply to believe. In the beginning, believing was a daily choice, not a feeling. As I practiced my new truth aloud, my thoughts began to change and miraculously so did my feelings! When that happened, the self-limiting, unwanted behaviors began to align with the truth I chose to believe about me. When the written down words became my truth, I began to confidently act and operate out of my design mode. It felt unnatural at first. It even took a great deal of courage for me to leave the known for the unknown. However when I did, I discovered many activities that once scared me to death were actually the very ones God designed as a part of my identity and destiny. Though I took baby steps at first, the people in my life began to notice the changes in me as I began to make strides toward my destiny. I even started speaking on a stage and loved it! It was like breathing to me.

Beloved. Belong. Believe.

This is the truth. You are a *beloved* child, created to impact and change this world. The truth is that you *belong* to something bigger than yourself. This truth gives you the courage and capacity to examine your negative narratives and get rid of self-limiting behaviors so you can choose to *believe* you were created to change the world.

You are a water walker, giant slayer, and history maker. It is your destiny. *Believe!*

I highly recommend you get out your package of 3x5 cards to write down your new truths. Your default mode is very familiar and easy, but it is not your design. Consult your Creator for your truth. Ask Him, "Who did you create me to be?" When He tells you, *"You are ..."* Internalize it as truth and write down, *"I am _____"* in the space below. I filled in the first couple of ones for you, the ones we have already discovered together:

- *I am a beloved child of God.*
- *I am fearfully and wonderfully made.*
- *I am delightful.*
- *I am a water walker, giant slayer, and history maker.*
- *I am planned.*
- *I am created on purpose for a purpose.*
- *I am _____ .*
- *I am _____ .*
- *I am _____ .*
- *I am _____ .*
- *I am _____ .*
- *I am _____ .*
- *I am _____ .*
- *I am _____ .*

Read these words of truth out loud at least twice a day. Will you choose this as your truth? _____ Will you choose to believe what your Creator says? ○ Yes   ○ No

Make these your vows. Live out of this truth. Your answer to these questions are so important and life altering because you *will* become what you believe. Remember, what you believe will produce emotions that produce behaviors. Therefore, this journey of purpose requires faith in what you do not see and what you may not feel quite yet. When you believe in yourself, when you begin loving yourself well, you will then have the faith to begin taking action steps toward your world-changing destiny.

Faith and belief—these are two very important requirements. Many people use the words *faith* and *belief* interchangeably. Dictionary.com defines it as:

"Belief that is not based on proof."

Sounds rather unintelligent, doesn't it? The Bible has a definition I like much better:

> "Faith is being sure of what we hope for
> and certain of what we cannot see."
> — HEBREWS 11:1

That is what we have been talking about in this chapter. Having confidence in what we cannot see at this moment but what we believe will be. That is having faith in your self.

This week has been about convincing you that *you are who God says you are*, and that *you have what it takes to do what He has created you to do.*

As we end this week and day of discovery, get your truth cards out and daily repeat the words you have written. Negative or positive repetition has the same outcome; it will become a well-worn path in your brain that will produce emotions that will affect your behaviors. It can be a negative rut you are stuck in or a positive path to your purpose. You can reverse the process of negativity with these truths..

Before time began, you were created on purpose for a purpose.
You have a great destiny awaiting you.

Examine what you believe and then why you believe it. Choose your truth. Change what you believe. You do have the courage to be you!

Repeat these words with me until you have the faith to believe:

I am beloved. I do belong. I have a destiny. I will believe.

That is what I want to give you. An invitation and the permission to be you—the you God created before time began. Do you have the courage to believe?

I want to remind you of this truth:

> *"You are unique, fearfully and wonderfully made."*
> — Psalm 139 (NIV)

You are an original work of art. Before time began you were known, planned, and loved. Long before your birth, God imagined you just as a painter imagines a painting he is about to create while staring at a blank canvas. You were no accident. It matters not the details of your conception or birth. You were meant to be. Even before your birth you were set apart for "such a time as this." God has plans for you, good plans meant only for you. My prayer for you today is that you will choose to believe it.

As we close out this week, I pray that as you work through your assessment, you will choose to believe God and only God for your truth. I pray that you will come to see that before the foundation of the world He planned you. He delights in you—the little child you once were and the person you have become. I pray that you will never settle for less than you were created for. You belong to him. You were adopted into His family and though the law says a biological child can be disinherited, an adopted child cannot. Your position is safe and your identity is eternal. Blessings, dear one.

You *are* created on purpose for a purpose!

Righteous Girlfriend/ Mighty Warrior

Beloved. Belong. Believe

– Day 1 –

Your behaviors stem from who you believe you are. What is extremely frightening is the fact that these beliefs may or may not be true! Reflect back over the first day of week four of the DDP. Share with your righteous girlfriends/warriors what behaviors may betray your beliefs about yourself?

– Day 2 –

What default behaviors did your Creator reveal to you that are based on erroneous beliefs? What emotions are produced by these behaviors? Did you have any "ah ha!" moments you would like to share?

– Day 3 –

What are some erroneous beliefs you hold about yourself? Do any seem absurd or ludicrous to you?

– Day 4 –

Were you able to identify an incident where you made a vow to change or adapt to the situation that may now be robbing you of your true destiny? Were you able to identify one of your key core narratives, "I am..., so I.."?

– Day 5 –

When you consulted your Creator for new truths about you, did He tell you anything new that you didn't already know? The purpose of identity boot camp is to convince you that you are who God says you are and that you have what it takes to do what He has created for you to do. Who does God say you are? What truths have you chosen to believe? Ask your group for their input or thoughts.

Pray for each other. Write down your prayer request on a piece of paper and pass it to the person on your right. Tuck their card into your Uniqueness Assessment so you will remember to pray each day. Believe God for this person as you learn to believe God for yourself.

Blessings, everyone!
I am personally praying for each of you.
You are going to change the world.

Week Five  Uniquely You

Body. Soul. Spirit.
PART ONE

Take a deep breath. You have done some hard work. I am so excited for you and where you are on this journey of purpose. I pray today you feel refreshed and filled with expectation after having applied truth to situations and negative beliefs that you may have held for years. I pray you have your 3x5 cards handy and begin today by reminding yourself who you are—beloved. You have been adopted into the family of God. You were created before time began for a specific and unique purpose. It is imperative you have the courage to be you.

Before I could be and do all God created me for, I had much to examine and assess. I had to understand the *me* God had created, so that I could fulfill my water-walking, giant-slaying, history-making destiny. To ignore any part of me could keep me from that destiny.

That is what we will be doing for the next week, more assessments. Are you ready? You will need courage.

"May God himself, the God of peace, sanctify you through and through. May your whole spirit, soul and body be kept blameless at the coming of our Lord Jesus Christ." — 1 THESSALONIANS 5:23

The essence of each of us is a sum of three parts—Body. Soul. Spirit.

Most of my life I've been rather confused about the "soul" and "spirit" part of this verse. Are they the same or different? If they are different, then what is the difference? This week and next, we will ask and answer those exact questions, while at the same time contemplate our bodies. We will be consulting our Creator to hear His truth, while assessing the health of our body, our soul, and our spirit. To fulfill our destinies all three must be strong.

The Body

The body is the external, material, obvious part of who we are. We and everyone else can see it and touch it. It is a combination of our eye color, hair color, height, and weight. Each body is an amazing, unique creation fashioned by God. However, not all of us love our bodies. This is why we need some truth about our bodies—"truth" that does not come from the T.V., a magazine, or our culture.

The Apostle Paul, our friend from the Bible, called our bodies "temporary tents" that will soon be put aside (2 CORINTHIANS 5:1–4). In theory, I know it is important to take care of my body, so that I can delay the "soon be put aside" part. We may all have differing beliefs with regards to God but not many of us disagree with the fact that we need to care for our bodies. The difficulty with this belief is putting it into practice. I agree with Mark, who said,

"The spirit is willing but the body is weak." — Mark 14:38

Amen. I need to, I mean to, I want to take care of this very important part of me, but in the end, I often neglect it, prioritizing other wants and needs in my life. It is a merry-go-round we have to get off of if we are to be and do all we were created for. We are going to need to be at our best. We must face this truth.

Our bodies were shaped and formed by God in the womb. However, once outside the womb, it becomes our responsibility to take care of them. We are to be good stewards of this amazing body we have been given. If you grew up going to church, you could not have missed the sermons on the mandate from God to be good stewards of your money. But were you taught this same lesson with regard to your body? I wasn't. I was never taught that my body wasn't my own. And I certainly wasn't taught the truth in the Bible that said people were supposed to see God in and through my body (1 CORINTHIANS 6). Does that make you want to cringe? People will see God through my body? Yikes! Now that is a huge responsibility.

I did grow up being taught that my body was the living temple of God—that my body housed the Spirit of God. During my teenage years, that was code for "Make sure you don't use that 'temple' to have sex before you are married." Or "Don't take that 'temple' into inappropriate places such as bars and night clubs." Now, as I consult my Creator and contemplate His words as a woman on the journey to uncover her identity and discover her destiny, it has different implications for me. In fact, I cannot mistake the mandate that I am to be an image-bearer of God—inside and out. Once I began to see all God created me to be and do, I was faced with the question, "How in the world am I ever going to carry out my purpose in this life if I am tired, lethargic, and overweight"? My answer came quickly and simply—I won't and I can't.

Friends, please hear my heart on this issue. The topic of our body is only about the things we can control—diet, exercise, sleep, and the choices we make in those areas. It is not about genetics or accidents or health issues we have no say in. It is about discipline and self-control. On my journey of purpose, I had to personally take ownership of those choices I was making in regards to my body if I was to ever become all God created me for. This is still a struggle for me, by the way. I am southern, and I like southern cooking. But I am not going to forfeit my destiny for twice-baked potatoes covered in cheese and butter!

It is common in Christian circles to judge, even condemn, those who abuse their bodies by drinking excessive amounts of alcohol or taking drugs, while many of us abuse our bodies by neglecting exercise or taking in too many calories. Walk into any church on a Sunday morning and you will see many people who are harming themselves in these ways, but we do not speak truth in love. Our doctors are warning us that America has a weight problem, and if we do not confront the truth, it is going to kill us. Please, again hear my heart. I am not addressing this issue to make anybody feel bad or hurt anyone's feelings. I am addressing this issue so that we can go and do and be all we were created for.

I do not want to move from your identity and destiny coach to a weight-loss coach. However, we must educate ourselves on the health risks associated with being overweight. This issue should not be avoided because we fear hurting someone's feelings. This issue needs to be addressed, because at the very least, people are not living life as God intended, and at the worst, people are dying. On days one and two this week, we are going to take an honest look at our bodies and consult our Creator about our health and our responsibility to be healthy. You may need some thick skin for these days.

The Soul
We are also made up of our soul, a part of us not as easy to see or make a determination of its health, like our bodies. This word is often used interchangeably with the word spirit, but I want to separate them and define them. When I researched the meaning of this tiny, four-letter English word *soul* in the Greek and Hebrew, I was amazed at the vast spectrum of other words offered. It is a rich, powerful word, just like our souls. I found it interesting that we need ten to twelve English words for this one little word from the Greek or Hebrew. It is a word packed with much meaning and has great implications in our self-assessment, as well as our journey in discovering our purpose.

alive, live, breath, to make alive, anger, courage, lust, heart, mind, emotions

Based on these definitions, it is apparent that our souls house our emotions, our will, and our intellect. Just like with our bodies, we can make healthy or unhealthy choices that affect this important part of us. We have already been doing a great deal of work on our souls as we searched through our memories and pasts for any negative core narratives, false belief systems, and default behaviors that were robbing us of our true identity and destiny. The days we spend on our soul will complement and enhance the work you have already done. Keep your 3x5 truth verses and affirmations handy for these sections. We will be pouring more truth on this part of ourselves, focusing on our emotions and what, if any, control we have over them. We will also see how out of balance or improperly aligned our thoughts and emotions can become when they are unhealthy, and how that can cause us to become derailed from a journey of purpose.

The Spirit
The third part of us is our spirits and we will examine and assess the part it plays in our identity and destiny. Again, we have touched a bit on this in previous weeks when we talked about God's Spirit testifying to our spirits that we are His children. We mentioned it when we talked about being created by the Creator before time began, even being known by our Creator before birth. These concepts are too big for our souls (our minds and emotions), so we must engage our spirit. We will define our spirits as *the eternal, immaterial essence of us.* Your spirit is the part of you that will remain when your body is gone. Your spirit knows and recognizes truth that does not need an explanation. Your spirit requires no words to communicate. Your spirit is the part of you that was known by God before the beginning of time and will go on into eternity.

This will be an exciting time as we tap into parts of ourselves that we often neglect. Our goal is the same today as it has been in weeks' past—we will make a careful assessment of who we are, so we can figure out what we are supposed to be doing and have the courage to just do it. We are solidifying our identity, our true identity as children of God, so that we will ultimately believe we have a water-walking, giant-slaying, history-making destiny—one that will change the world.

We are very complex, intentionally created beings, so consulting our Creator throughout the next two weeks for His insight into who we are and who He created us to be will remain a priority.

Week Five  Uniquely You

Body Work

Daily Discovery Process

Consult Your Creator
Today we begin by consulting our Creator with regard to His plans and His truth for our bodies. Read these words and let what they say about your body sink in.

"Or didn't you realize that your body is a sacred place, the place of the Holy Spirit? Don't you see that you can't live however you please, squandering what God paid such a high price for? The physical part of you is not some piece of property belonging to the spiritual part of you. God owns the whole works. So let people see God in and through your body." — 1 Corinthians 6:18 (MSG)

"For you created my inmost being; you knit me together in my mother's womb. I praise you because I am fearfully and wonderfully made; your works are wonderful, I know that full well. My frame was not hidden from you when I was made in the secret place. When I was woven together in the depths of the earth, your eyes saw my unformed body. All the days ordained for me were written in your book before one of them came to be. Such knowledge is too wonderful for me."
— Psalm 139 (NIV)

Uniquely You

Day One

"Each of you should learn to control his own body in a way that is holy and honorable." — 1 Thessalonians 4:3–5

In the space below, journal your thoughts regarding your body. Do you make caring for it a priority? Do you like your body? Journal about the concept that your body is not your own, and our Creator expects us to be *a good steward of the one He has given us*. Do these concepts challenge you to think differently about your body?

_____

_____

_____

_____

_____

_____

My Story

When I first typed these words, my dad was in Africa feeding widows and orphans. He was seventy-one and had been to Africa five times within the last three years. Now as this assessment is getting ready to go to press, he is seventy-eight and has made ten trips to Africa since his sixty-ninth birthday. He is planning another trip next month. Each time he makes the trip, he takes a twenty-six-hour flight from Mississippi to the continent of Africa. When he is there, he walks most everywhere he goes covering five to ten miles each day. When he does go further and needs a ride, he hitchhikes on the back of gravel or pick-up trucks. He has slept on a dirt floor in a mud hut deep in the bush, squatted over a hole in the ground for a toilet, and eaten food that has not been approved by the FDA. He also hiked Mt. Kilimanjaro at the age of seventy-three. My dad is walking on water! He is smack dab in the middle of his destiny. He has built a church by hand, started two sewing centers, feeds thousands of widows and orphans monthly, started a school, sponsored more children than I can count, preached the word of God at countless church services, and led baptisms afterwards. My dad did not start this adventure until he was sixty-nine years old!

My dad is able to do all of this, because he has taken care of his body every day of his life. At his age, he cannot just rely on a good gene pool! He has practiced and continues to practice good stewardship of his body. Those widows and orphans in Africa do see God through his body. What if he physically could not go? What if he was not physically able to do what God has called him to? The answer is quite simple. People would starve. My dad has changed lives, because he took care of his body. Their eternity is different, because he was physically able to go. His spirit and soul could have been willing and able, but it would have been impossible for him to endure the physical requirements of the trip without a healthy, well-cared-for body. There was something for him to do that only he could do, and he had prepared his entire life for it simply by keeping his body healthy. When God issued him his purpose papers, he was ready.

What about you? If you are not being and doing all you were created for, then there is an unmet need and an unanswered prayer in this world. Fellow warriors, not only is creation eagerly awaiting for you to be you, so are others. My dad's ability to make these trips to Africa is a direct result of how he cares for the body he has been given. He exercises, watches what he eats, gets plenty of rest, and doesn't put unhealthy things in his body. It isn't complicated. It just isn't easy—at least for me.

My weight is a rollercoaster issue in my life. I have a twenty-pound variance. When the number is low, my self-esteem is high. When the number is high, my self-esteem is low. I have wrestled with this since I quit smoking. In 1993, I decided to stop slowing killing myself. (Don't tell my dad I ever smoked—he would kill me!) It was a good decision, but I received a new problem. Now that I didn't smoke, food tasted so much better! So I just ate more. I am not an emotional eater. My problem is that I am Southern and we just like our food fried with lots of butter. In my home, I am the cook, and in that role, I only cook what I like. I just can't understand why you would spend any time cooking something that doesn't taste good. So each night I am confronted with a plate full of food that I love, prepared just the way I like it; my family of men gets up from the table and I am left there buttering just one more piece of cornbread. When I dare to look at what a "normal" portion of food really is, I am shocked at the small amount "they" expect me to live on!

I hate this struggle. I hate feeling so defeated in this area of my life. When I made a careful assessment of myself in this area, I knew I would need help and accountability. I chose to ignore my feelings of embarrassment, and instead I brought the issue to my Creator and my righteous girlfriends so I could move closer to my destiny. My desire to be and do all I was created for forced me to get my head out of the sand and face my naked body in the mirror. Now that took some courage.

Through this part of my assessment and journey, I learned I could trust my Creator with any issue. God's word is applicable to every area of my life, even this one. I discovered that every weight loss program in the country has built their program around a biblical principle.

> *"Confess to each other and you will be healed."* — JAMES 5:16, (NIV)

What does every successful weight loss program have in common? Accountability. It does not matter if it is Jenny Craig, Weight Watchers, or one of the numerous Christian weight loss

programs. A key element of each program is the weekly weigh in. I hate weigh-ins, but I have come to appreciate the accountability and effectiveness of the process. My negative core belief and fear of embarrassment raises its ugly head every time I contemplate accountability in this area of my life. However, I now know the source of this lie, so I choose to act out of my true identity and face what I need to face. Let's face some facts about our health and our body.

Do you know the health risks of being overweight?

If you are overweight, you are more likely to develop health problems, such as heart disease, stroke, diabetes, certain types of cancer, gout (joint pain caused by excess uric acid), and gallbladder disease. Being overweight can also cause problems such as sleep apnea (interrupted breathing during sleep) and osteoarthritis (wearing away of the joints). The more overweight you are, the more likely you are to have health problems. Weight loss can help improve the harmful effects of being overweight. Studies show that you can improve your health by losing as little as ten to twenty pounds.

How do you know if you are overweight?

Ask your doctor or use the weight-for-height chart below. Find your height in the left-hand column and move across the row to find your weight. If your weight falls within the moderate to severe overweight range on the chart, you are more likely to have health problems. Take into account that this chart does not factor in your age or body type. It is simply a reference point for us. The Internet provides more detailed information, but the best source for establishing your healthy body weight is your doctor.

Weight-for-Height Chart

Another key indicator of good health is your waist measurement. If you are a woman and your waist measures more than thirty-five inches, or if you are a man and your waist measures more than forty inches, you are more likely to develop heart disease, high blood pressure, diabetes, and certain cancers. I am not trying to scare, embarrass, or humiliate you. I want us all to be aware and take the blinders off about our bodies and its relationship to our health. We cannot do what God has called us to do if we are sick, tired, and overweight. I understand there are some health issues totally and completely out of our control, but typically our weight is not one of them.

I have to confess that at the writing of this assessment I was "mildly overweight" according to the chart above. Though I hate the label, I am immediately encouraged that only a slight loss in weight can improve my physical health and reduce my chance of disease. What about you?

Assessment

Find your height and weight in the above chart. Don't guess. Weigh and measure yourself. Circle the appropriate statement.

- I am underweight.
- I am at a healthy weight for my height.
- I am overweight for my height.
- I am obese.

Now let's consult our Creator. Many people never consider consulting God for help in this area of their lives. They feel defeated and embarrassed. Friends, if this is how you feel, there are some core-beliefs at work in your life buried deep within. Ask God to reveal them to you. Overeating is very often a symptom of a behavior caused by a lie. God is ready and willing to apply His power to this area of you life. You just have to ask. The Bible says, "You don't have because you don't ask or you ask with the wrong motivation." Let the motivation of your heart be for a healthy body and *not* so you can fit into a smaller pair of jeans. Journal about where you are today regarding your health and your body.

_____
_____
_____
_____
_____
_____
_____

If you are ready to commit to good health, then read this prayer out loud:

> *Lord, I acknowledge my body is yours. Forgive me for acting as if it were my own. This is such a struggle for me. I want to eat healthy and exercise but just feel so defeated in this area of my life. I am scared to try again only to fail. I cannot do this on my own, so You are going to have to help me. You say that in my weakness You are strong. Forgive me for not relying on your power and your strength in this area of my life. I want to be free, Lord. I don't want to be held captive by anything. Set me free, Lord. I want nothing holding me back from all You created me for. Thank you, Lord. Thank you for your grace and your mercy. Thank you, Lord, that you don't condemn me; now help me not to condemn myself. I am fearfully and wonderfully made. Amen.*

Now for the scary part. Call someone who loves you and tell him or her about your commitment to get healthy or share this news with your small group at the end of the week. Ask them to hold you accountable in a very practical way. Have them call you and ask you daily if you exercised. Keep a food journal and read it to them daily. Find other ways to be accountable to your partner. God says that we are more than conquerors—we are victorious. You can have victory in this area of your life.

My accountability partner is: _____

> That is my prayer for us as we end this day of discovery,
> that you will pursue health inside and out.

Week Five  Uniquely You

Assessing Your Physical Health

Daily Discovery Process

We could spend the next six weeks of this assessment talking about our bodies and getting healthy. We could set goals to achieve a healthy weight and healthy lifestyle. We could set up accountability and motivation exercises. We could search the Bible for Scriptures for the responsibility of caring for our bodies. We could and we should. However, as I explained in the beginning of this assessment, sometimes the best thing a coach can do for you is to recommend an expert in a certain field. There are numerous weight-loss and exercise programs aimed at addressing the body. Do whatever you need to do to get healthy, whether it's hiring professionals in this area, joining a gym with group classes, or putting on those walking shoes and hitting the road. I highly recommend consulting your doctor if you have not exercised in a while or had a recent check-up. As for our purposes today, we are going to make a careful assessment of our bodies, find out what we need to be doing, and then make a commitment to *just do it!*

We need to commit to being disciplined physically, so we can be healthy and strong as we prepare to fulfill our water-walking, giant-slaying, history-making destinies. Ephesians 6 tells us that we are to put on our armor daily for protection against our enemy. My friends, do you know how heavy armor is? Let's do this. Make a careful assessment.

 Day Two

Physical Health Assessment:

When was the last time you had a physical? _____

Women only:

    Pap smear? ◯ Yes ◯ No Date: _____

    Over 40: Mammogram?

        ◯ Yes ◯ No Date: _____

How much do you weigh? _____

On the chart listed above, how was your weight classified?
- ◯ Healthy weight
- ◯ Moderately overweight
- ◯ Severely overweight

Waist measurement: _____

    Ladies: more than 35"? ◯ Yes ◯ No
    Men: more than 40"? ◯ Yes ◯ No

Take all your measurements and list below.

    Chest _____

    Waist _____

    Hips _____

    Upper Thighs _____

Do you smoke? If yes, how many packs per week? _____

Do you use unhealthy coping mechanisms when in pain?

    ◯ Yes ◯ No

If yes, circle which ones and/or include any not listed.
- ◯ drugs
- ◯ alcohol in excess
- ◯ obsessive exercising
- ◯ excessive food intake
- ◯ controlling food intake

List any others: _____

Exercise Assessment:

Heart (cardio)

Do you exercise five days a week for at least thiry minutes each day where your heart rate is so high it is difficult to talk?

○ Yes   ○ No

What type of exercises do you do? _____
_____
_____

Muscle (strength)

Do you do any strength exercise or training?

○ Yes   ○ No

How often? _____
What type? _____

Nutritional Assessment:

Do you eat three meals a day?

○ Yes   ○ No

If not, why not? _____
_____
_____

Do you eat a diet that is high in protein, vegetables, fruit, and fiber?

○ Yes   ○ No

If not, describe what your diet consists of:
_____
_____
_____

What is your greatest unhealthy food weakness and how often do you indulge?
_____
_____

 Uniquely You

Do you struggle with portion control (you keep eating even when you are full)?
　　○ Yes　　○ No

Are you an emotional eater?　　○ Yes　　○ No

Do you ever eat out of boredom, loneliness, fear, rebellion, or any negative/positive emotion?
○ Yes　　○ No

Do you consider food comforting?　○ Yes　　○ No

Do you ever hide to eat?　　○ Yes　　○ No
If yes, why? If not, why not? _____
_____
_____

Personal Grooming Assessment:

Do you shower daily?　　○ Yes　　○ No

Do you shower more often if you have had physical exercise or physical labor?
　　○ Yes　　○ No

Do you wash your hair daily?　　○ Yes　　○ No

Do you keep it cut and styled?　　○ Yes　　○ No

Do you use deodorant products for your body?
　　○ Yes　　○ No

Ladies, do you shave your legs and underarms regularly?
　　○ Yes　　○ No

Do you always wear clean clothes?　○ Yes　　○ No

Do you know how to determine if an outfit is suitable for an occasion?
　　○ Yes　　○ No

If you answered "no" to any of the above questions, indicate the reason below (i.e., financial, depression, not knowing how, etc.).
_____
_____

List what you consider to be your weak areas with regards to your body.

Goal Setting:

Now we will list goals for each area above. They must be specific, measureable, and attainable, and they must have a begin date and a review date. These goals can be as simple as making all recommended doctor's/dentist appointments, losing ten pounds, preparing for a marathon or strenuous hike, learning to ride a horse—be creative! Consult your Creator in this. When thinking about exercise, factor in the things you love to do and those that are convenient for your life style, financial situation, etc. Some people can hire a trainer or join a gym to facilitate their goals, while others may need to enlist the help of a walking partner to join them every day on a strenuous walk.

HEALTH GOAL:

Start Date: _____

Results you intend to achieve by the end of each week?

Results you intend to achieve by the end of the month?

Results you intend to achieve by the end of the quarter?

After 6 months?

After 1 year?

What do you believe you need to be successful to attain this goal?

EXERCISE GOAL:

Start Date: _____

Results you intend to achieve by the end of each week?

Results you intend to achieve by the end of the month?

Results you intend to achieve by the end of the quarter?

After 6 months?

After 1 year?

What do you believe you need to be successful to attain this goal?

NUTRITION GOAL:

Start Date: _____

Results you intend to achieve by the end of each week?

Results you intend to achieve by the end of the month?

Results you intend to achieve by the end of the quarter?

After 6 months?

After 1 year?

What do you believe you need to be successful to attain this goal?

PERSONAL GROOMING GOAL:

Start Date: _____

Results you intend to achieve by the end of each week?

Results you intend to achieve by the end of the month?

Results you intend to achieve by the end of the quarter?

After 6 months?

After 1 year?

What do you believe you need to be successful to attain this goal?

ACCOUNTABILITY PARTNER:

Who is going to be your accountability partner for these goals?

_____

When will you review these goals with them and ask for their help?

By: _____

How often will you talk with them to review your progress?

(Circle one)

    Daily   Weekly   Monthly

I recommend keeping a journal listing these goals to track your progress, noting the date of each accountability conversation and milestone. Remember to celebrate your successes.

My prayer for you as we end this day and the topic of our bodies is for you to believe you can have victory in this area of your life. I pray you choose to believe you are fearfully and wonderfully made as you take responsibility for the care of your body. I want you to have all the strength and energy required to be and do all God created you for. I pray people will begin to see God in and through your body.

Soul Work

Daily Discovery Process

My soul is me. It includes my heart, my mind, my emotions, and my beliefs. It can be swayed, influenced, and inspired. It is my personality, my likes, and my dislikes. I can love and hate from my soul. My soul is all the parts of me you can't see or touch, but they are the parts that make me *me*.

> *I am an extrovert. I love to talk. I am loud. I love Mexican food. The Blues make me dance. I love to dance. I love deep conversations—soul conversations. I love the sun. I hate the cold, but I love to see snow. I choose still, quiet streams over the roar of the ocean. I love trees. I love green. I hate blue. I love to be up high looking out into wide-open spaces but I hate heights. I love to hike. I hate extreme sports. I hate to go fast. I like to feel safe. I like to feel strong. I love completing a task. I hate starting one. I like to stay at home. I'd rather decorate my home than my body. I love being with people. I love having people in my home. I love being alone. I love change. I hate to be bored. I have child-like faith in God. I am generous. I hate being wrong. I am embarrassed easily. Me. That is me.*

Your Story
You caught a glimpse inside my soul all in one paragraph. What about you? Have you ever given much thought about your soul? Yes, we are back to the *"Who am I?"* question. What do you like, what don't you like? There are no right or wrong answers. You get to be you. Try it. Describe your personality, your soul. What do you like? Love? Hate? Who are you?

Consult Your Creator

The Bible has a lot to say about our souls—our emotions, our will, and our intellect. Here is a quick reference guide. I encourage you to look up and read each verse. Grab your 3x5 cards and write down any of the verses that seem to jump out at you. It may be a truth your heavenly Father wants you to know.

- You can love God with all your soul. (Deuteronomy 6:5)
- You can serve with all your soul. (Joshua 22:5)
- You can pour out your soul. (1 Samuel 1:15)
- Your soul can be strengthened. (Joshua 5:21)
- Bitterness can enter your soul. (1 Samuel 1:10; Job 3:20; Job 7:11)
- You can devote your soul to something. (1 Chronicles 22:19)
- You can seek something with your soul. (2 Chronicles 15:12)
- Your soul can grieve. (Job 30:25)
- Your soul can loath. (Job 33:20)
- God can redeem your soul. (Job 33:28)
- Your soul can be in anguish. (Psalm 6:3)
- God can revive a soul. (Psalm 19:7)

- God can restore a soul. (Psalm 23:3)
- You can choose whom to give your soul to. (Psalms 24:4, 143:8)
- Your soul can boast. (Psalm 34:2)
- Your soul can rejoice. (Psalm 35:9)
- Your soul can pant and thirst for God. (Psalm 42:1–2)
- Your soul can be downcast. (Psalm 42:4–6)
- Your soul can take refuge in God. (Psalm 57:1)
- Your soul finds rest in God. (Psalm 62:1–5)
- Your soul clings to God. (Psalm 63:8)
- You can lift up your soul to God. (Psalm 86:4)
- Your soul can be full of trouble. (Psalm 88:3)
- God can bring consolation and joy to your soul. (Psalm 94:19)
- You can praise God with your soul. (Psalms 103, 104)
- You can sing and make music with your soul. (Psalm 108:1)
- God can deliver your soul from death. (Psalm 116:8)
- When your soul is weary, it can be strengthened with God's word. (Psalm 119:28)
- Your soul waits with hope. (Psalm 130:5)
- You can still and quiet your soul. (Psalm 131:2)
- Wisdom and knowledge are pleasant to your soul. (Proverbs 2:10)
- Pleasant words are sweet and healing to your soul. (Proverbs 16:24)
- You can guard your soul from evil. (Proverbs 22:5)
- Your children can bring delight to your soul. (Proverbs 29:17)
- Your soul can hate. (Isaiah 1:14)
- Man can kill your body but not your soul. (Matthew 10:28)
- You can be overwhelmed with sorrow in your soul. (Matthew 26:38)
- Your soul can glorify God. (Luke 1:46)
- God's word can penetrate your soul. (Hebrews 4:12)

Journal about the complexity of your soul.

_____

_____

_____

The Power of Choice

As I read through the descriptions of the word *soul* from God's Word and my own description of myself (my soul), I am struck with the *power of choice* we have been given. The words above say I can choose what to feed my soul, what to give my soul to, who to worship with my soul, and how to strengthen my soul. They say that though my soul can be overwhelmed to the point of death, filled with sorrow, grief, and bitterness, I can choose to seek God for His presence, and His Word can bring peace, rest, wisdom, restoration, and healing to my soul. I am not at the mercy of circumstances good or bad. My soul responds to my Creator.

As I researched this little word *soul*, what I found very interesting is that we can actually talk to our soul. King David was so good at this. I learned a lot about my soul studying David and the account of his life in the Bible, especially the rawness of his words in the Psalms. He deals with his emotions privately and honestly before God. He does not give them to anyone else and he certainly does not sugar coat how he is feeling. As I read the intimate words of the Psalms, I am struck by how God welcomes the exchange and especially the transparency. It is almost like David has 3x5 cards he has written down and is talking to himself in the mirror like we have been.

> *"Why are you downcast O my soul?*
> *Why are you so disturbed within me?*
> *Put your hope in God for I will yet praise him."*
> — Psalm 42:5 (NIV)

In this verse, David is having a dialogue with his own soul, questioning his emotional state. He actually tells his own soul what to do in spite of his emotions and the circumstances producing them. *He made a choice contrary to his feelings.*

The author of Lamentations does the same. He went through a process where he examined what he was thinking about, reflected on his emotions, then called to mind other thoughts that produced a different emotion. In the end, *he made a choice opposite of his disturbing emotions.*

> *"I remember my affliction and my wandering, the bitterness and the gall.*
> *I will remember them and my soul is downcast within me."*
> — Lamentations 3:19–20 (NLT)

First, he thinks about the bad stuff—the affliction, the situation, abuse, or betrayal. As he recalls them all, he then reflects on how his soul has become downcast. But there is more:

> *"Yet this I will call to mind and therefore I have hope,*
> *because of the Lord's great love we are not consumed,*
> *for his compassions never fail, they are new every morning;*
> *great is your faithfulness. I say to myself, 'The Lord is my portion;*
> *therefore I will wait for him. The Lord is good to those whose hope is in him,*
> *to the one who seeks him; it is good to wait patiently for the salvation of the Lord.'"*
> — Lamentations 3:21–25

He resolves to think on something different than his circumstances. He begins to think on all that God has done for him, and thus, a different emotion is produced—hope.

It seems David and the author of Lamentations learned a great secret that will be of great value on a journey of purpose. When your soul is feeling down, sad, or lonely, you have the ability to tell your soul what and on whom to focus. It seems there is a direct correlation to our feelings and our ability to thank God for our blessings. Try it with me.

Grab your Bible, computer, or smart phone. Read all of P‍salm 42. Write a note to your soul. Ask it, *"Why are you down, sad, or depressed?"* Be very honest about your current circumstances and feelings. List all of the struggles you are having. Then in the next paragraph, make a list to remind yourself of all you have been given and all you have to be thankful for. Instruct your soul to put its hope in God, and then praise your Creator for all He has given you. See if a flicker of hope is produced. If you are not struggling with any life circumstances right now, save this exercise for when troubles come.

List any reasons why you are downcast, sad, or depressed.

_____
_____
_____
_____
_____
_____

Now, list all that you have to be thankful for. Tell your soul which of these you will focus on.

_____
_____
_____
_____
_____
_____
_____
_____
_____
_____

Overcoming Emotions

The truth is that sometimes we want to feel sorry for ourselves or have someone else feel sorry for us. We may want pity or to make someone else responsible for how we feel. However, this is not a healthy soul response. This will not take us down a path of purpose. We must take responsibility for our own thoughts and emotions; we must take responsibility for a healthy soul if we are to be and do all God created us for.

Now the question becomes "how"—how do we stop being ruled by our emotions? It is simple but not easy. Our souls, our emotions, are powerful. How do we make a choice in spite of negative beliefs that can be so strong and emotions that can "feel" so overwhelming? We take every thought captive and ask Jesus what He thinks about our situation so we will know how to feel about it.

"... we take captive every thought to make it obedient to Christ."
— 2 CORINTHIANS 10:5 (NIV)

Sound impossible? You may be thinking, "Wait a minute; we were talking about my emotions, not my thoughts. I can't control my thoughts much less my emotions." However, God's words tell us something different. We are not victims to our thoughts and emotions. We are in control of them; they are not in control of us. They are part of our souls, and as we mentioned before, we have choices with regard to our souls and keeping them healthy.

To understand the richness of these words, let's consult the original Greek language.

- *captive*—to be led away by force.
- *thought*—"root word midriff of the body; it means sympathy, feelings, sensitive nature and the mind, cognitive facilities and understanding. Your will to exercise, to rein or curb, to fence in, stop, block or silence the mind or a sentiment or opinion, set your affection on, feelings."

Do you see what I saw? Is your heart racing? The word *thought* in the Greek is not just your mind, but is also your emotions and your will. Wait for the surge of revelation as you read the literal translation of Paul's words quoted above from 2 CORINTHIANS 10:5.

"Take your perception of the situation, how you perceive it, understand it and HOW YOU FEEL about it, and stop it, block it, restrain it, and forcefully lead it away and make it obedient to Jesus."

In the churches where I grew up, as well as the ones I have attended as an adult, I heard numerous sermons on "taking our thoughts captive," as we should. However, I have never once been taught that God has given me the same power to "take my emotions captive and by force lead them to Jesus for His perception of the situation." I was astounded and excited by this revelation. I could control what I think, thus what I feel. I could talk to my soul and it would respond. Need more evidence? I did when I first made this discovery. Here's what I found.

"Those who live according to the sinful nature have their MINDS set on what that nature desires; but those who live in accordance with the Spirit have their MINDS set on what the Spirit desires. The MIND of the sinful man is death but the MIND controlled by the Spirit is life and peace." — ROMAN 8:5–6 (NIV)

Now for the literal translation of Paul's words in Romans using the Greek definition of *mind*. I love this!

"To those of you who live according to your sinful nature, you are exercising your mind to have your opinions, feelings, cognitive thoughts, and affections set on your selfish wants and desires, but those of you who live in accordance with the spirit exercise your mind to have your opinions, feelings, cognitive thoughts, and affections set on what the spirit desires. The thoughts and feelings of the sinful man are death, but the thoughts and feelings that are controlled by spirit is life and peace."

Mind in the Greek is the same as *thought*. It is your thoughts, feelings, opinions, and emotions. It is your soul. My footnote for this verse in the NIV Bible says, "Paul is describing the mindset of a son of sonship." We have to think like God's children, or as the Bible says, we are to have the mind of Christ. This means, if we have the identity of children of God, then we have the power to control our thoughts and emotions, not be controlled by them. You can act out of WHOM you are, not how you feel.

I can provide more proof.

"Do not conform any longer to the pattern of this world, but be transformed by the renewing of your MIND. Then you will be able to test and approve what God's will is - his good, pleasing and perfect will." — ROMANS 12:2 (NIV)

My spirit quickened over the word *transformed* in this verse, so I looked it up. I loved its meaning, which is literally to be changed or transfigured to the *intended* state by what you think about. This word *transformed* is where we get our English word for *metamorphosis*.

So the literal translation of Romans 12:2 is:

"Do not conform to the pattern of the world but changed into your true self (transformed) by reversing the damage (renew) of your thoughts, will and feelings THEN you'll be able to figure out what God's will is for your life," (i.e., your destiny!).

I so wanted to add to that translation and say, "When you are NOT looking through the lens of your past, your circumstances, or your feelings."

I am so filled with excitement because these verses reverse the lie we have been told and even repeated ourselves: "I can't help it—it is just the way I feel!" Oh, yes we can change and we can make different choices..despite the way we feel about it, what others say, or what our past has been like.

Okay, I just can't quit. Sorry, I hope you are still tracking with me. All of these verses are confirming what we have been learning about our true identities. At times, your own soul is at war with the identity bestowed upon you by God. However, you have the power to convince your soul of your true identity. Stay with me a bit more, please.

"May God himself, the God of peace, sanctify you through and through. May your whole spirit, soul and body be preserved blameless until the coming of Jesus."
— 1 Thessalonians 5:12

In this verse, the word *sanctify* jumped off the page at me. I had no idea what the literal translation was so I went back to my *Strong's Exhaustive Concordance*. I found only one Hebrew word *gadash* and only one Greek word *hagiazo* or *hagos*. When I read their meaning, I almost fell out of my chair again! The English word **halo** was staring at me! Halo is an object that goes around your head—your mind. It's often used as a symbol of holiness. The Hebrew and Greek meaning of these words are "to make innocent, purify mentally, a holy spot."

When the writer used, *sanctify you through and through,* he was saying, *"make your thoughts innocent through and through."* Isn't that encouraging? No matter what we have seen or what we have done God can purify our thoughts so that different emotions and actions can be produced.

Then I looked up all the words used in this verse to uncover the treasure, the literal meaning of the words *preserved* and *blameless* as they are used in this verse in 1 Thessalonians. Literally translated, it says,

"May God himself, the God of peace, purify you completely, perfectly, in your mind, making it innocent, a holy spot, so that your entire spirit, soul (intellect, will, emotions, and body) will be guarded, kept a close watch over so that you will be irreproachable, faultless till the coming of Jesus." — 1 Thessalonians 3:11–13

Be encouraged those of you (us) who believed we had no choice! For us who call ourselves "children of God," we are made innocent/holy (sanctified) through our minds and our thoughts. How? God purifies (puts a halo around) your mind so that your spirit, soul, will, and emotions will be guarded. He keeps a close watch over them so that you can be faultless (able to make good choices)! So how does this sanctification process happen for us? What is the magical formula? There's no magic. Just truth—God's truth alone.

"Sanctify them by the truth; your word is truth."
— John 17:17 (NIV)

Essentially, this says—putting the Word of God into your mind will make a halo around your thoughts, which will then change (purify) your emotions, your feelings, and will! The implication here is that the Word of God can purify not only your thoughts, but also your emotions, thus changing your choices and actions!

Oh, let it be as you say, God!

A few more verses providing evidence of this truth when translated with the literal meaning.

"We have the mind of Christ."
— 1 Corinthians 2:16

We literally have the thoughts, feelings, and will of Jesus!

> *"Be not shakened in your mind."*
> — 2 Thessalonians 2:2

Do not be shaken in your emotions!

God has given us the power to not only control what we think about, but He has also given us the power to control our emotions instead of being controlled by them.

This is going to take practice, taking our thoughts and emptions captive. Often, we feel hijacked by very real circumstances that are scary and beyond our control. It is hard to hear when that happens.

> *"... but they did not listen to him because of their discouragement and cruel bondage."*
> — Exodus 6:9

Ever felt that way? I have. My circumstances have been so difficult at times that I couldn't hear anything encouraging because my thoughts were screaming "We are going to die!" Feelings produced by thoughts based solely upon our circumstances are a double whammy, which make it extremely difficult to hear God's truth and His promises for us in those same circumstances. Those circumstances are very often designed by our enemy to get us off the path of purpose and keep us from walking in our destinies. However, we must take control over our souls. We must take every thought captive and ask God for His take on our situation. He has given us this power as His children—we must use it.

My prayer for you as we end this day of discovering is that you are beginning to see who you are, who God created you to be, and that you have a choice to consult Him daily. I pray you are beginning to hear His voice through His Word, and that you are receiving and believing them as truth. Let it penetrate your soul! You do have control.

Gaining Emotional Control

Daily Discovery Process

That was a long day yesterday and today will be the same. This topic and truth is so important to our destinies. You must get control. You do have control. A teenager shouts at his parent, "I don't feel like it!" A woman accuses her husband, "You hurt my feelings." "I feel worthless," a husband confesses after losing his job. An elderly woman prays, "I feel useless." I feel! I feel! I feel! As I type those words, I smile as I imagine a three year old in the midst of a temper tantrum kicking and screaming with an intense, uncontrollable, overflow of emotion and feelings. This eruption of emotions does not apply to just toddlers, does it?

When I speak on this topic, I start out by asking the audience this question,

> *"How many of you have had your feelings hurt today?"*

Consistently, over a third of the audience raises their hands. Interestingly enough, most all responders are female. I then ask,

> *"How many of you have had your feelings hurt this week?"*

Hands fly up! Now more than half of the women in the room have their hands proudly raised. When I get to,

> *"How many have had your feelings hurt this month?"*

Most every woman in the room is waving her hand victoriously! (If they haven't by now, they are being "encouraged" by their significant other's elbow jabbing them in their ribs!)

Men, I apologize. We, women sling these words around like a weapon for any perceived offense, intended or not. The slight that elicits these words can range from "You forgot my birthday," to "You didn't like my spaghetti sauce." "You hurt my feelings" is definitely a chick phrase and one I must confess I used early in my marriage to manipulate my husband. Yes, I said manipulate. If I am honest, my own insecurities caused me to grovel to my husband on many occasions for his lack of sensitivity, a sensitivity that is not often found in the male species. In addition, I had a preconceived list of ways for him to atone for his sins while proving his undying love for me in ways I deemed appropriate.

What was worse, I could go from "you hurt my feelings" (often for things my husband had no idea he had done, because God forbid I tell him as if he was supposed to look into his crystal ball and figure it out; well, at least he would if he loved me enough), to pouting for five days if necessary to make my point. (I think during the first few days of pouting, my husband was just thankful I wasn't talking so much and had no idea I was mad at him or that "my feelings were hurt.") It sounds ridiculous when you actually say it out loud, doesn't it ladies?

Well, it isn't only ridiculous; it is deadly. It is emotional blackmail. And it is wrong. It kills intimacy. It kills unity, marriages, and relationships, as well as your purpose on this planet. We have got to stop being controlled by our emotions. It is a lie to say, "I can't help it; it is just how I feel"! There is no biblical reference for that statement, nor is there a psychological one. This issue of emotions or "hurt feelings" is a soul issue and one of the reasons we ladies are not leading lives of purpose and passion! I love this quote by Nancy Leigh DeMoss—she hit the nail right on the head:

> *"A lot of women end up crippled emotionally and spiritually because they are relying on their feelings to be an accurate barometer of what is true."*
> – Nancy Leigh DeMoss

Gentlemen don't get too puffed up, as you are not immune. Each of us must take our emotions captive before they enslave us. Some of us are literally being held in bondage by our hurt feelings. We are choosing to be offended.

Hear my heart. I am not asking you to ignore your feelings. That strategy would be a ticking time bomb! I certainly don't want you exploding. I am not asking you to pretend you haven't been hurt, because all of us have in one way or another. I am not asking you to fake it or to pretend you don't feel. I know many, many women and men, within the church and those who don't go, who are dealing with oppression, depression, and hideous circumstances. Emotions

and feelings are real. There is a time to mourn and a time to cry. But God has promised to be bigger than our circumstances and our emotions. We must resolve to not think and dwell on our negative circumstances and feelings, because this path leads us to death—physical death, spiritual death, and the death of our dreams and destiny.

What I'm asking you to do is deal with your hurts, emotions, and feelings in a healthy manner. I am asking you to confront them, take them to your Creator, and let Him put His perfect lens of love on them. We must consult our Creator on this issue of our emotions if we are to be and do all we were created for.

Did you know there is no Hebrew or Greek word in the Bible for the English word *emotion*? At least in the four translations and the *Strong's Exhaustive Concordance* I referred to there isn't. However, www.dictionary.com defines it as simply "strong feelings." Interesting. Though I didn't find *emotions* in the Bible, I did find the word *feeling*. Did you know that in the entire Bible, the word feeling is only used seven times and of those seven passages there is not a single reference to "hurt feelings"?

Thus the statement, *"I can't help it; it is just how I feel!"* is an untrue one. You **can** help how you feel and I'm going to prove it to you. Remember, what we believe about something may have nothing to do with truth, thus your feelings are not an accurate **barometer of truth.** You can decide in advance and resolve to not let your emotions about a circumstance or a situation derail you from living out of your true identity and fulfilling your destiny.

I love the word *resolved*. I ran across it in my Bible the other day.

"But Daniel resolved not to defile himself..."
— DANIEL 1:8 (NIV)

In the King James translation of this verse, "purposed in his heart" is used instead of "resolved." I love the literal translation from the Hebrew word for *resolved*. "Widely used for emotions, it is where wisdom and courage come from but it was from his mind, his intellect."

In essence, Daniel made up his mind in advance to not defile himself or be influenced physically or emotionally by his circumstances. He talked to his soul. He was in control, not his emotions. He acted out of who he was, not the circumstance he found himself in, which he had no control over.

Daniel was a slave, held against his will. He was in a very difficult, emotionally disturbing situation, far from the support, love, and security of his family and home. If anyone had a right to be emotional, it was Daniel. However, he did not give in to his emotions. He resolved (made up his mind in advance) that his emotions and his circumstances would not deter him from changing his world.

Over and over, the Bible records Daniel praying. I am sure he poured out his heart and often-overwhelming emotions to his God until his soul was comforted. We see Daniel making a huge impact in his world in spite of what he felt or what was fair.

What do you do with your emotions to maintain a healthy soul? I have a theory that most of us fall into one or two camps with this issue of emotions. Either we are *feeling givers* or *feeling takers*.

I am a feeling taker. You don't even have to ask; I'll just come looking for them. For most of my life, I have assumed responsibility for other people's feelings. Much like false identities bestowed upon us by others, taking on other people's feelings is exhausting, but I liked it much better than people being sad or being mad at me. It took me consulting my Creator on a daily basis to realize it takes a great amount of energy just for me to control my own emotions and that I can't take on everyone else's or I will never be and do all He created me for. It felt like a news flash; at least it was to me. It is not my responsibility to make sure everyone is happy. Bigger news flash..God began to show me that if I am really walking in the destiny that He has called me to as a water walker, giant slayer, and history maker, then my obedience to Him is going to hurt people's feelings, disappoint many more, and make some very mad at me because I can't or won't put their needs and wants above God's plans for me. I hate that, I really do. But I have to admit, it is so freeing to just make sure I am being and doing what God created me to do, while pointing others to God for their answers instead of feeling like I've got to produce them.

There is another camp—the feeling givers. These are the people who always want to give away their feelings and make someone else responsible for them and their happiness. In Christian circles, they very often quote the verse in Matthew that says if someone "offends" you that you are to go to them and point it out. The problem with this is that the word *offends* means when someone "sins" against you, wrongs you, or has given great offense to you, not simply "hurt your feelings." This is such a misuse of God's Word. I love that this verse puts the burden upon the one who believes they have been offended. While some feeling givers want to give their feelings away, others never find the courage to go and talk to the person that they believe has wronged them. Instead they pout, invoke the silent treatment, and bottle up their feelings, until one day there is an explosion disproportionate to the current situation. Neither of these are good scenarios.

Which one are you—a feeling giver or feeling taker? Circle one. Or are you an equal exchanger? You give your feelings away and make other people responsible for them, while at the same time you take on everyone else's emotions, feeling responsible to fix them or make them happy.

Have you ever considered why? Which is easier for you, sharing or taking? Why do you believe others are responsible for your emotions? Why do you believe you can be responsible for someone's emotions?

List your predisposition and describe why you believe it is your default reaction.

_____
_____
_____
_____
_____
_____
_____

Do you get your feelings hurt easily?   ◯ Yes   ◯ No

If yes, do you beat people up with your feelings, getting angry instead of vulnerable? Do you share your feelings without blaming, or do you invoke the silent treatment, not speaking for hours, days, or weeks until someone finally asks you, "What's wrong?" Describe your default reaction when your feelings get hurt.

_____
_____
_____
_____
_____
_____
_____

Some of us do not react emotionally but intentionally numb or stuff our emotions, denying they even exist. Is this a common reaction for you?

◯ Yes   ◯ No

Why? Do your emotions frighten you? Why or why not?

_____
_____
_____

Uniquely You

Day Four

_____
_____
_____
_____

How do you currently feed your emotions in positive ways? (Hint, hint, what you think about produces your emotions.)

_____
_____
_____
_____
_____
_____
_____

Negative ways?

_____
_____
_____
_____
_____
_____
_____

Goals for Your Emotions

We need to set goals in this area of our life just like any other if we want to be healthy and reach our full potential and purpose.

Which emotions do you need to control?

_____
_____

Which emotions do you need to feel?

What emotions do you need to share?

What is your tangible plan for putting these into practice?

I will begin today by:

Once a day I will:

Once a week I will:

Who do you trust to hold you accountable in this area of your life? Who will you let speak truth into your life to ensure your emotions aren't lying to you? Call them now!

c2bu.com/vid6

We have got to take responsibility for our own emotions. We have got to resolve to not be controlled by our emotions. We have got to resolve to not blame others for our feelings, nor act out of emotions. We must learn to act out of who we are, the identity as beloved, children of God, and not what we feel due to our thoughts, circumstances, or perceived slights or offensives. That is my prayer for you today.

Acting Out of Who We Are

Daily Discovery Process

Dear mighty warriors and righteous girlfriends, my prayer for you is a healthy soul. To have one, we must feed our souls truth. There is no biblical reference, directive, or instruction in God's Word that we should ever base our belief, our truth, and certainly not our choices or actions on our feelings. Nor is there a single reference in God's Word to "trust" our feelings, or that we have a right to react if someone "hurt" them. We must learn to act out of who we are, not what we feel.

We are emotional beings. I'm not saying otherwise. The Bible says that God experiences emotions, too. We all "feel." However, to base your value, your self-worth, and your choices on "feelings" is a recipe for disaster. In the last twenty-four hours, I have probably "felt" fifteen different emotions, some pleasant and some not so pleasant. Some are based on the reality of a situation and some are based on my own inaccurate perceptions, not to mention the ones based on the fact that I'm in full-blown menopause!

We are created in God's image. God is not coy about expressing his emotions, his anger, and his hurt over his disobedient children's choices, the Israelites. I am sure he has the same emotional reaction to some of mine. Jesus felt deeply as he walked this planet in the skin of a man. He wept, he got frustrated with those he loved, and he wrestled with severe anxiety as he contemplated his destiny, the journey to the cross. The Bible tells us that the Holy Spirit can be grieved just as we humans experience grief. We are emotional beings. We feel. Feelings can be

good, bad, right, or wrong, but they are just "feelings." They cannot be trusted to make decisions. They are not good indicators of reality.

In fact, very often they do not have a thing to do with truth but only our perception or inaccurate perception of a situation. They should not be trusted, nor be the basis and/or justification for our decisions, our actions, and our behaviors. So many times, I have heard people use their "feelings" as an excuse to not move forward into their destinies. Feelings are deceitful. I have a newsflash for many of you: your emotions are robbing you of your identity, destiny, and purpose. This is not only my opinion, but also the words of the prophet Jeremiah.

"The heart is deceitful above all things, and desperately wicked: who can know it? I the LORD search the heart, I try the reins, even to give every man according to his ways, and according to the fruit of his doings." — JEREMIAH 17:9–10 (KJV)

Same verse. Another translation.

"The heart is deceitful above all things and beyond cure. Who can understand it? I the Lord search the heart and examine the mind to reward a man according to his conduct according to what his deeds deserve." — JEREMIAH 17:9–10 (NIV)

I bet you are thinking, "This woman is crazy!" Nowhere in that verse does it mention the word "feelings" or emotions. Wait for it. The Hebrew word for "heart" is *leb*. Consider the definition, "Used widely for **the feelings**, the will and even the intellect of an individual; the center of anything, **the "heart" is the source of various emotions** like courage."

Drum roll please. Though I could not find the word *emotions* in the Bible, I did find the Hebrew word for *heart*, which includes, but is not limited to, our *feelings*. Consider the literal translation of Jeremiah's words in Chapter 17.

"Our feelings, will and intellect are fraudulent, deceitful and polluted in addition to being desperately feeble and frail. Who can understand it? But, I the Lord, dig deep, investigate, put on trial your emotions, your will and thoughts and according to the course of action chosen by man, by our actions he will be rewarded!"
— JEREMIAH 17:9–10

I love this. Jeremiah agrees with me! He says right here we cannot trust our emotions. They are fraudulent. Deceitful. Polluted. Feeble. Frail. "Who can understand them?" I know how Jeremiah "feels." I often have a hard time understanding my own emotions. I love how God jumps in here and basically says, "but I am going to reward you on your 'course of action,' your choices—not on what you are feeling." Do you see the implication? We **can** make choices that differ from how we feel! We can! We must if we are ever to be and do all God created us for.

But wait a minute. If our emotions and thoughts are not to be trusted, if our "heart" is not to be relied upon, then what do we base our choices and actions on? Simple. We base them on our identities as children of God. God said this very same thing of Himself in Ezekiel.

"I seriously considered unleashing my anger on them right there in the desert.
But I thought better of it and acted out of who I was not by what I felt,
so that I might be honored and not blasphemed by the nations
who had seen me bring them out." — Ezekiel 20:14 (MSG)

"But dear Israel, you'll also realize that I am God when **I respond to you**
out of who I am, not by what I feel *about the evil lives you've lived, the corrupt*
history you've compiled." — Ezekiel 20:44 (MSG)

Did you hear that? God acts out of *who he* is not how he feels! God had been betrayed over and over by the people He created, the people He loved, the people He rescued, the people He chose. He had a right to His feelings but He didn't act out of them. He acted out of who He is and who He continues to be. What about you? Do you act out of how you feel or who you are? Do you respond to people out of your God-given identity or your inflamed emotions? Re-read the verses above and journal your thoughts here.

_____
_____
_____
_____
_____

Who are we? We are God's children. Period. Therefore, we must choose to act like it. If we are ever to fulfill our God-given destinies, we have got to stop giving so much weight to our "feelings." Quite honestly, it doesn't matter if you "feel" like a child of God; it only matters whether you choose to believe it and think on it. Your feelings will follow what you think on.

Your life and your emotions will literally change when you choose to believe that you are the precious princess daughter of the king or courageous warrior son. Over and over, as I study this topic of emotions and feelings, as I study my personal heroes in the Bible and the ones who have walked or are still walking this planet, I am convinced and have seen evidence that God has given us the power to make choices in spite of how we "feel." In Deuteronomy, God says to his people,

"I have set before you life and death, blessing and curses. Now choose life so that you and your children may live and that you may love the Lord your God, listen to his voice and hold fast to him." — DEUTERONOMY 30:19–20A

It's a choice. The passage doesn't say one word about "trusting your feelings" or "only do it if you feel like it." It is a choice. Who do you trust more about a situation—your identity, God, or your feelings?

_____
_____
_____
_____
_____

In JUDGES 6, we find a man wrestling out this very concept. Gideon. Gideon was a man hiding out in a winepress, fearing for his life. His identity and his destiny had been stolen because of circumstances beyond his control. He didn't believe he had any choices until an angel showed up on the scene. The angel didn't change Gideon's circumstances. He did not miraculously take away all of Gideon's problems or ask him to share his feelings. No! He showed up to tell Gideon who he was! He bestowed his identity upon him and that changed everything in Gideon's life.

"You are a mighty warrior." — JUDGES 6:12 (NIV)

The God of the Universe had just intervened into his circumstances. After a little convincing by the angel, Gideon started acting out of that identity, like the mighty warrior God created him to be. He made a choice opposite his circumstances and emotions. He started to focus on the identity bestowed upon him by God instead of the labels put on him by man and the very real emotions that were being produced from his thoughts about his circumstances. Very soon, not only was he participating in changing his circumstances, he was leading the charge to invoke change for an entire nation—all because he was choosing to live and act out of a new identity. Do you see this truth? Gideon could not participate in his destiny until he was free from his emotions. He went from victim to victorious simply by believing the identity that had been bestowed upon him! We can all learn from Gideon. We do not have to be victimized by our emotions, our feelings, or our circumstances! Nothing changes until we change how we think about something. Sadly, for some people, even long after their circumstances change and the abuse stops, they are still held captive by their thoughts, which produce negative emotions, which lead to poor choices.

This is far from God's plan for our lives. We are children of the King. You have a new identity! We are to be his ambassadors to this world for every situation we find ourselves in. We literally represent God in every situation we show up in. That is why how we act and how we respond matters.

Describe your current circumstances and how embracing your identity as a child of God would cause you to make different choices in spite of your feelings.

_____
_____
_____
_____
_____
_____
_____
_____
_____

I have taught my children that they have my name and God's name on their back whenever they go to someone's house or out in this world. Their behavior is a reflection on all of us! Weighty, huh? Our behavior is a reflection on God. We have got to stop acting out of our emotions and resolve to be and do all God created us for in spite of how we feel or the circumstances we find ourselves in. Creation is waiting for the sons and daughters of God to be revealed. The world is waiting. Destinies are at stake—your water-walking, giant-slaying, history-making destiny.

As we end this chapter, let's courageously pray this verse.

"Search me O God and know my heart, try me and know my thoughts. See if there is any wicked way in me and lead me in the way everlasting." — Psalm 139:23

Literal translation. (It takes courage to pray it!)

"Search me thoroughly, deliberately examine me O God, and know my emotions, my thoughts and my will. Test me and know if I am anxious, double-minded, divided in my mind, skeptical or have wrong opinions about the situation. See if there is any wicked or grievous way in me, point out anything that is offensive to you or that displeases you and then guide me into the glorious, bright victorious future you have planned for me! Amen."

Take a few minutes to "chew" on this verse. Make it your prayer as you read the words out loud. Sit still and meditate on each word. See what springs to your "mind."

Record your thoughts. Are there any anxious thoughts that spring to mind? Write them here.

_____
_____
_____
_____
_____

Ask God to show you where you have been double-minded or divided in a situation and record them here.

_____
_____
_____
_____
_____

Is it a possibility that you have wrong opinions or feelings about a situation or a person? Ask God to give you his opinion about it, him, or her. Record your thoughts after you ask for God's perfect lens on the situation.

_____
_____

_____
_____
_____

You've probably mentioned some people or situations that are negative; now ask God to show you anything that is negative or offensive in you; anything that you are doing that displeases Him, anything that you are responsible for contributing to the situation. Record those thoughts and make them a prayer of confession to God.

_____
_____
_____
_____
_____

Now read your prayer out loud. Ask God if you need to contact the person and apologize directly. Do you? ◯ Yes ◯ No

If yes, stop what you are doing and either pick up the phone to make the phone call or write a letter. If the person cannot be contacted directly because they are no longer alive or if you have lost contact, still write the letter as if you could talk with them. Tell them they no longer have a hold on your thoughts, your emotions, or your choices.

This exercise is really about examining your soul, examining what you allow into your thoughts and mind. It is a very important exercise because what you are depositing into your "soul" (your mind) will produce emotions, which will produce actions.

How do you feed your "soul"? Have you ever thought about it? I really want you to take a look at what you are consistently allowing into your mind. I believe once you become aware of what you randomly let it, you can change how you feel if you instead become very intentional about the process of feeding your mind. I believe this is the easiest way to "take every thought captive."

Things to consider:
- Music
- T.V.
- Books
- Conversations
- Internet
- Social media, like Facebook
- E-mail

Can you describe in very simple terms whether most of the input allowed into your brain on a daily basis is consistently negative or positive? (Circle one)

List what you tend to feed on.

_____
_____
_____
_____
_____

What about people? Are most of the people in your life positive or negative? Are they positive and life giving, or are they negative, feeding you a diet that poisons your soul?

_____
_____
_____
_____
_____

Do you focus and think on the good in your life or is your focus on the bad? Let's take a little test to see.

Please list twenty-five things you are thankful for in less than five minutes.

1. _____
2. _____
3. _____
4. _____
5. _____
6. _____
7. _____
8. _____
9. _____
10. _____
11. _____
12. _____

13. _____
14. _____
15. _____
16. _____
17. _____
18. _____
19. _____
20. _____
21. _____
22. _____
23. _____
24. _____
25. _____

Was the exercise easy or difficult? (Check one) ○ Yes ○ No

Did you struggle to write twenty-five things in five minutes? Take your soul pulse.

How do you "feel"? (Check one) ○ Good ○ Bad ○ Indifferent

Now, go back and take the time to think about each item you listed for thirty seconds; I really want you to ponder each one for thirty seconds. Picture each item, each person, each "blessing" you listed. This exercise should take you about ten or fifteen minutes.

Thinking on the positive things in your life produces positive emotions, which produces positive actions. After this exercise, take your feelings pulse. Can you detect a change in your feelings after meditating on the blessings, the positive things in your life? Write down any reflections.

_____
_____
_____
_____

Do you ever have imaginary conversations with yourself where you chew on or think about instances, people, and experiences where you believe you have been wronged? Do you begin to feel sad, mad, or aggravated? Remember that thoughts are either produced by you, God, or Satan. A thought produces emotions, which produces an action. If you want to change

 Uniquely You

something in your life, don't focus on the action or emotion; go straight to your thoughts! Take every thought captive.

List any negative thoughts and/or situations you have been pondering and reflecting on.

___

Which of those situations do you have the power to change?

___

Which of those thoughts about the situation do you not have the power to change?

___

Do you see that you have more control over your thoughts than you do situations and/or other people? What tangible steps can you take to stop pondering those thoughts/situations when they "pop" into your mind? Be creative. Take a walk? Write down the things you have to be thankful for? Read a book? Talk to a friend? You do have the power to take thoughts/emotions captive. Use it! Write down your ideas.

___

In what ways do you positively feed your soul to keep your thoughts positive?

_____
_____
_____
_____
_____

List any negative ways.

_____
_____
_____
_____
_____

Goals for Your Mind

What new thing would you like to learn or do?

_____
_____
_____
_____
_____

List your career goals.

_____
_____
_____
_____
_____

List the educational resources you'll need to achieve those goals.

_____
_____

 Uniquely You — Day Five

List the financial resources you'll need to achieve those goals.

List what it will require of you to obtain this goal. (i.e., taking a course, going back to school, additional financial resources, getting financial aid, quitting your job, managing your time better, eliminating other activities from your life, etc.).

To the best of your ability and knowledge, go back and review your goals, then arrange them in the order they would need to be accomplished.

1.
2.
3.
4.
5.
6.
7.
8.
9.
10.

Identify and describe any feelings associated with any of those actions required to obtain your goal.

_____
_____
_____
_____
_____

In spite of those feeling, think about one positive action step you can do to implement this goal into your life today and list below (i.e., research classes on the Internet, look for a part-time job to get the financial resources necessary, tell a friend your goal, etc.). Be creative!

To achieve this goal in my life today, I will:

_____
_____
_____
_____
_____

Then, once a week I will:

_____
_____
_____
_____
_____

Then, at least once a month I will:

_____
_____
_____
_____
_____

Repeat this exercise for every new thing you want to learn as a positive way to feed your mind.

List the person you will contact to ask them to hold you accountable in your action items.

_____

Call them now!

Goals for Your Will and the Choices You Make

What choices are you currently making that are negative/unhealthy and you need to give-up with regard to your:

Body

_____
_____
_____

Soul

_____
_____
_____

What positive choices do you need to make with regards to your:

Body

_____
_____
_____

Soul

_____
_____
_____

Again, who is your accountability partner in this important area of your life?

_____

When will you contact them to discuss your soul goals?

_____

I must warn you about something before we continue. As you pursue a journey of purpose, the people in your life will notice. Some will be cheering you on, some will even join you, but some will be threatened by your choices and the positive impact of those choices in your life. The pursuit of your destiny will cause people to say, "You hurt my feelings," while others will become disappointed because your new choices may change the dynamics of your relationship. Be ready. Some people in your life may even get downright mad at you. It is very important that you are aware of these potential scenarios. I have encountered them all.

Consult your Creator

Be gentle with those you love but do not let them manipulate you by making you responsible for their feelings. Don't take them! They are not your responsibility. Do not let anyone stall or distract you from your world-changing destiny.

I pray and hope you are falling in love with yourself or at the very least starting to like the way you were made. I pray that you are truly realizing what an amazing creation you are. When you begin to see yourself the way your Creator sees you, the way He created you, then and only then will you believe the plans He has for you.

Righteous Girlfriend/ Mighty Warrior

Body. Soul. Spirit.

PART ONE

– Day 1 –

Share honestly with your RG's or MW's your "view" of your body. Please stay focused on the verse that says God is to be revealed to others through our bodies. Keep your discussion on the healthiness of your body not on your weight. Discuss any health issues you are having that can be addressed by your choices. If you can, relate any unhealthy behaviors you have towards your body to any erroneous core beliefs you hold. Our mighty warriors or righteous girlfriends can often help us see this parallel.

– Day 2 –

Discuss some of the health goals you set for yourself for exercise, nutrition, and grooming. What changes will you make? Who will be your accountability partner and have you contacted them yet?

– Day 3 –

As a group, discuss how we have let our souls control our choices. Also, share with your righteous girlfriends or mighty warriors which part of you is "fed" the most: body, soul, or spirit.

– Day 4 –

Are you a feeling giver or a feeling taker? What is your default reaction when you get your feelings hurt? How do you feed your emotions in positive or negative ways?

– Day 5 –

Describe your current circumstances and how embracing your identity as a child of God would cause you to make different choices in spite of your feelings. Share with the group how the thankfulness exercise impacted your thinking and feeling.

Before writing out your prayer requests and passing to your righteous girlfriend or mighty warrior on the right, give each person one minute to share a victory they have had this week in regards to their identity and one struggle they have had in the same area. Remember, no advice giving, but cheerleading and encouraging is welcomed! Before leaving, write down your prayer request on a piece of paper and pass it to your RG/MW on your right.

Please commit to praying each day for your righteous girlfriend or mighty warrior. Tuck their card into your Uniqueness Assessment so you will remember to pray for their need to God each day. Believe God for them as you learn to believe God for yourself.

Blessings!

 Uniquely You   Overview

Body. Soul. Spirit.
PART TWO

More soul talk. Your soul has unique needs, wants, and values. Identifying them is an exercise in making a careful assessment of yourself and ensuring your soul is healthy for your journey of purpose. You are an exceptional work of art. You are special, unique, and original. If all that is true, then why in the world do we strive so very hard for most of our lives trying to look and act like everyone else? We spend more time attempting to reinvent ourselves rather than getting to know ourselves. That is just plain wrong. It is critical that you know *you*, love *you*, and value *you* so that you can be and do all you were created for!

Your needs, wants, and values are indicators designed to escort you into your destiny and keep you on course. Knowing these three things about yourself will accelerate your journey to your destiny. Have you ever considered what you need to get out of bed every day? What do you need to motivate you to be and do all you were created for? What do you need in place in order for you to do your best, to never quit, and to never give up? What do you need to fight for your true identity and destiny? What about your wants? What do you want out of life? What do you want your legacy to be? What do you want to be when you grow up? What do you want people to say about you after you leave this planet? Have you ever considered what you value? What is most important to you in life? What is non-negotiable and why? We will dig for these answers in days 1, 2, and 3.

Besides what our soul needs, wants, and values, we must remember there is a spiritual side of us that needs to be tended and cared for, too. Your spirit is the eternal essence of you—the part of you God knew from the beginning. God's Spirit testifies to our spirit about *who* we are and *what* we are supposed to be doing. We just have to learn to recognize and trust its truth. In Days 4 and 5, we will look at what we need to do to tend to and care for our spirit, and something called spiritual gifts. These are our innate skills, talents, and abilities He has empowered us with to carry out His purpose for our lives. When we discover and understand our spiritual gifts, we will begin to see why certain aspects of our lives are natural, normal, and easy, while others remain a struggle.

Soul Needs

Daily Discovery Process

Needs are conditions, things, and feelings that you *must* have to be satisfied in life, to be content, to experience fulfillment, and to experience happiness in spite of your circumstances. Often, needs are the things that must be met before you can really get on with life. When we have unmet needs, we tend to get stuck in a rut of a particular behavior or thought pattern and are more susceptible to being sad, depressed, angry, or resentful.

When I say the word *need*, I'm not talking about air to breathe, food to stay alive, and shelter from the elements. Of course we need those to stay alive. I'm talking about the things you need in order to be you, in order for you to soar. The needs I am talking about are not selfish ones; they were part of how you were crafted before time began. These types of needs are unique to us as individuals. For some of us, it can be acceptance, accomplishments, acknowledgments, compliments, being loved, being needed, having security, clarity, accuracy, comfort, communication, control, responsibility, freedom, peace, order, power, recognition, safety, work, or significance. These are the things that are critical to our motivation, and they are things most of us never contemplate. Think of it as a shot of adrenaline in our arm.

When these needs are withheld or we believe they are, we can easily fall prey to despair, disillusionment, depression, disappointment, and discouragement—the Big D's! Left unexamined, our unmet needs can stop us from ever being and doing all we were created for.

My Story
When I began this process, I believed with all my heart that I needed comfort and security. However, during this process of discovering my identity and fulfilling my destiny I actually found out those needs were false and being placed on me by culture and society. I came in

agreement with that belief. I incorrectly believed comfort and security would keep me safe. However, when I pursued and focused on them, they actually kept me from my destiny. It was so fascinating to discover through the process of consulting my Creator that even my real needs were put within me to help motivate me and propel me to my true identity and destiny. Ascertaining my needs was a critical exercise that ultimately launched me into my destiny.

Here are a few things I discovered about myself. While you are reading these, consider what you believe you need to be you and then consult your Creator to see if they are true.

> *I need to matter. I need to know that what I am doing has a purpose and matters in the grand scheme of things. I need to be a part of something bigger than myself. I need to bring people together for a purpose. I need to hear my Creator's voice. I need to lead. I need to speak up. I need courage to be and do all I am created to be and do. I need to encourage everyone I meet. I need to be doing something. I need wide-open spaces. I need to be in authentic relationships.*

I discovered I needed these things like I need the air I breathe. I needed them to be me. What about you? What do you need to be you? What are your optimal conditions in a day, in a job, in a relationship? Take the time now to journal some thoughts.

_____
_____
_____
_____
_____
_____
_____
_____
_____
_____

Love Languages

We all have the need to be loved. When we are loved well, then we can love well. As we discussed earlier in the assessment, we are commanded to love others as we love ourselves. Making a careful assessment of who we are is an important part of learning to value and love ourselves so that we can love others—well. Our purpose on this planet includes loving others.

"Be imitators of God, as dearly loved children, live a life of love." — EPHESIANS 5:1

Many of us have not been loved well by the humans in our life. That is why God adopted us into his family—to lavish his love on us so we can lavish it on others. Be imitators of God. Live a life of love. It sounds so simple, doesn't it? I have discovered that on my own I just don't know how to love others well. How do I love them in a way that speaks to their soul?

Knowing your love language and the love language of everyone in your life is the most amazing tool I have found in "loving well." Generally, we tend to love others in the way we long to be loved. Gary Chapman's book *The Five Love Languages* teaches you to love others in their own language, in the way they feel loved. I highly, highly recommend this book. Every married couple, every parent, and every friend should read this book. It is truly life changing. After you buy the book, take the assessment in the back to determine your love language. After I read it and took the assessment, I then gave it to my husband, my children, and my best friends—anyone I was in relationship with. This book transformed my relationships, but more than that, it helped me understand my needs and myself. Knowing your own love language enables you to keep your emotional tank full because out of a full tank, you can love others well. When you are empty, it is impossible to love anyone in a healthy way. You cannot give away what you don't have.

Here is a re-cap of Mr. Chapman's five love languages. Circle the ones that best apply to you.

A = Words of Affirmation. If you have this love language, then words can lift you up or tear you apart. A person who has Words of Affirmation as their primary love language feels most loved when words are used by another to affirm them.

B = Quality Time. If you have this love language, then to feel loved you need someone to give you undivided attention. Togetherness is a must. I call it breathing the same air. Often words are not required. Focused attention communicates the importance of the individual.

C = Receiving Gifts. If you have this love language, then the receiving of gifts says to you that you are important enough to be thought of and the gift is a symbol of that thought. The cost does not matter. Without frequent visual symbols of love, a person who has Receiving Gifts as their primary love language may question whether or not they are loved—the symbol confirms this for them.

D = Acts of Service. If you have this love language, you feel loved by the act of service. An act of service is someone doing something to please you and serve you in a way that is unique to you. The act is symbolic and demonstrative. Something you need to feel loved.

E = Physical Touch. If this is your love language, then holding hands, back rubs, hugs, touching as you talk, running hands through hair, or sitting close enough to touch are all required for you to feel loved. Physical intimacy is very important to you and you require frequent and consistent doses to feel loved.

Day One

Contemplate your love language. Get the book and do the assessment in the back. Write down what you need to feel loved. Is this primal need being met in your life? If so, write down how and by whom. If not, reflect on ways you can share your need with those who love you.

_____
_____
_____
_____
_____
_____
_____
_____
_____
_____
_____
_____
_____
_____
_____
_____
_____

Your Creator made you. Allow Him to love you in your specific, unique language. That love may come in the form of words of affirmation through His word or through the words of another. That love may come to you as you spend time alone, taking a walk outside with your Abba Father, or breathing in the beauty of His creation. He may love you by giving you a gift that is uniquely for you—a breathtaking sunset, an unexpected answer to a long-prayed prayer, a new opportunity to be you, or maybe resurrecting a dream you thought was long buried. His love may come to you in a physical way with a hug from a friend or a family member. He may love you by meeting a need or desire you have long been struggling with. I pray God opens the eyes of your heart so you can see and feel His love for you in a tangible way today.

My prayer for you as we conclude this day is that you are learning to love yourself, and that out of that love, you can love others. I challenge you to share your love language with the people in your life so that they can learn to love you well. Be patient with them, dear one. Remember they are only human. Your heavenly Father is the only one that can love you unconditionally. Go to Him often for that love.

Exploring Our Wants

Daily Discovery Process

Wants are distinct from needs. We are often made to believe that needs are necessary and wants are selfish. I disagree. Wants are conditions, things, or experiences that you feel would optimize your life. Wants can come from past experiences, upbringing, or advertising. Wants, just like needs, can be the motivator that gets you out of bed every day. The things you want, when processed with your Creator, can give you a glimpse into the destiny you have been created for. Define your wants and then review them periodically.

When you were a child, what did you want to be when you grew up? At one point in my life, I thought I wanted to be a fashion model .. let's just say it didn't happen. At another time I wanted to be a mom and a missionary. As I grew up and experienced more of the world, I wanted to be an interior designer, event planner, a psychologist, and a chiropractor. After beginning a journey of purpose, I realized that some of the jobs I thought I wanted, when examined, gave me clues to my identity. I liked being on a stage, thus the fashion model title. I am a nurturer and encourager, which can be described as a mom. I want to have beautiful, peaceful surroundings so I explored interior design. I have the gift of hospitality and love to entertain so I thought about event planning. I want deep relationships and to understand human behavior so I once explored being a psychologist. I want to help people live a life free of pain and I loved my chiropractor, so I considered that as a career. Sometimes a job that appeals to us can be clues to our unique identity and destiny.

A friend of mine once told me that she always wanted to be a lawyer. Her family encouraged her because she argued all the time. As she grew older, she realized that she had what I call the "justice gene." She argued all the time at any injustice she encountered. She didn't become a

lawyer; she became a social justice advocate. Early in her childhood, she didn't have access to this title or job description so she chose one she recognized. Another friend of mine wanted to be an astronaut when she was little. That dream never happened, but later in life, after going on her own journey of purpose, she realized the title "astronaut" was one she used to describe her desire, her want to travel and explore—both of which she did.

As for me, as I continued going through this process with my Creator examining what I wanted, I realized deep within me were wants I didn't have words for as a child, but my Creator helped me articulate them as an adult. From a very young age I wanted to be a world changer. I hate for things to stay the same. I want to experience change. I am an agent of change. I want to realize my full potential. I want to lead people to their Creator. I want to see their lives change. I want to be known. I want to leave a legacy for my children, grandchildren, and great-grandchildren in which my ceiling becomes the floor of their life. I want people to say that my life, my journey, encouraged them on their own journey. I want to do something that no one has ever done before in a way that no one has done it. I want my Creator to get all the credit. I want to help you begin your own journey of discovering your true identity and fulfilling your destiny.

What about you? What did you want to be when you grew up? List all the job titles you remember. Ask your Creator to help bring those to mind.

_____
_____
_____

Did you become any of them?   ◯ Yes ◯ No

If yes, describe the sense of satisfaction you get from being and doing that job. Does that job give you clues to your identity?

_____
_____
_____

If you did not become who you wanted to be when you were little, consult your Creator and ask Him if there are clues to your identity in those job(s) you thought you wanted. Write down any insights here.

_____
_____
_____

What do you want to be known for? What is the legacy you want to leave? What do you want out of your relationships? Ponder these questions for a moment and then journal your thoughts. Don't edit them or make them pretty, just write. Give yourself permission to think of your wants. Think of these as motivations.

_____
_____
_____
_____
_____

Here are several other assessments I recommend, which may help you determine your needs, wants, strengths, and values, all which help you fall in love with you. Some of them require a fee for the assessment, but I highly recommend making the investment in you.

> *"Hide not your talents. They for use were made.*
> *What's a sundial in the shade?"*
> —Benjamin Franklin

StrengthsFinder 2.0™ by Tom Rath

Do you have the opportunity to do what you do best every day? Chances are you don't. All too often, our natural talents go untapped. From the cradle to the cubicle, we devote more time to fixing our shortcomings than to developing our strengths. We need to focus on our strengths.

This one of my very favorite assessment tools because it focuses on your natural God-created strengths instead of your weaknesses; it uncovers what you have instead of what you don't. This book shows you how to develop these raw strengths into excellence. You can purchase the book on Amazon. I encourage you to buy the book and use the code provided on the back using your computer to take the assessment. When you complete StrengthsFinder 2.0, list your top five strengths below.

1. _____
2. _____
3. _____
4. _____
5. _____

Did your top five strengths surprise you? Journal your thoughts about this aspect of your identity, then consult your Creator as to the parts of you He has created on purpose for a purpose that you have yet to recognize.

___

The Enneagram

Richard Rohr and Andreas Ebert developed a Christian perspective of the Enneagram, a personality assessment tool, which has been particularly valuable to me in understanding my own default reactions. *The Enneagram: A Christian Perspective* is my favorite version of The Enneagram. I love this book. I highly suggest ordering it. It can be found on Amazon. There is a separate online test available at www.enneagram.com. At this same site, there is a free sample test that is a bit abbreviated but can still provide insight.

The enneagram is a set of nine distinct personality types. It is common to find a little of yourself in all nine of the types, although one of them should stand out as being closest to yourself. This is your *basic personality type*.

Read the descriptions below, reflecting upon which of the nine titles and descriptions fits you best most of the time. Circle any words that would describe you in any of the nine descriptions.

1. The Reformer
The Rational, Idealistic Type: Principled, Purposeful, Self-Controlled, and a Perfectionist.

2. The Helper
The Caring, Interpersonal Type: Demonstrative, Generous, People-Pleasing, and Possessive

3. The Achiever
The Success-Oriented, Pragmatic Type: Adaptive, Excelling, Driven, and Image-Conscious

4. The Individualist
The Sensitive, Withdrawn Type: Expressive, Dramatic, Self-Absorbed, and Temperamental

5. The Investigator
The Intense, Cerebral Type: Perceptive, Innovative, Secretive, and Isolated

6. The Loyalist
The Committed, Security-Oriented Type: Engaging, Responsible, Anxious, and Suspicious

7. The Enthusiast
The Busy, Fun-Loving Type: Spontaneous, Versatile, Distractible, and Scattered

8. The Challenger
The Powerful, Dominating Type: Self-Confident, Decisive, Willful, and Confrontational

9. The Peacemaker
The Easygoing, Self-Effacing Type: Receptive, Reassuring, Agreeable, and Complacent

"No one is a pure personality type:
everyone is a unique mixture of his or her basic type
and usually one of the two types adjacent to it
on the circumference of the enneagram.
One of the two types adjacent to your basic type is called your wing.
Your basic type dominates your overall personality,
while the wing complements it and adds important,
sometimes contradictory, elements to your total personality.
Your wing is the 'second side' of your personality,
and it must be taken into consideration to better
understand yourself or someone else,"

(Rohr and Ebert, *The Enneagram: A Christian Perspective*).

The best way to understand the influence of your wing is to read the full descriptions of your type and its wings in the Personality Types page of www.enneagram.com. You can also read the descriptions of the two types adjacent to your basic type and decide which best applies to you.

 Uniquely You — Day Two

At first glance, what number best describes you on the enneagram scale?
_____

What appears to be your wing?
_____

What descriptive words from the material above led you to choose that number? If you took the online test, record your results in the space below. What did you learn about yourself from the enneagram? What did you learn about yourself in making this careful assessment?

_____
_____
_____
_____
_____
_____
_____
_____

Consult your Creator. Thank God for how He made you in your journal. Reflect again on Psalm 139. Are you beginning to feel fearfully and wonderfully made? It is time for you to choose this truth.

_____
_____
_____
_____
_____
_____
_____
_____

My prayer for you today is that you are awed by you. You are unique. You are special. You are delightful and you have been created specifically on purpose for a purpose.

What Do You Value?

Daily Discovery Process

Values are strong foundational beliefs that anchor our lives. They are the things that matter most to us. They are the non-negotiable characteristics that best describe who we are and what we live for. They are important to our souls. If your "needs" are met then you can more easily live out your values. Values are not needs. If you need something, it is not a value, even though it may appear to be. Once you experience your needs being satisfied and met, you see this distinction more clearly. Values are what you do or how you express yourself after your needs are met.

Think about where you spend most of your time and effort. When are you the happiest and most fulfilled? Examine what frustrates you. Frustration can sometimes show you where your life is out of balance and how you are not making time for the very things you value. Here are some words to get you thinking about what you value:

Adventure. Authenticity. Beauty. Collaboration.
Comfort. Community. Compassion. Competence. Competition.
Control. Consistency. Creativity. Determination. Diligence.
Efficiency. Elegance. Encouragement. Excellence. Faithfulness.
Family. Freedom. Fun. Gentleness. Genuineness. Good taste.
Gracefulness. Growth. Hard Work. Harmony. Honesty.
Humility. Humor. Impacting People. Independence. Influence.
Integrity. Joy. Love. Laughter. Loyalty.

Uniquely You — Day Three

Making Money. Marriage. Obedience. Orderliness. Organization. Patience. Peace. Perfection. Performance. Persistence. Physical Vitality. Productivity. Purity. Quality. Recognition. Relationships. Relaxation. Respect for Earth. Respect for life. Respect for people. Responsibility. Risk-taking. Romance. Security. Self-discipline. Self-control. Self-expression. Sensitivity. Service. Sexual fulfillment. Silence. Sincerity. Solitude. Spiritual growth. Spirituality. Stability. Success. Tolerance. Tongue control. Tranquility. Trust. Truth. Unity. Vision. Water-walking. Winning. Worship.

Did some of the words jump off the page at you? Highlight them, circle them, or write them down in your journal. Contemplate the *why* behind them. This exercise was so difficult for me when I first attempted it. I spent most of my time staring at the words. What *did* I value? I spent so much of my life pleasing everyone else that I was not even sure of what I valued, what mattered the most to me.

When I read the list again, I got hung up on picking words I should pick, things I believed I should value if I were a good person. Honesty. Peace. Service. Going to church. Whew! My head was spinning. Consulting my Creator was mandatory for even figuring out what I value, for what He created me to value. I discovered mine are unique to me and will lead me to my destiny. Yours will, too.

List the words from above you circled. Now, go back and re-read them, put a line through the ones you do not really value, you just believed you "should have picked."

_____

_____

_____

Now list the top five in order of importance.

1. _____

2. _____

3. _____

4. _____

5. _____

Here are my top five words, with a description after each. (I combined a few words to come up with my five; please feel free to do the same.)

1. AUTHENTIC RELATIONSHIPS

My number one core value is having authentic relationships with my Creator and with the people in my life. I discovered I have no time for chitchat, small talk, or mindless conversations. I want to know my Creator and the people I love deeply. I want to know them and be known by them. I do not have time for anything else.

Years ago, I would have defined my values as God, family, and others—all relationships. While that is still true, I learned they must be deep and transparent. I need relationships where I can just be me. I have been designed with a large capacity for relationships: meaningful, direct, and authentic ones. These are critical to my identity and my destiny! I need purpose in everything, even in my relationships. I discovered this is why I hate to play games. I would rather have deep, meaningful conversations instead. You may describe this value as communication. You are right. I love to communicate on a transparent, authentic, deep level.

2. MARRIAGE AND FAMILY

I value my marriage and my family. Sounds trite, huh? Most of us would list our family as something we value—or at least we believe we should. However the way I value them is a bit different. That is why I list them separately from authentic relationships. In my StrengthsFinder 2.0 results, I am called a *maximizer*. If something is good, I want it great; if it is great, I want it grand; if it is grand, I want it grandiose! I love bigger and better. Relationally, I am the same. I want more from my marriage, more from that relationship, more for and from my husband and our sons. I want us all to be better because of each other. I want us to spend time together because we want to be together, not because we have to. I want my Creator to use our family to change the world. My greatest fear is that individually or collectively we will settle for less than they were created for. (Yes, I drive all of them crazy!) This value of marriage and family also includes the people in our lives that aren't biological but that we have chosen to call family.

3. GROWING/LEARNING

My second value is all about growing and learning so I reach my full potential. Then I want to replicate, duplicate, and impart all that is within me. I hate being bored. I want to be stimulated. I want to feel alive, and through my times of intimacy with my Creator, I was shown this is an important part of my destiny—to be fully alive, growing daily, and producing "fruit" that lasts an eternity. Without consulting my Creator day by day, I do not think I would have been able to state this as a value.

At first glance, my life and past did not seem to reflect this value. I did not go to college and did not have a great deal of desire to excel when I was in school. However, my Creator reminded me that I love to read. I literally devour books. Reading is learning. I love to go to conferences. I love to listen to speakers. I love to hang out with people who are smarter than I am. Though my life choices took me from a path of structured learning, I appease my hunger for knowledge in a more unstructured way. I long for knowledge that produces personal growth. For years now, I have asked my Creator to be my teacher, and daily I try to learn something new. I am now so thrilled to be entering college at the age of fifty-five!

4. ACTION

I value doing something, anything—even if it is wrong. I am not scared of failure, but I am scared to death of sitting by and doing nothing. I hate sitting still. I hate being bored. I hate worrying and wringing hands. I hate problems with no answers. I like action. It is so affirming to have your Creator show you the very thing that often drives people crazy about your personality is the very thing placed inside of you to ensure that you will fulfill your destiny! It is incredibly encouraging to know that you are created on purpose for a purpose—even if you are often misunderstood or told to sit still. I love making decisions and taking action.

5. SOLITUDE AND MORE

Solitude, wide-open spaces, aesthetically pleasing environments, influencing, respect, and responsibility round out the top ten values of my life. I have others that I also try to be intentional about living from, but these five are the core values that drive me and influence my decisions and choices.

List your five words again, and this time, write a description of each and why it is important to you. Also, list your current level of satisfaction in making this a priority in your life using high, average, low or non-existent.

1. _____

_____

_____

_____

Level of Satisfaction _____

2. _____

_____

_____

_____

Level of Satisfaction _____

3. _____

_____

_____

_____

Level of Satisfaction _____

4. _____

_____

_____

_____

Level of Satisfaction _____

5. _____

_____

_____

_____

Level of Satisfaction _____

If you list something as important to you as a value, but you are not making it a priority, then your level of satisfaction in life may be low and you are out of balance. When your values are out of balance, you can get stalled in your journey of purpose. You will get stuck and your soul can become unhealthy.

Your needs, wants, and values can be used to give you clarity on what to say yes to and what to say no to in life. I can always tell when I have made choices that do not reflect my core values, needs, or wants. I become overwhelmed, irritable, and frustrated. My soul is out of sorts.

Aligning these three things—your needs, wants, and values—with the way you spend your time is vital to living out of your true identity and discovering your destiny. This is literally what it means to stay true to your self. This is what it means for our souls to be healthy. Often, you will need to recalibrate your schedule and make sure you are operating out of your values. Be kind to your soul.

Consult Your Creator

"And this I pray: that your love may abound yet more and more and extend to its fullest development in knowledge and all keen insight [that your love may display itself in greater depth of acquaintance and more comprehensive discernment], **so that you may surely learn to sense what is vital, and approve and prize what is excellent and of real value** *[recognizing the highest and the best, and distinguishing the moral differences], and that you may be untainted and pure and unerring and blameless [so that with hearts sincere and certain and unsullied, you may approach] the day of Christ [not stumbling nor causing others to stumble]. May you abound in and be filled with the fruits of righteousness (of right standing with God and right doing) which come through Jesus Christ (the Anointed One), to the honor and praise of God [that His glory may be both manifested and recognized]."*
— Philippians 1:10 (AMP)

"For physical training is of some value (useful for a little), but godliness (spiritual training) **is useful and of value in everything and in every way,** *for it holds promise for the present life and also for the life which is to come."*
— 1 Timothy 4:8 (AMP)

A Satisfied Soul

As I reviewed the words I had written about myself, I actually laughed out loud. What a complicated, complex, convoluted individual I am! What was my Creator thinking when He made me? I remember wondering that in the early days of making a careful assessment of myself. Today, I see how uniquely I have been crafted on purpose for a purpose. I am just right for the task I have been given, and you are, too.

My prayer for you as we end this day is that you will begin to make choices and decisions on that which you truly value. I pray you will consult your Creator for the values He has placed inside of you that will be breadcrumbs toward you and your destiny.

Week Six — Uniquely You

Spirit. The Eternal Essence of You

Daily Discovery Process

"Now we have not received the spirit [that belongs to] the world, but the [Holy] Spirit Who is from God, [given to us] that we might realize and comprehend and appreciate the gifts [of divine favor and blessing so freely and lavishly] bestowed on us by God."
— 1 Corinthians 2:12 (AMP)

God's Spirit testifies to our spirit that we are His children. Your spirit knows this truth. Your spirit recognizes this truth. God says when you believe Jesus is His son and you begin a personal relationship with Him, then the Holy Spirit comes and resides inside of you (Romans 8:15; Galatians 4:6). This is what has been happening throughout the assessment when I have asked you to consult the Bible for your truth. God's Spirit testifies to our spirit about *who* we are and *what* we are supposed to be doing! That concept totally blows me away. It is just too big for my soul (my mind) to comprehend, but in my spirit, I recognize it as truth.

Grab your Bible and look up the following verse, recording the words in the blanks.

 Day Four

JEREMIAH 1:5 says,

"_____

_____

_____

_____"

After you finish, say the words out loud. Internalize them with your spirit. Let them pass through your soul (your mind) and let them go straight to your spirit. Now say them out loud again, this time putting your name in the blanks below.

"_____, before I formed you in the womb I knew you. Before you were born _____, I set you apart."

Our need to be known, our need to matter, to belong, and to make a difference is so strong within souls. I believe our souls ask the question "Who am I?" and "Why am I here?" And because of my own personal journey and because of God's own words in the Bible, I believe He implanted the answers deep within our spirit long before time began.

Look at these verses again. They say you were known before you were formed. Who was known? Both your soul and your body were formed in the womb. But God says he knew you *before* that. So who did he know? Your spirit, the eternal essence of *you*.

My Story: I needed to be known
How I wish we could sit down for a cup of coffee and just chat. I'd love to hear your stories as I am typing my own. I have to confess. This writing is difficult. I have so much of my journey in my heart but I have never taken the time to write it all down. As I type, I imagine you reading my words. I imagine my granddaughters and grandsons also reading them. It is what keeps me sharing my heart, my longings, and my stories. Deep within me is the need to be known.

I woke up early on the morning of November 7, 2003. It was my 43rd birthday and my 11th wedding anniversary. Aside from those momentous occasions, the day began much like any other—a cup of coffee and a prayer for guidance, provision, and protection. It was the normal rhythm of an ordinary day, or so I thought! A friend of mine called me to say *happy birthday*, but she added mysteriously, "The Lord has a special surprise for you today." Well that was intriguing! No one had every said anything like that to me. I was filled with child-like expectancy.

The reason I woke up early that morning was to savor the sweet silence of my sleeping children so could open my birthday cards and presents alone. It was a luxury to sip my coffee and read the words lavished on me from my family members and friends. I had almost an hour to myself before I heard the stirring of my precious boys. "One last card. Should I open it or wait?" I thought. Hurriedly, I tore it open hoping I could read it before the boys made it downstairs screaming "I'm hungry!" The words on the card went straight to my spirit.

> *"On your birthday, I wish for you one perfect moment when you are utterly yourself, when you are convinced you are God's own child ... when you realize that everything is within your grasp."*
> — Maya Angelou

I felt Maya had written those words just for me! How I wanted to ponder those words. I tucked the card into my purse so I would have it with me all day. My children were now dragging daddy half-awake down the stairs bestowing homemade cards, birthday wishes, and lots of kisses! I loved being a mom. As I cooked the boys' breakfast, my mind was visualizing my day. Lunch with the girls, phone calls from faraway friends, grocery store, takeout for the kids, and finally a romantic evening dancing in the city with my husband and close friends. Now that was a birthday present I was looking forward to. I love to dance! My husband doesn't. Nor does he like mushy romance. But for some reason he was feeling both! I didn't need to analyze it; I just received it and picked out a new outfit to celebrate. I was loving my birthday!

With the kids off to school and a slew of my errands completed, I had a few minutes to shower and meet my friends for lunch. I grabbed the mail before running out the door just in case more birthday cards arrived. I love words, especially words to me about me. In the pile of bills and catalogues I recognized my favorite handwriting on a particular envelope. It was from one of my most favorite people in the world, my aunt Dean.

My aunt had been sending me birthday cards for as long as I could remember along with a long letter filled with news from her life. She was such a constant in my life, a constant source of love. We have always been close. I named my middle son after her and my grandfather. I anxiously opened her card. Strange. Instead of the long letter I had grown accustomed to, I pulled out a short note in her handwriting. "I am sure I have told you this before but the reason I believe we share such a special bond is because you were born on Granny's birthday (Eleanor—the woman who rescued my Mimi from the orphanage) and I was born on Daddy Ben's" (Eleanor's husband and the namesake of my youngest son). I had never known that truth about myself. My spirit felt saturated with love. I burst into tears. I was going to be late for lunch. This moment was too good to rush through. It was worth savoring.

My Mimi had given me Eleanor's wedding band years ago. I treasured it, tucking it away safely in my jewelry box. Eleanor, who I knew as Granny, was one of the first people on this planet that held me as an infant, loved me as if my parents' wedding and my subsequent birth were no accident and told me Jesus loved me. As I grew older, I learned of how she rescued my Mimi. I always loved her though I have no memory of her—just old, faded black and white photos of me sitting on her lap. Today, I wear her wedding band as my own. My husband placed it on my finger on that very day, eleven years prior. As I said before, my wedding day is also my birthday. And now after forty-three years, I discovered it was also Eleanor's! I felt like I had been given an extraordinary gift from God. Even the day I was born was planned. I was no accident. I wonder why we continually need to hear that truth. Do we really feel that insignificant? I thank God that He never stops reminding us of who we are and the importance of our life and our destiny. I was planned. That truth resounded to a new level. My spirit rejoiced! Now I really felt like dancing.

I was finally beginning to see how I was created on purpose for a purpose. I was beginning to appreciate why God made me untalented, but instead loud, talkative, bossy, empathic, nurturing, and passionate about people. God's Spirit was confirming to my spirit that I was born at this time, in this place, for a very specific purpose. I saw how my parents, grandparents, and great-grand parents were responsible for giving me a high ceiling to stand upon. I saw the rich heritage of generations and generations of strong, water-walking, giant-slaying men and women, who believed God for themselves and others. I even saw why we bought a particular house in a particular neighborhood. On my birthday, God was wowing me with the details of my life. The whole birthday thing almost sent me over the edge and it wasn't even noon yet!

I had begun a journey of finding my purpose to discover why I was on this planet. Somewhere along the way I fell in love with God and myself. It was an amazing experience and journey to this place, to this moment. I wish I could tell you the discoveries made my life perfect. It didn't. In fact on that particular birthday in 2003, my circumstances were very difficult and very stressful. My husband had lost his job. We were being sued in federal court. We decided to start our own business. I quit my job and came to work for my husband. Yes, the two of us were working together every day in the same house and still are today. At the same time, my middle son was diagnosed with crippling arthritis, my oldest son had announced he had eloped three months prior to a girl he had only known for six weeks, and my youngest son came home from school crying every day because learning was such a struggle for him. However, because of all we have learned together in this assessment, I realized these were just my circumstances. Daily, I was on the most amazing, supernatural, life-giving adventure with God. Daily, I was uncovering my identity and believing God for my destiny!

It took me a while to figure out God was using my circumstances to get my attention in a new way. It seemed God had a new lesson for me, one He wanted me to master completely. He and my circumstances certainly had my attention because they just kept getting worse. As I spent more and more time alone with God, I learned He wanted to take me to a new place—a place called *abandon*. It seemed God wanted my complete trust and He wanted me to prove it by stepping out in faith in new ways. I was taking baby steps toward my destiny and that scared me to death!

During this time, I came to an awareness that I was settling for less than I was created for. God showed me how I had carefully constructed a mask to hide parts of myself I deemed undesirable, how I had crafted a comfort zone that I was unwilling to take risks from. He showed me my excessive desire to be in control at all times and the lines I had drawn in the sand that I refused to cross. God and I were at a crucial crossroad. He asked me to give up control, take off my mask, abandon myself to His plans, cross over from the known to the unknown, and ultimately get out of my boat and walk on water. Again I felt His loving whisper as He challenged me, "Do you have the courage to be you—the *you* I created"? *I thought I was already doing that*, my soul cried! God answered that I was only being me when safety was guaranteed. "Why?" I asked. "Why?"

The restlessness returned and so did the fear. God had ruined me for the ordinary so turning back at the proverbial crossroad was not an option for me. Deep in my spirit I knew there was more. And I wanted it all! I wanted to experience everything God had planned for me before time began. But I was scared. I was scared in a new way and in a new place inside of me. I was scared of appearing crazy to everyone I knew. I was scared God was going to ask me to do something that would cause me great pain or embarrassment. I was scared my marriage would suffer and that my kids would not love me. I was scared I might speak in tongues! I was scared God wanted me to knock on doors and hand out tracts. I wondered what might God ask me to do. Why was this so hard? What was at the bottom of my fear? Why was I so tempted to settle for mediocrity, stability, and familiarity? What was I still longing for after all God had given me?

These questions were all fighting for answers inside of me as I left my birthday lunch with my friends. It was delightful, but as I was laughing and smiling with them, God kept pressing me for my answer and I kept pressing Him for mine. To pause the thoughts, I turned on the CD player in my car to listen to what my children call my "God music." I turned my thoughts to my date with my husband, while at the same time praying, "I'll do it, Lord. I'll do anything if you will give me the courage to be me. Why am I so afraid?"

Immediately, the volume to the music in my car was mysteriously turned up. I looked at my radio. It was as if an invisible hand reached in to my car to ensure I didn't miss this particular song. I'm sure I had heard the song before but now the words seemed to come from my own heart.

In the song "Hungry" by Kathryn Scott, she sings of how God's love doesn't ever run dry when I come to him hungry and empty. He alone satisfies my hunger and thirst. It's a beautiful song. The words and melody became one as they entered and physically surrounded my body, my soul, and my spirit. The familiar words produced an ache and urgency that was not of this world.

With mere words I will never adequately be able to describe what happened next. Tears began to flow down my cheeks as the song played. The notes were hitting chords deep within my spirit. I was truly hungry for that which is not food. Time stood still and liquid warmth began to pour over and through me. My quiet tears became sobs. My eyes became the lens of a camera and I saw two dancers. I literally saw them. (Yes, I was still driving.) One of the dancers was me, a perfect me. I was in the outfit I had planned to wear that evening with my husband. But my perfection did not come from my outfit. I was beautiful in a way I knew I could never be. I felt beautiful for the very first time in my life. I was dancing, as I was being held close. My partner was dressed in a tuxedo. I knew him but I could not see his face. He knew me in a way I had never been known. He led me around and around the ballroom. I was weightless and graceful and many other things that I am not. The moment was intensely intimate. I was being loved in a love that is pure and unconditional. It is a love that is beyond words. Stronger, deeper, and more complete than any love I had ever felt before. I finally pulled my car off to the side of the road. The vision continued. I keep hitting rewind on the song so it would never end, but eventually it did. My sobs subsided.

I sat there alone in my car. There was no concept of time. It just didn't exist. The moment was surreal but I knew it had happened. I have no idea how long I continued to sit in my car on the side of the road. I had no words. I had no previous experience to compare it to so I didn't even try. I just reveled in the knowledge that I was known—completely known—and was still loved. Everything I was and everything I would never be was known. I was loved in spite of them. My secrets were all exposed and I was still loved. It had been Jesus. I heard Him whisper to every part of me, "This is what you have been longing for. You will never find it in the approval or praises of others. You will never find it by playing it safe. You will never know love like this apart from me. You have been searching all this time for *me*, for the love and approval only I can give you. Love, not based on what you do but for who you are. Be still and know *my* love. My life-changing love."

As I became conscious of time and the passing cars, I knew I had been given another incredible gift from God on my birthday, on my great-grandmother Eleanor's birthday, and my wedding day. I danced with my destiny. It was the birthday wish on my card. I had one perfect moment when I was utterly me and I realized as I never had before that I was a child of God and that absolutely nothing was beyond my grasp. I now had the courage to be me because I had experienced true love. God had taken what I knew in my head and applied it in full Technicolor to my heart and to my spirit!

My very next thought was of you! How would I tell you, the men and women I have become so passionate about, that Jesus wants to dance with you, too? God knows I cannot keep quiet about anything that happens to me or when He teaches me something. In fact, I have come to believe that He counts on me to do exactly this. Paul said in 2 Corinthians, "I am absolutely crazy for God but dead serious for you." That is how I feel on most days. You may want to commit me to the psychiatric ward after reading this story. But it is true. It happened to me. I just had to tell you because I know Jesus wants to dance with you, too. He is calling your name and asking, "May I have this dance?"

Consult Your Creator

*"David **danced** with great abandon before God."*
— 2 Samuel 6:12

*"In God's presence I'll **dance** all I want! Oh yes, I'll **dance** to God's glory—more recklessly even than this. And as far as I'm concerned, I'll gladly look like a fool."*
— 2 Samuel 6:20 (MSG)

*"David and all Israel worshiped exuberantly in song and **dance**, with a marching band of all kinds of instruments."*
— 1 Chronicles 13:1

*"You did it: you changed wild lament into whirling **dance**; you ripped off my black mourning band and decked me with wildflowers. I'm about to burst with song; I can't keep quiet about you. God, my God, I can't thank you enough."*
— Psalm 30:11 (MSG)

*"Oh, visit the earth, ask her to join the **dance**! Deck her out in spring showers, fill the God-River with living water. Paint the wheat fields golden. Creation was made for this! Drench the plowed fields, soak the dirt clods with rainfall as harrow and rake bring her to blossom and fruit. Snow-crown the peaks with splendor, scatter rose petals down your paths. All through the wild meadows, rose petals. Set the hills to dancing. Dress the canyon walls with live sheep, a drape of flax across the valleys. Let them shout, and shout, and shout! Oh, oh, let them sing!"*
— Psalm 65:0 (MSG)

 Uniquely You — Day Three

*"You own the cosmos—you made everything in it, everything from atom to archangel. You positioned the North and South Poles; the mountains Tabor and Hermon sing duets to you. With your well-muscled arm and your grip of steel— nobody trifles with you! The Right and Justice are the roots of your rule; Love and Truth are its fruits. Blessed are the people who know the passwords of praise, who shout on parade in the bright presence of God. Delighted, they **dance** all day long; they know who you are, what you do—they can't keep it quiet! Your vibrant beauty has gotten inside us— you've been so good to us! We're walking on air! All we are and have we owe to God, Holy God of Israel, our King!"*
— Psalm 89:4–6 (msg)

*"Oh! Teach us to live well! Teach us to live wisely and well! Come back, God—how long do we have to wait?— and treat your servants with kindness for a change. Surprise us with love at daybreak; then we'll skip and **dance** all the day long. Make up for the bad times with some good times; we've seen enough evil to last a lifetime. Let your servants see what you're best at— the ways you rule and bless your children. And let the loveliness of our Lord, our God, rest on us, confirming the work that we do. Oh, yes. Affirm the work that we do!"* — Psalm 90:12 (msg)

*"Let Wilderness turn cartwheels, Animals, come **dance**,
Put every tree of the forest in the choir."* — Psalm 96:12 (msg)

*"Be good to your servant, God; be as good as your Word. Train me in good common sense; I'm thoroughly committed to living your way. Before I learned to answer you, I wandered all over the place, but now I'm in step with your Word. You are good, and the source of good; train me in your goodness. The godless spread lies about me, but I focus my attention on what you are saying: They're bland as a bucket of lard, while I **dance** to the tune of your revelation. My troubles turned out all for the best— they forced me to learn from your textbook. Truth from your mouth means more to me than striking it rich in a gold mine."* — Psalm 119:65 (msg)

"With your very own hands you formed me; now breathe your wisdom over me so I can understand you. When they see me waiting, expecting your Word, those who fear you will take heart and be glad. I can see now, God, that your decisions are right; your testing has taught me what's true and right. Oh, love me—

Week Six  Uniquely You

*and right now!—hold me tight! just the way you promised. Now comfort me so I can live, really live; your revelation is the tune I **dance** to. Let the fast-talking tricksters be exposed as frauds; they tried to sell me a bill of goods, but I kept my mind fixed on your counsel. Let those who fear you turn to me for evidence of your wise guidance. And let me live whole and holy, soul and body, so I can always walk with my head held high."*
— Psalm 119:73 (MSG)

"Hallelujah! Sing to God a brand-new song, praise him in the company of all who love him. Let all Israel celebrate their Sovereign Creator, Zion's children exult in their King. — Psalm 149:1 (MSG)

*Let them praise his name in **dance**; strike up the band and make great music! And why? Because God delights in his people."*
— Psalm 149:1 (MSG)

*"Let them praise His name in chorus and choir and with the [single or group] **dance**; let them sing praises to Him with the tambourine and lyre!"*
— Psalm 149:3 (AMP)

*"Dear child, if you become wise, I'll be one happy parent. My heart will **dance** and sing to the tuneful truth you'll speak."*
— Proverbs 23:15 (MSG)

*"A time to weep and a time to laugh, a time to mourn and a time to **dance**."*
— Ecclesiastes 3:4

*"Their lives will be like a well-watered garden, never again left to dry up. Young women will **dance** and be happy, young men and old men will join in. I'll convert their weeping into laughter, lavishing comfort, invading their grief with joy."*
— Jeremiah 31:10

*"One final word, friends. We ask you—urge is more like it—that you keep on doing what we told you to do to please God, not in a dogged religious plod, but in a living, spirited **dance**."* — 1 Thessalonians 4:1

> *"God told them, 'I've never quit loving you and never will. Expect love, love, and more love! And so now I'll start over with you and build you up again. You'll resume your singing, grabbing tambourines and joining the **dance**.'"*
> — Jeremiah 31:2

Your Story

Dance my dear, dance! Dance with abandon. Dance in freedom. Dance because Jesus loves you unconditionally and with wild abandon. That is the truth that should make us dance!

For a very long time I was afraid to dance. I couldn't abandon myself to God's plans for my life. I couldn't leave my comfort zone or take off my well-crafted mask until I experienced the dance of unconditional love. I wish I could bottle that love and pour it all over you. I know how much God wants you to experience it. I know how much you long for it. God promises to give us the desires of our heart if we delight in Him. Doesn't dancing feel delightful?

Journal your thoughts today. What is God calling you to abandon? How is God calling you to abandon? Is he asking you to take a step or a leap of faith? Is your comfort zone more precious to you than your destiny? Have you taken off the mask you crafted and carry around for yourself? How can you dance in abandon with all the baggage you are carrying around? Lay it down and dance! Pour your heart out to God. Tell Him all your weaknesses, all your insecurities, and all your fears. Tell Him who you are and who you aren't. Tell him of your longing to feel beautiful and significant. Wait for Him. Wait for Him to love you unconditionally. Your destiny awaits you.

Week Six — Uniquely You

My prayer for you as you end this day is that you will dance. Dance into the arms of the only One that will love you as you are longing to be loved. You, my friend, are loved. When you close your eyes to go to sleep tonight, let that be your last thought. *I am loved.*

Tending to Your Spirit

Daily Discovery Process

Have you ever been moved to tears over pure beauty—the beauty of an evening sunset that lit the sky up with brilliant colors or a waterfall that cascaded down the face of a mountain spraying off a mist that was a multi-colored prism of rain? Perhaps it was when you watched your child sleeping and a smile spread across his mouth leaving you to wonder what he dreams of. Maybe it was a specific melody of music or the words of a song that cut straight to the core of you that describe feelings or thoughts you recognized but couldn't have articulated? Was it a time that you saw pure innocence in the eyes of a child? Did your tears surprise you? Sunsets, waterfalls, music, lyrics, babies, and beauty, all travel past the logic of soul and go straight to our spirits, communicating a truth that we recognize but cannot name with mere words.

Words go straight to my spirit. When I consult my Creator, I always insert my name in the blanks of the paper. As it becomes surrounded by the ancient words of God, tears come to my eyes as my spirit recognizes the truth my soul often cannot—that before time began I was known, truly and intimately known and loved. And from that great love a unique destiny was planned for me and me alone. Ah, how my spirit recognizes this truth. And before my logical soul tries to work it out, I just choose to believe.

Which part of you is the strongest? I will give you a hint—it is probably the part you pay the most attention to. Circle one:

Body   Soul   Spirit

I would dare to say that our spirits get the least amount of attention. Our bodies are fed daily and rightly so, because if we did not eat, we would die. Our souls are constantly being fed a diet of wants. "I want what I want when I want it." The Bible refers to this as our "flesh" and it cannot always be relied upon for what is "good and pleasing." But our spirit is the eternal essence of who we are and God's Spirit can communicate truth directly to our spirit. We just have to learn to recognize and trust its truth.

To feed my spirit, I need time alone in equal doses to the amount I am with people. I give energy to people, so I must receive energy for my spirit in other ways. For me, a few of my favorites are hiking to a waterfall, inhaling the scent of the trees, journaling while sitting in a house high up in the mountains so I see the tree tops as I write, and long walks on the beach breathing in the ocean air as I listen to the roar of the waves. Being totally still, waiting for my Creator's Spirit to whisper my name and tell me I belong. Listening to music that touches my core and makes me stand to worship my Creator. Seeing beauty that takes my breath away. Participating in deep, authentic, transparent conversations, where I am just myself. Opening up God's Word. Reading the ancient text speaks to my spirit. It provides answers to prayers I never even knew I was praying. Words leap off the page and speak to my spirit inspiring me, encouraging me, convicting me, and providing me wisdom well beyond my knowledge and experience. The words become personal as if written only for me. They strengthen and enlarge my spirit. Sometimes my spirit feels too big for my body and I feel I could fly.

These are the first things to come to my mind that feed, strengthen, and enlarge my spirit. I have learned that my busy life will choke them out, so I must be intentional about scheduling them in my week, or else I get grumpy.

In what ways do you pay attention to and feed your spirit?

_____

_____

_____

_____

_____

_____

 Day Five

How often do you need to feed your spirit before you get grumpy?

What are your goals in this area?

1.

2.

3.

How will you attain them?

When will you attain them?

Who will keep you accountable?

When will you contact them?

Spiritual Gifts

Children love to get gifts! And parents love to give them to their children. Our heavenly Father is no different. The Bible says that not only has God created us "on purpose for a purpose," but that He has also empowered us with the spiritual gifts needed to carry out that purpose. Spiritual gifts are innate—they transcend our skills, talents, and abilities. When we discover and understand our spiritual gifts, we will begin to see why certain aspects of our lives are natural, normal, and easy, while others remain a struggle. These innate, spiritual gifts need to be mined from the details of our lives. Once discovered, they can be developed and strengthened. For most of us, a handful of gifts will be evident at any point in our lives. In different situations and seasons of our lives, however, new gifts may emerge as others recede. God's Spirit blows where it wills—what is strong in us today may become secondary tomorrow. What remains constant is that our gifts are from God and are to be used to draw us into our destiny and benefit others—just like Queen Esther.

If you have never attended a church or served in a church ministry, then these questions may not apply directly to your life. Don't worry or stress over your answers. This is a process. I remember when I first took my spiritual gift assessment, I didn't have the gifts of "leadership" and "teaching" because all the questions were geared toward leading or teaching in a church. I kept thinking they should ask questions such as "Have you ever taught aerobics?" or "Have you ever lead a PTA committee?" Then my gifts would have shown up! But God directed my path and fulfilled His purposes for me—now they show up on the assessment.

Your Story

If you are at the beginning of your spiritual journey, don't worry if this spiritual gifting is new to you; just use this first assessment as your baseline. Go to one of the following websites and take your spiritual gifts inventory:

www.buildingchurch.net (click on Gifted2Serve).
or www.spiritualgiftstest.com

If you have already identified your spiritual gifts, please list them below to share with your Righteous Girlfriend or Mighty Warrior group at your next session. If you are unfamiliar with this topic, click on either of the links and take your free spiritual gifts assessment. I take a spiritual gift assessment every year or so. As I daily walk with God and grow into the woman He created me to be, I have seen my gifts change and rearrange.

Write down your spiritual gifts and your scores. As with this entire assessment, the spiritual gifts test is just another tool for you to be aware of who you are and what you are to be doing. Answer as you are now, not as you feel you should be or want to be.

Uniquely You — Day Five

List your top five spiritual gifts:

1. _____
2. _____
3. _____
4. _____
5. _____

Journal your thoughts about the gifts God has given you. Do you see them in your life? If so, how? Did you think you were "gifted" in a certain area but it didn't show up on the assessment as one of your top five? As you journal your thoughts, write them as a conversation and a prayer to your heavenly Father, asking for His input.

_____
_____
_____
_____
_____
_____
_____
_____
_____
_____

God's Word says that He has given you everything you need to be you. Everything has been planted in your spirit before the creation of this world.

> *"Praise be to God our Father and to Jesus our Lord who has blessed us in the heavenly realm with every spiritual blessing. For he chose us in him before the creation of the world."* — EPHESIANS 1:3

Today as we finish, I just want you to journal your thoughts about *you*—your body, your soul, and your spirit—as we end this day and this week. Who are you now in these three areas, and who did God create you to be? Is there a difference? Continue to ask God to reveal any lies you have believed in any of these three areas of your life. Think about where you receive your truth—from your soul or your spirit. Have you begun to make different choices about who you believe for your identity? Are you beginning to see a picture of who God created you to be? Are you starting to believe you are fearfully and wonderfully made, an adopted son or daughter

Week Six    Uniquely You

of the King belonging to His royal family ready to be launched into your unique destiny? Just write the words that are in your heart at this point in the assessment. Ask God to testify to your spirit any truth He wants to communicate to you. If you don't "hear" in your spirit just yet, flip back through the pages of your assessment and read out loud any truth verses you have highlighted, circled, or personalized for yourself. Ask your heavenly Father to reveal to you everything you need to know about who you are and what you are to be doing. As we end today with your story, I pray you will seek God will all your body, your soul, and your spirit. I pray, dear one, that your identity has been uncovered and that you are ready to discover your destiny! I can't wait for you to share with your righteous girlfriends or mighty warriors all you have learned about yourself and God this week!

___

My prayer for you as we end this day and this week is that you are beginning to see what a generous, loving, heavenly Father you have. He has perfect plans for you. Good plans. Plans to give you hope and a future. I pray you are beginning to see His invisible hand in your past and are beginning to trust Him for your future. Blessings, my righteous girlfriend, or mighty warrior!

Righteous Girlfriend/ Mighty Warrior

Body. Soul. Spirit.

PART TWO

– Day 1 –

What do you need to feel loved? What are your Love Languages and are they being met in you?

– Day 2 –

What did you want to be when you grew up? Did those childhood dreams give you any clues to your identity? Did you order StrengthFinder 2.0? What about the Christian perspective on the Enneagram? If you took the Enneagram assessment online, share with your RG or MW's what your number is, your number's description, and the wing that best describes you. Explain any ways these assessments this week helped you make a "careful assessment of yourself." Share any "ah ha!" moments from this week.

– **Day 3** –

What words did you select that best describes what you value? Did they change after you went through them a second time? Share your top ten values with your group. Was this difficult for you to articulate?

– **Day 4** –

Use this time to share with your righteous girlfriends or mighty warriors examples of what your spirit knows that you are just beginning to know in your soul.

– **Day 5** –

How do you currently or will begin to tend to your spirit? Share your spiritual gifts with the group. Were there any that were surprising to you? Did you have any "ah ha!" moments when you did the gift test?

Six weeks. You have been meeting with your group for six weeks already! I pray your time together has been rich.

Continue praying for each other.
Continue cheering each other on.

Welcome to Boot Camp

c2bu.com/vid7

For the last six weeks, we have focused on you—on who you are, your identity. I pray I have convinced you that a strong and accurate sense of your identity as a unique creation is a must before you can believe and achieve your water-walking, giant-slaying, history-making destiny. It is imperative that you know and love yourself. It is crucial that you see who God created you to be and that you take courage, along with the necessary steps, to live out of that identity daily. The success of your mission hinges on your confidence in that God-given identity.

I was discussing the topic of identity, destiny, and purpose with an army staff sergeant friend of mine before she departed for her third tour of duty in Iraq. I told her I had made a *secret* discovery about the importance of knowing your identity before fulfilling your destiny. She just laughed at my revelation. I was shocked when she told me that the United States Army had employed "my secret" for years as a part of new recruit training. It is called *boot camp*.
The U.S. Army's boot camp is where a civilian recruit is transformed into a soldier. I wanted to learn everything I could about that transformation, because I had a sense it could be critical in learning to embrace my own identity and training others to embrace theirs. In great detail, my soldier friend outlined how much time, effort, and training the army spends in reinforcing a soldier's collective identity as a member of the U.S. Army before they ever divulge that soldier's destiny, what they call their *mission*.

During the first week of the ten-week boot camp, new recruits receive hours of classroom instruction in the army's heritage, the seven core values of the U.S. Army, the code of military justice, and the soldier's creed. All of this information, combined with weeks of rigorous training, leads to their transformation. As my staff-sergeant friend talked, I imagined a long line of new army recruits on the first day they report for duty. I can feel their nervousness as they contemplate the unknown. They are so young, probably nineteen or twenty years old—way too young, in my opinion, to sign up to defend our country and possibly go to war. This is my default, fearful mom opinion. In reality, I would be a proud mom if any of my sons enlisted in the armed forces, just as many other moms and dads have proudly watched as their sons and daughters have volunteered to fight for and protect our freedom in this country. This is a high calling and grand purpose.

These young recruits are all so different when they enlist. They fit no mold. They have diverse educations, aspirations, and experiences. They come from different family environments and histories. Yet they have all signed up for the same thing: to serve their country, to be a part of something bigger than themselves. I admire them. It takes a great deal of courage and faith just to enlist.

Do you think these young recruits actually know what they have signed up for? Do they really understand what they have committed their lives and future to? I doubt it. They may have signed up because they want to do something that has meaning and purpose. Maybe they want to be a part of something far bigger than their individual selves. They may have joined to follow family members or continue a family tradition. The reasons may vary for joining, but they all end up in the same place—boot camp. Boot camp is designed to provide these young soldiers with a collective water-walking, giant-slaying, history-making identity and destiny.

Soon after enlisting, I am sure some of these young people may question their decision or even wish they could run back home, while others are gung-ho and eager to begin their journey of purpose. Either way, by enlisting they have begun a journey of faith—faith in the U.S. Army. They have given up their individual rights and the control of their own lives for the privilege of being identified as a soldier in the United States Army. It is an honor.

Now it is the army's responsibility to train and transform these young civilians into soldiers.

Do you think on the first day of boot camp the army distributes weapons and discloses missions to these new recruits, sending them out to the front lines with a pat on the back and a *"You can do it!"* cheer? I don't think so. These new soldiers would have no chance. If they did not get themselves killed immediately, they might succeed in getting half their unit blown up. If, on that first day of boot camp, all of those anxious, out-of-shape, untrained recruits were given battle plans without any instruction or sense of what it means to be a soldier in the U.S. Army, chaos and mayhem would ensue and most would quit or die on the first day they started.

Thus the army has a different plan, a tried and true method. It is called boot camp.

Recruits begin an intentional, intensive, and repetitive process designed to teach each new solider his or her individual and collective identity as a member of the U.S. Army. While missions are given based on assessments of individual ability, strengths, and aptitudes, the identity of a U.S. soldier is common to everyone who survives boot camp.

Do you think the army lets new recruits define or determine their own identity? Do you think the army polls each new recruit and asks, "What do you think the identity of a soldier should be?" Do they put it out for a vote? Of course not. The army, and only the army, defines the identity of its soldiers. It is constant and does not change. In both word and deed, the army begins the time-honored process of bestowing the new recruits' identity upon them. It is woven throughout the ten weeks of boot camp.

> *"Treat a man as he is, and he will remain as he is.*
> *Treat a man as he could be, and he will become what he should be."*
> —Ralph Waldo Emerson

That is what the army does. It teaches the new recruit who he or she can be.

The process cannot be rushed. The army stresses and repeats who they are and how they are expected to behave when bearing their new identity. The bar is high and the training intense for this transformation to occur. It takes time for the army recruits to believe in and trust their new identity. The officers know it will take a while before the recruits' behavior mirrors this new identity. That is why repetition is important. The soldiers memorize and recite, out loud and often, their creed and core values to make the army's belief system and values their own.

The army knows what I have learned: If recruits believe they are U.S. Army soldiers, they will act like U.S. Army soldiers. That is why so much time and money is spent on training, on repetition, on boot camps, and practice drills—to solidify their identity in such a way that when they are in the middle of their mission, they will never question who they are or what they were trained to do.

The recruit is taught to trust that training.

By the time they graduate and leave boot camp, they have become a U.S. soldier. The creed is no longer something they just recite; it is who they are and a part of them. It defines them. It is a statement of their collective identity. Notice the creed as you read through it, has many sentences beginning with *I am*. Those are the identity sentences stressing who they are. The other sentences tend to begin with *I will*. Those sentences reflect the behaviors they have chosen to demonstrate in advance of their circumstances, in advance of being given their mission. We worked through these same exercises earlier in this assessment.

Week Seven  Uniquely You

The Soldier's Creed

I am an American Soldier.

I am a warrior and a member of a team.

I serve the people of the United States and live the Army values.

I will always place the mission first.

I will never accept defeat.

I will never quit. I will never leave a fallen comrade.

I am disciplined, physically and mentally tough, trained, and proficient in my warrior tasks and drills.

I always maintain my arms, my equipment, and myself.

I am an expert and I am a professional.

I stand ready to deploy, engage, and destroy the enemies of the United States of America in close combat.

I am a guardian of freedom and the American way of life.

I am an American Soldier.

I felt like one of those eager, untrained, clueless young recruits when I first said yes to being who I was created to be and fulfilling my destiny. Like them, I had no idea what I had signed up for. I had no idea my life was not my own. I had enlisted for a mission of purpose, not knowing where it would lead, or the training it would require. I was both scared and excited. However, although I had said *yes*, I was in no way ready for my Creator to reveal His plans for me, because I was struggling to grasp and act out of my new identity. If I had known what my destiny would entail before fully coming to terms with my true identity, I would have fallen on the floor in laughter. If I would have seen the battles I have been required to fight, I might have quit before I started or turned tail and run for the hills.

In the beginning stages, just like our new army recruits, I had not yet embraced my true identity. I was more comfortable with who I was instead of who I was created to be. My past looked like it disqualified me from a future of divine purpose. I had no obvious talents. I talked too much, listened too little, and spoke with a Southern accent, frequently butchering the English language. I write like I talk, I hate to leave home, and I have no college degree. I have been divorced, despise math, and am frightened to death to try anything I'm not good at. When I looked at me through my own eyes, I did not see much potential; my identity screamed *mediocrity*. Like our young army recruits, I needed to go through an identity boot camp if I was ever going to be who I was created to be, and you needed to do the same. The first half of this assessment was our identity boot camp. We learned who we are in anticipation of receiving our purpose and mission. For the next few days, we'll see if what we learned has truly become a part of us. Let's recap what we have learned before we get our marching orders.

Our Creed

Daily Discovery Process

My Story
After I read the Soldier's Creed, I decided I needed one, too. I needed a powerful statement of identity that I could repeat often to myself when doubt crept in. So I wrote the following:

I am a beloved child of God.

I am lavished with love.

I am fearfully and wonderfully made.

I am a masterpiece woven together by God in my mother's womb.

But even before that, I was imagined and crafted by the God of the Universe on purpose for a purpose.

Good plans have been designed especially for me.

I have a destiny that will transform lives, change history, and answer prayers.

I am a child of God. I will live like a well-loved child.

I embrace that identity. I trust in that identity.

I will not allow anyone else to ever tell me who I am, except my Maker.

I will only consult my Creator for my identity and my destiny.

I am a water walker, giant slayer, and history maker.

I refuse to quit.

I will change the world.

I will have the courage to be me.

Your Story

Taking into consideration all you have learned about yourself during the last six weeks, I would like you to write your own creed. Consult your Creator, your 3x5 cards, and all your journal entries you've written up to this point. Answer the question, "Who am I?"

_____
_____
_____
_____
_____
_____
_____
_____
_____
_____
_____
_____
_____
_____
_____
_____
_____
_____

The path to your purpose requires you to embrace your identity. It must be unshakeable. No more self-doubt or low self-esteem. Going through boot camp will make your identity stick. It is designed to make you ready for your water-walking, giant-slaying, history-making destiny.

You need to know that you can trust yourself when the battles come. You need to know you have what it takes to succeed at your mission. You need to trust that when things get tough, you will not quit. Your boot camp is a test, designed uniquely for you by your Creator. It is meant to strengthen you and prepare you for your water-walking, giant-slaying, history-making destiny. It is also designed to test your faith in your Creator. Will you move when He says move, even when you do not have all the answers? Will you go when you do not have the exact location? Will you be willing to be alone or have people think you are a little crazy? Your boot camp will answer these questions for you and for your Creator. He has to trust you are ready. Having said all of that, I must warn you that on some days, your boot camp will look and feel a lot like war!

Trust Your Commander

Daily Discovery Process

I have to tell you a secret: No one feels qualified to do what they are created and called to do. I certainly do not on many days. I still feel like the poster child for ordinary. Boot camp is difficult, but it is a necessary precursor to receiving our marching orders. It is there where we are prepared for our purpose. It makes us better and it makes us stronger. It establishes and reinforces our belief in our identity, but it does so much more. Boot camp establishes a deeper trust between you and your Creator, or as the Army calls it, your Commander.

My Story

When my oldest son Austin was in the fourth grade, I was asked to teach his Sunday school class. The lesson that day was on trusting our Creator. I wondered all week how to illustrate this lesson in a way that rowdy fourth grade boys could embrace. I read through several inspirational books and pondered several ideas before tossing them out. At the very last minute, I received divine inspiration.

When the boys arrived to class and finally got settled in their chairs, I asked them to come up and form a line in front of me. I asked Austin to go last. One by one, I asked the boys to come and stand about two feet in front of me, with their backs to me. I then asked the first boy to close his eyes and cross his hands over his chest.

Then I told him to fall backward.

His eyes flew open and he turned around, shocked. I repeated the instructions, got him in place again, told him to close his eyes, and again said, *"Fall backward."*

He could not do it.

Hands flew up and all fifteen of the other fourth grade boys screamed, *"Let me!"* bravely adding, *"I can do it!"*

But they also could not.

Not a one, except for my son.

Confidently, he stood in front of me, back turned, eyes closed, and arms crossed, and with complete trust he fell back into my arms without hesitation. All the boys cheered. He smiled. He was able to do what the others could not do because he *knew* me. He had experiences with me in which I had been faithful. He had a history and a relationship with me, thus he was able to completely trust me.

Trust cannot be rushed. It is evidence-based. It is established through experience; you could say it is a boot camp-like experience. We learn to trust another person or even a product over time. Trust is birthed from a history of faithfulness. Trust is a peace that settles in our soul and originates from a deep, intimate relationship or knowledge of another. Trust is achieved slowly during the routine daily dialogue of our lives.

The more trust that has been established between two individuals, the more the other person is invited to speak into our lives and our circumstances. In order to follow another, trust must be built. That trust is built when someone consistently follows through on what he or she has said.

Military boot camp exercises and drills are designed for the purpose of establishing and cementing trust between peers and those in authority. Trusting that leaders will do what they say and provide the resources needed to fulfill the mission is critical to success. Boot camp shows us whom we can trust. And it also teaches us to trust our training and ourselves. God's boot camp is no different.

Journal about your ability to trust your Creator. Is it easy or difficult for you? Explain why or why not.

_____
_____
_____
_____

In general, is trust easy or difficult for you? Explain why or why not.

Your ability to trust your Creator has a direct bearing as to whether or not you trust people. Be patient with yourself through this process. Your identity boot camp is what God often uses to forge a bond of trust. Experience, relationship, answered prayers, and conversation all are tools that can lead to establishing trust between you and your Creator. Trust is based upon evidence, but it can also be a choice, like belief. A little reminder here .. your feelings are often not trustworthy.

> *"Trust in the Lord with all your heart and lean not on your own understanding. In all your ways acknowledge him and He will direct your path."*
> — Proverbs 3:5–6

To fulfill the world–changing destiny assigned to you, you must have complete trust in yourself and your Creator. You must have complete trust that you are prepared for your purpose. You must have complete trust that provision of resources will be there for you to succeed in your mission.

In addition, you must *earn* the trust of your Maker. He must also trust you. That is another aspect of your identity boot camp. Can your Creator trust you to stay the course, get fit, believe in the mission, and not quit? Explain why or why not.

When we put our trust in our Creator, believing we are who He says we are, He will direct our path. However, just like the U.S. Army puts its young recruits through boot camp to solidify their new identity before providing their destiny, God must do the same for you. As I read the pages of my Bible, I discovered many forms and lengths of boot camp. Abraham's boot camp lasted for nearly seventy years and required belief when there was no evidence. Noah's lasted close to one hundred and twenty years and required him to work hard and to stand against an entire community alone. Moses's was about forty years of solitude away from the place he called home. Joseph's involved family betrayal and prison. David's involved being chased by a jealous, murderous king for nearly ten years. Esther's involved being orphaned and being caught up in a virgin roundup that included rape. Nehemiah's held slander, criticism, and disappointment. Daniel's a new country, slavery, and a lion's den. Jesus' involved leaving a heavenly kingdom of perfection to die on a cross. Mine involved losing our home, financial ruin, and a new location. Boot camp is biblical. Boot camp is designed to look and feel a whole lot like war. It is necessary to prepare you for your water-walking, giant-slaying, and history-making destiny. I thank God every day for mine.

Are you in boot camp? Consider any current, difficult circumstances you are going through right now. Attempt to view them through the lens of a boot camp designed to prepare you for your destiny. What do you think God is trying to teach you and/or prepare you for? Consult your Creator. Pick one of the stories I listed above and read the account in your Bible. Journal your thoughts when you are finished.

My prayer for you as you end this day of discovery is that you will see the loving hand of your Creator in your circumstances, who is preparing you for your water-walking, giant-slaying, history-making destiny.

Weeding Out the Quitters

Daily Discovery Process

Boot camp situations are designed to go beyond our ability to fix them and will require divine intervention. It seems delayed answers to prayers, unexpected circumstances, and problems with no immediate solutions are all exercises and drills used by our Maker to ascertain our level of faith and trust in His leadership and our new identity. It seems He has to do this.

We are competent people. We get up, go to work, earn a paycheck, and then drive the car we bought with our hard-earned money to the local store to buy groceries so we can feed ourselves. We like being independent, problem-solving people. All of these actions are done without any outside help, we proudly claim. On any given day, we human beings can fight fires, save lives, get an education, buy a home, get a job, build a house, paint a picture, invent a device, and have a baby, all without divine intervention. We are wonderfully and fearfully made. However, if we are to attempt world-changing destinies, we are going to have to tap into the divine. We will need to be trained in how and when to attempt the impossible. Your Maker must know that you can be trusted to finish the task He assigns and to not quit when things get tough. *Boot camp weeds out quitters.*

Before you ever start on this journey of purpose, you have to resolve within yourself that quitting is not an option. I often play mind games with myself to bring clarity to situations. I treat every obstacle, every problem, and every opportunity in my life as either a test to be won or a battle to be fought. Both situations require my commitment to the calling on and purpose for my life. Both require that I not quit when things get tough.

Before you are given the details of your destiny, you will be put through rigorous situations and war-like circumstances to determine if you will quit or not. Our Creator designs situations to teach, test, and strengthen us. We want to pass, win, or succeed in the first test, because that particular lesson is required to move us into the strategic position our Creator has designed for us. The test brings out the best in us and fully prepares us for our future trials and circumstances. The lesson can also reveal any weaknesses we may still have. In fact, if we don't pass the test the first time, we can be sure we will get to take it again until we pass! The test teaches us to fight so we are competent and deadly when the battles come. It is designed to give us confidence in ourselves and in our Maker and to demonstrate that we can be depended upon when things get tough—we will not quit.

Sometimes, a situation may present itself that is not from my Creator, rather it is a battle designed by my enemy to rob me of something that is rightfully mine. Boot camp prepares me for this. Now instead of quaking in fear, the situation puts steel in my spine, makes me angry, and causes me to fight for and take back what is rightfully mine. I feel much stronger when I see myself as a warrior in battle rather than a victim of my circumstances. Through boot camp and war-like situations, I have been trained to fight. I am confident. I am prepared to face my enemy. I have been guaranteed victory. In both of these scenarios, we must resolve in advance to not quit when things get difficult. There is much at stake. One of my greatest fears is to realize that I was a day away from victory or promotion but I gave up and quit one day too soon.

Boot camp has taught me that winning simply means not quitting. During some of the most difficult days of my life, the only prayer I could utter—through clenched teeth and with tears running down my cheeks—was, *"I will not quit!"* I had to resolve and make up my mind in advance that no matter the test I have been given or the battle I was fighting, I would not quit. I wanted to matter. I wanted to change the world. I wanted to walk on water, slay giants with stones, fly on the wings of eagles, do the impossible, and make history. To achieve that, I would not quit. What about you? Have you resolved to not quit? Journal your thoughts about your resolve to not quit.

_____
_____
_____
_____
_____

Say it with me: ***I will not quit.***

My prayer for you today is that you will vow to never quit, to never cease to be you, and to vow to fulfill your unique destiny. People are waiting on God and praying prayers, and He is waiting on you to fulfill them.

Preparing for Battle

Daily Discovery Process

News flash! There is a war being fought over you and your destiny. God's boot camp and subsequent tests are designed to prepare you for that war. To fulfill your purpose, you will be required to fight for your life. Boot camp teaches you how to respond when you are in that battle.

Expect Friendly Fire

"When you are being fired upon, take cover immediately. Then take a tactical pause. Be still and do nothing. Then you must ascertain if the fire is enemy or friendly. If it is enemy fire, you give them all you've got. Fire away and call for reinforcements. However, if it is friendly fire take cover, stay put and do nothing until it is over."
— Jenny Williamson

"What? I'm going to be shot at by friends, by those I love?" I said aloud after my Army buddy said these words to me.

This was probably the hardest lesson I have had to learn. I expected to be shot at by the "bad guys" but not by the good ones. I guess what I found even more surprising than being shot at with "friendly fire" was that those closest to me were the betrayers. I was unprepared for this reality of my destiny. I am not going to spend an enormous amount of time on this topic except to say this really happened. I have experienced it, and so will you in your journey of purpose.

Week Seven  Uniquely You

You will be betrayed. Expect it. Train for it. Prepare for it. The army does.

You do not respond to friendly fire the way you do enemy fire. When you have determined that the good guys are firing upon you, take cover and do not fire back. That means keep your mouth shut. Go underground. Wait until it stops. Do not hunt them down or murder them with your mouth. Take a tactical pause. Determine who is still loyal to you and the mission, and stay loyal to them. Regroup. Reassign positions if necessary. Then get back to work. Friendly fire is a part of war.

I wish someone had taught me this lesson early in my boot camp. It was a lesson I learned much later. I learned the hard way that it is wise to be slow in letting people be members of a team or giving them pieces of your heart. As we discussed earlier, trust is built over time. *People must earn trust.* When they do, then they are given more responsibilities. This is the way the army does it. You advance through a series of well-defined job responsibilities and roles. Promotions occur when you have shown yourself to be capable and trustworthy. It would be wise for us to do the same. Promoting people into the inner circle of our hearts and lives should occur only as they prove trustworthy.

I let people into my heart, my life, my home, and the non-profit I founded very easily. I am extremely naïve and trusting, thus it is extremely upsetting to me when I am fired upon or betrayed by friends. I spend an enormous amount of time expending energy into conversations that take place only in my head, instead of holding people accountable for their actions. I give grace and second chances, only to be fired upon again. My strength is my weakness. I believe in people. I am inclusive. I see potential. I invest a lot in my relationships. It is hard for me to let go and leave people to their own choices.

What about you? Have you ever been betrayed by someone you love and trusted? How did you respond?

_____

_____

_____

_____

Because of the identity boot camp that my Creator had put me through, when I was blindsided by friendly fire, I knew to take cover and a tactical pause. I acted out of who I was, not what I felt. I consulted my Creator and gave Him all my feelings of hurt and betrayal. As I listened to His still, small voice, I heard these words,

> *"Since it is so hard for you to let people go, then be slower at letting them in."*

I can do that? It is not mean?

Somewhere in my Southern and Christian upbringing, I thought you had to let everyone into your life and inner circle. I was taught to be nice at all costs. I was taught confronting someone about their unhealthy or bad behavior was bad manners. However, I now realize this is not true and it can be very dangerous to remain silent. Remaining silent in the face of bad behavior is often taken as agreement, and trusting the wrong people can lead to betrayal, friendly fire, and a sabotage of your journey of purpose.

We need a battle plan for both instances.

When betrayed by those we call family or friends, what the army calls "friendly fire" must be fought with a tactical pause and silence. They are the most effective *weapons* at our disposal. Without them, you can easily be derailed from fulfilling your destiny. To minimize these types of attacks, you need to use wisdom and seek discernment about adding people to your life. Before giving them access to your home, your heart, your family, and the destiny you are fulfilling, you must do all you can to find out if they are trustworthy. Do background checks, talk to those with whom they have worked for or worked with, and do not be afraid to do your due diligence. If the individual is offended, that should be considered a red flag. Here are three simple things to keep in mind before allowing people access to your life.

- Go slow
- Consult your Creator
- Guard your heart

While we cannot judge a person's heart, we can judge their fruit. So be careful. Watch out for friendly fire. Their purpose is to stall your plans and make you quit. When you learn to use the weapon of a tactical pause, you will be unstoppable. Always keep in mind that "friendly fire" is a part of your boot camp to train and prepare you to fulfill your destiny. When your training is complete, you will be a fierce warrior!

What would it mean for you to take a tactical pause in the situation you listed above?

_____
_____
_____

If you used this weapon, do you think there would have been a different outcome? Why or why not?

_____
_____
_____

When those we love or are in relationship with display behaviors that are unhealthy or cruel, we must take courage, speak up, and confront them. Remaining silent only adds fuel to the fire of the behavior. Often we remain silent because we do not want to deal with the emotional conflict. But we must. These behaviors and our lack of loving confrontation become a means of manipulation that we are not even aware we are engaged in and, again, can derail us from our world-changing destiny.

How do you handle conflict? Is it effective?

_____

_____

_____

Get a Battle Buddy

Boot camp trains you to be the best you that you can possibly be. You learn to trust your training and not your feelings. Boot camp, especially God's boot camp, prepares you for your purpose and gives you new tools to fight for identity and destiny. A tactical pause is one and having a battle buddy is another. Boot camp teaches us that we cannot complete our mission alone. We must depend upon others for success—this lesson I learned from a retired veteran. He had tears in his eyes when he shook my hand after a Sunday evening service where I spoke; he thanked me for the encouragement I had given from the stage. I was talking about the purpose of boot camp. He told me I was correct about the benefits of boot camp but that I had left out the most important thing you receive in boot camp—a battle buddy.

> *"The guys I went through boot camp with, and the ones I continued to fight beside to execute our missions, were the closest relationships I have had in my life, outside my wife and children. When you train with someone, fight with them, and believe in a mission that is bigger than yourself, it binds you together in a way nothing else can. Some of those men are gone now and some I have not seen in over thirty years, but I will never forget the influence and impact they had on my life and our mission."*

Well said, my new friend.

A battle buddy is someone who goes through boot camp with you, someone who holds you accountable, encourages you not to quit, and believes in the mission that you would sacrifice your time, your talent, your treasure, and even your life for.

I, too, have experienced those relationships and know that without them I would have quit a long time ago. When you come to grips with your water-walking, giant-slaying, history-making destiny, you will be graciously surrounded with very strategic people and relationships—ones that will sustain, nourish, and support you during the difficult days of boot camp and through the dangers of war. These relationships are ones that you will be grateful for all your life. They

become a part of you, even if you have not seen or talked to these people for years.

When Hurricane Katrina hit the Mississippi Gulf Coast and New Orleans area in 2005, my heart broke. Mississippi is my home state. I was moved not only with compassion, but also with a great desire toward action. I immediately volunteered to go with a group from San Carlos, California, to do relief work.

When we began preparations for the trip, we were a group of strangers. By the time we returned home from our mutual experience ten days later, we were lifelong friends, bonded by an experience that is difficult to describe unless you were there to participate in it with us. It was difficult and at the same time immensely satisfying. Together we made a difference. Together we did more than we ever could have done alone.

The army is intentional about putting a young new recruit with other recruits who are starting out in the same place as they discover their identity prior to embarking on their mission. This common journey is an incredible bonding process. It is true that "we are better together."

Your Story

Write about a time when you were with complete strangers, but through a series of events you became very close because of a common purpose or mission.

_____
_____
_____
_____
_____

Do you have someone whom you would describe as your battle buddy? What is their name? Describe what they mean to you and an instance when they believed in you when you could not believe in yourself?

_____
_____
_____
_____
_____

Take a moment to write them a thank you card or pick up the phone to call and tell them exactly what you wrote in the space above.

If you do not have someone in your life you would call a battle buddy, then consult your Creator. Ask Him to provide you one. As we end this day of discovery, it is my prayer for you to experience this type of relationship that is built on a common language and common purpose.

Lessons from Boot Camp Needed to Fulfill Your Mission
A few lessons I'd like to highlight about fulfilling our missions:

Big, impossible, life-changing, world-altering, incredible purposes and missions cannot be accomplished alone.

There is a power that multiplies whenever human beings collectively agree on anything, whether good or bad—it is the power to do the impossible.

Our team at Courage Worldwide has lived this truth firsthand. We all agree it is wrong for a child to be sold for sex. It is our common language. Because of that common belief and our core value and emphasis on unity, we believe that we can do what some would call impossible. We believe we can build a home, a Courage House, for victims of sex trafficking in every city in the world that needs one. We believe we can engage a million people to build a thousand homes in a hundred countries during the next ten years so that hundreds of thousands of children can be rescued, restored, and told the truth that they, too, were created on purpose for a purpose.

Every day, five or six days a week for hours a day, we work toward this common goal, speaking the same language, engaged in the impossible. These individuals that I have the honor of working with at Courage Worldwide are my family, my battle buddies, and my fellow warriors.

They have my back and I have theirs. Without them, I could not do what I am created to do. Together we are able to accomplish more, faster, than any of us could alone. Our collective power, energy, and creativity astounds even us, but we have been brought together using our unique purposes to further an eternal purpose. It is an honor to be a part of a team like this.

You have an enemy who wants you to fail at accomplishing your purpose and your mission.

Your enemy knows that if you ever realize your true identity, then your chance of success in your destiny increases. The enemy will attack you very early and frequently when you embark on a journey of purpose. Your finances, relationships, and health will all be attacked. These attacks are designed to distract you, to make you forget who you are, why you are fighting, and what the mission is. You need to be reminded by other people.

You are going to need courage, but you are also going to need somebody to watch your back. It is much easier to *take courage* when others surround you with their weapons. Your battle buddies stand with you when you are fighting. They have resources and experiences that you do not. Because they are not emotionally involved in the battles that are personal to you, it is easier for them to encourage, support, and believe in you when you can't yourself.

Small groups forge bonds that allow members to see in us what we cannot see in ourselves.

We all need someone to believe in us, cheer for us, and kick us in the butt when we get stuck. Our battle buddies do this for us. I find it fascinating that the people I work and serve with see my potential much easier than I do. They encourage me when I get down. They pursue me when I doubt. They challenge me when I am tempted to give up, and they love me even when I fail. They help me "change the world," and your battle buddies will, too.

When a group discovers that its collective identity and destiny are more powerful than the members' own individual ones, they will accomplish more than they dared to ask or imagine. They will literally change the world around them. While doing this work and pursuing the impossible, a bond is forged that is extremely strong and rarely broken. I am so thankful for the encouragement and company of those who are called to the same mission I am. I cannot imagine doing what I do without them. They make me better.

Expect and Prepare for Friendly Fire.

One form of friendly fire requires silence and a tactical pause. The other requires loving but firm confrontation.

Pray for a Battle Buddy.

A battle buddy is someone who has a common purpose with you, who will hold you accountable and cover your vulnerable places. It is a person who will believe in you and your mission when you do not have the strength to believe for yourself.

My prayer for you today is that you will embrace the lessons of boot camp and that they will strengthen and serve you well on your journey to fulfilling your destiny.

Obey Without Question

Daily Discovery Process

In the military, there are clear lines of authority. You learn immediately to say, "Yes, sir!" and not question commands or orders given by your superiors. There is an extreme level of trust that is required in order to obey without question. Without that level of trust, a situation can become abusive and destructive. As we talked about previously, boot camp is designed to build that level of trust.

In the family I was raised in, it was exactly the same way. My dad was the head of the household. There were no majority votes or soliciting of opinions. Everything worked well if we just did what we were told. Now, my dad was not abusive. He was not a dictator. Repeatedly, he had demonstrated his love for his family, his integrity, and his ability to provide for us. He had a vision for our family and we all had important parts, but at critical and stressful times he had to know he could depend upon our instant obedience. We were able to do that because we had complete trust in him. Because of his character and love, obeying was easy, even if I didn't have all of my *why* questions answered.

I believe our Creator requires the same of us if we are to be and do all that our destiny requires.

My Story
One morning, I felt these words penetrate to the core of my being: *"Sell your house."*

What? Are we moving? I thought.

Silence followed. It was decision time for me. Do I obey what I have come to trust and what I have learned is the direction of my Creator? After much discussion with my husband and family, we decided to "step out in faith" even though we did not know where we were moving to or what we were supposed to do. Yes, people thought we were crazy. Even I thought so on some days. However, we did as we were ordered *without* having all our desired answers.

When my husband gave his blessing—it took two weeks for him to wrap his brain around all of this—I then called a realtor who put the house on the market. It sold in a week. I resigned from my volunteer positions at church and school, told all our family and friends, informed my pastor, and began packing boxes—all without having any idea where we were going. I had children in elementary and middle school at the time. I had no idea where they would be in school the following year. It was June. I figured I had three months until it was an issue.

People asked me over and over, "Where are you moving?"

I said, "I have no idea." I continued to pack and prepare to move until I received additional orders.

I could do all of this because I had gone through boot camp. I had proved I could be trusted, and I knew that my Creator could be trusted as well. I had complete faith that my family and I were being strategically moved to where we were supposed to be. I knew this was an exercise in obedience. Would I obey without having all the answers now that trust was being put to the test? It was a test I desperately wanted to pass, and I truly believe my destiny hinged on it.

Weeks later, after the house was sold, the moving van ordered, and the last boxes packed, I was given an address through divine provision. I was delirious. We were moving! I felt I had just received my marching orders and was heading straight into my long-awaited destiny. Was I scared? Yes! But I chose to take courage and trust my Creator. I had been through boot camp. I was prepared. Though our family was going through a difficult financial crisis, I did not trust my feelings or my circumstances. I vowed I would not quit. I just said yes to the unknown. I believed that was where my destiny was—in the midst of the unknown, far away from my comfort zone.

Your Story

Are you in a situation where you do not have all the answers but sense your spirit is leading you on a journey of faith? Are you scared and sense excitement all at the same time? Describe your situation.

_____

_____

_____

Consult Your Creator

In your Bible, read Genesis, Chapter 12, verses 1–4. Write the words in the space provided below.

_____
_____
_____
_____

Tell me what strikes you about these verses? What words or phrases jump out at you?

_____
_____
_____

For me it is these words, "The Lord said to Abram, *'Leave your country, your family, your friends and go to a place I will show you.' So Abram left."* Period. God said *go* and Abraham went. No answers. No directions. No strategic plan.

Would you do that? Just go? When you believe God is saying *jump*, do you jump or stay put? That is what boot camp prepares you to do. Trust and obey your creator. Is there a situation you are in right now that you are hesitating to make a move or a decision because it is too risky, or you don't have all the answers and need more assurances? List the situation below.

_____
_____
_____

When we read Abraham's story we get the luxury of the ending. In our own, we do not. It is a daily journey that requires faith to be and do all we were created for. This type of faith flies in the face of our culture that promotes security and low risk. Here, 401k's, college funds, and sure things are celebrated as wisdom. Our western culture often does not line up with water-walking destinies. Consider the circumstance you listed above. Why won't you go? What is holding you back from trusting God and making a move?

_____
_____
_____

What is the worst thing that can happen?

_____

Uniquely You — Day Five

_____
_____

What is the best thing that can happen?
_____
_____
_____

What are the real chances of the worst scenario happening?
_____
_____
_____

What about the best?
_____
_____
_____

What do you think is keeping you from taking a leap of faith? Lack of trust? Fear of the unknown? Your comfort zone? Need of comfort and security? Sit quietly and ask your Creator to reveal to you the answers. Journal your thoughts below.
_____
_____
_____

Without the squeeze of our financial situation, I don't know that I would have left my home or friends that felt like family to move to the unknown. God knew what type of boot camp I would require to leave my comfort zone. It took a great deal of courage. I could only take courage because I trusted my Creator above my circumstances.

Read Psalm 25:12. Write the words in the space below and on a 3x5 card. Read the words out loud.
_____
_____
_____

God promises to instruct you and lead you in the way He has chosen for you. It is my prayer as we end this day of discovery that you have enough evidence to trust the One who created you; to believe He will be with you as you leave the comfort of the known for the adventure awaiting you in the unknown. It is where your destiny lies.

Ready for Your Mission

Boot camp. Rigorous physical and mental training is required to prepare army recruits and us for our grand purposes. It cannot be avoided, diminished, or rushed. Oh, how I wish it could!

The days, months, and—yes—even years of boot camp can seem long and often uneventful, but be encouraged! You are being prepared for action; your time is coming. During this arduous process of preparation, something amazing will transpire, or may have already. It is difficult to detect at first. But wait for it. It is worth it, I promise.

My move, the one I didn't know where I was going, was the very place I needed to be to start a home for young girls rescued from sex trafficking. My financial situation was the test and impetus God used to get me from where I was to where He wanted me to be. To make that move, I had to first trust in Him as my Creator and heavenly Father. That trust enabled me to get out of my comfort zone and walk into the water of the unknown.

Somewhere along the way, the forced training and discipline of our identity boot camp start to become a habit instead of a chore. Our bodies, minds, and emotions begin to reflect the identity and training that have been bestowed and inflicted upon us. We see evidence of our new identity—evidence of who we were meant to be. At that point our behaviors begin to betray our belief. Just like a young army recruit, we begin to act out our true identity.

Now you are ready to learn of your mission. You are finally ready to hear and believe what was planned for you before time began. Not only that, but because of the new confidence in your identity and your partnership with your Creator and your battle buddies, you will actually start to believe that you can accomplish the impossible—the mission assigned to you.

My hope is that now you are beginning to understand for the first time that who you are has a direct correlation to ***what you are to do***. Not just anyone can do what you have been assigned to do. It is your very own unique purpose.

I end this section as we began it .. that before time began, you were created on purpose for a purpose. Now that you know your identity, you can be released into your water-walking, giant-slaying, history-making destiny. Take courage!

Righteous Girlfriend/ Mighty Warrior

Welcome To Boot Camp

– Day 1 –

As you answered the question *"Who Am I?"* were you able to make for yourself a *Soldier's Creed*? Please share any new discoveries about who God says you are.

– Day 2 –

What trust issues do you have or have had in the past? Do you find it easy or difficult to trust God? Other people? Why or why not? If you are in boot camp, what current or difficult circumstances are you going through?

– Day 3 –

Have you resolved to not quit? Have you experienced tests or battles that you were victorious in not quitting?

– Day 4 –

Have you experienced friendly fire before? How did you handle it then? How will you handle it differently in the future? Do you have a battle buddy? Describe him or her and why he or she is a good battle buddy for you. Are you preparing for your mission?

– Day 5 –

Are you ready to obey God for your mission instructions? Have you learned to trust Him enough to obey without question? Are you being led on a faith journey? Is there anything holding you back? Are you ready to begin your mission?

Before you end your time together as a small group,
ask for prayer requests and then pray together as a group.

PART TWO

Your Destiny

Just Be You

c2bu.com/vid8

Congratulations!
You made it through identity boot camp.

I pray you are daily embracing your identity as a child of God, confident that your Creator will lead you in the path He has chosen for you. Keep those 3 x 5 cards nearby. You will need your new vocabulary to silence the negative tape that has been playing in your mind for years. We will silence it with truth. Do not be surprised or discouraged when your new identity is challenged as you embark upon your journey of discovering and fulfilling your water-walking, giant-slaying, history-making destiny. Now that you know *who you are*, it is time to ask, *"What am I supposed to be doing?"* It starts with you—the *you* you were created to be.

"Therefore as dearly loved children, live a life of extravagant love."
— EPHESIANS 5:1

Kayla's Story

She literally plopped in my lap completely startling me. "An angel!" was my first thought. "Delightful!" was my second. In that moment, I would have told you that her arrival was totally unplanned, maybe even random if I believed such things. But I would have been wrong. Time would reveal that this encounter was extremely intentional and full of purpose. This delightful, pint-sized angel would be more than just a gift for the moment: she was a tender reminder of someone I lost a long time ago.

I was alone and operating in full mommy mode prior to this divine lap landing. My middle son had band practice at our church. His first public guitar performance was scheduled for the next evening, and I had the mundane task of carpooling. I comforted myself with the thought of two uninterrupted hours of inspired reading to pass the time while I waited. I had just claimed my seat on the floor with a few other carpool-weary moms. I was just about to get lost in my book when a swirling blond vision caught my eye. Without warning, but to my utter delight, the lovely little girl plopped into my lap.

My senses were overwhelmed as her strawberry-scented hair covered my face and obscured my view. I was literally wrapped in angel hair. Her tiny hand caressed my face and she laughed as she freed her hair from mine. What came into view was clearly a beautiful angel masquerading as a three year old only inches from my face. Without hesitation or a proper introduction, she threw her arms around my neck and stared intently into my eyes. With stillness uncommon to children her age, she held my gaze hypnotizing me. Though neither of us spoke we communicated perfectly in the silence. An eternity later, she broke the spell when she asked, "Will you be my friend?" Though it was the most ordinary and common of child speak, the words were spoken with eloquence and sophistication causing me to feel somehow chosen for a great honor. My reply of yes delighted her so much that she hugged me as if she had known me her entire life. Captivated, I fell completely and madly in love. The rest of the evening I spent willingly engrossed in her and her world. Joy bubbled up from my soul and tangibly displayed itself as tears in my eyes. I giggled (which is much different from laughing) out loud, for I knew without a doubt that I had just been ambushed in the ordinary and thrown headfirst into the extraordinary.

In retelling the story, I am still amazed how the little girl, whose name I came to find out is Kayla, plopped so confidently into my lap. It amazes me that she did so without any fear of rejection. I guess being so young, she had not yet felt the sting of that particular emotion and I never wanted her to. So I wrapped my arms tightly around her, burying my nose deep in her hair while she talked non-stop. As she shared her angel secrets, I noticed a very serious little boy hovering nearby. I was about to speak to him when Kayla whispered in my ear, as three-year-old little girls do, that this was her big brother. By the look on his face, it was obvious he was extremely wary of my close encounter with his little sister. Suddenly with great drama, he cupped his hands around his mouth and loudly proclaimed, "Stranger! Stranger!" to anyone who would listen—especially me. His body language actually screamed the different message of "Danger! Danger!" But my little angel ignored her brother's warning, possessively wrapping her arms tighter around my neck. Her love for me was not cautious but instead extremely extravagant. I felt bathed in it, even if her brother was not amused.

The room we were in was large and had been cleared of all chairs for the concert. There weren't many people in the room except those on stage. The stage was covered with instruments, amplifiers, and look-a-likes of my son, nervous adolescents eager, yet scared to death to perform in their first concert. No one paid any attention to Kayla and me—except her brother. And her other brother—another had shown up by this time. This one, however, wasn't fazed at all by my love affair with his little sister. He was content to sit beside us quietly reading a book. The concerned oldest brother continued to hover nearby just in case Kayla needed to be rescued. We all listened to the band play. The music was exceptionally beautiful. This place and time seemed enchanted.

After a while, in spite of our mutual love, my little angel got antsy and needed to move her body through space. As quickly as she entered my lap, she left it. But before I could feel the ache of missing her, she reappeared in front of me, this time not to sit with me but to perform for me. I was honored and thrilled! My little angel turned into a dancer and began spinning in circles—round and round and round. She never once got dizzy, a fact she was quite proud of. It was one I remembered accomplishing myself long, long ago. She danced uninhibited to the young band's music confident they played only for her. When they paused, she ran as fast as she could across the room, flying, so she claimed, with arms outstretched, jumping in the air like a ballerina. I clapped and cheered loudly as if I birthed her from my own body. I never once took my eyes off of her. She kept looking at me, making sure I was looking at her. I was her audience of one and that greatly mattered. My delight in her grew as she performed with an abandon common only to three year olds. She danced with all her heart and suddenly I had the desire to do the same. Quickly, like the mature adult I am, I suppressed the urge and remained anchored to the floor.

Several times during my angel's performance I wondered where her parents were. I was reluctant to break the spell of this magical dance, so I didn't allow my thoughts to become words. Finally, my own Mommy Mode proved stronger than the moment and I asked, "Where are your mommy and daddy?" She turned, pointing proudly toward the stage, to a man doing sound check. Mystery solved, my angel continued her performance. The now identified daddy of my angel eventually wandered over to introduce himself. Or maybe he thought we were being a little too intimate for strangers and wanted to make sure my intentions were honorable. If that was the case, I truly wanted to ease his fears. So before he spoke, I blurted out that I had fallen madly in love with his daughter. It is a wonder he didn't think I was certifiable! But he only smiled and nodded as if this was a most common phenomenon with his daughter. Was I not the first to be so captivated? I rejected the thought, choosing rather to believe that I had been specially chosen.

We chatted some more, and I guess I passed the stranger safety test because my friend's daddy returned to the stage, confidently leaving Kayla and I to walk hand in hand to the ladies' room. Her trust in me had no boundaries. Like good girlfriends do in the bathroom, we shared some lip gloss and a hair brush after we washed up. As we walked back to the auditorium, my angel-turned-dancer decided that walking was way too boring. She suggested we skip. With only the slightest hesitation on my part, we did just that. When we burst—and I mean burst—through the door, we were laughing louder than the band was playing! Suddenly, Kayla went totally still and quiet. I wondered at the abrupt change in her demeanor. I followed her gaze to the stage. Then I saw what she saw and heard what she heard. It was her daddy. He was singing.

She dropped my hand and ran straight for the stage. As I watched her run from me, the room changed and I felt transported into a realm of reality that was not of this world. I was completely frozen and could actually feel time slow. The band's music became a background symphony to what seemed an epic movie playing before me. Everything swelled in crescendo as my little angel climbed boldly onto the stage. The camera in my mind's eye zoomed in on her as she collected herself and walked quietly over to her daddy. Regally, she stood still beside him, molding her body against his. He never stopped singing. I loved that he did not shoo her away or give her a stern "don't do that" parental look. Instead, he put his arm around her, welcoming her to the stage beside him as if it was her rightful place.

I held my breath, now realizing there was a divine purpose to this evening and it was about to be revealed. Without missing a note, my angel's daddy bent down and handed her a microphone. She acted as if she expected him to do just that, as if she were waiting on it. With the poise of a professional she began to sing. Angelic was the sound. Though tiny in stature, she was the only star on stage. She sang without one ounce of self-consciousness and I longed for things I had no words to express. She sang of God's love and it surrounded me. His presence became tangible in that room. For the second time that night, I felt joy in its purest form.

Overwhelmed, a tear slipped down my cheek and the joy I felt morphed into a profound sadness. An urgent prayer erupted unexpectedly from my soul. "Protect her Lord! Don't let this world or some circumstance or cruel words steal her essence from her. Right now she is her truest self!" As I watched her, it became obvious to me that she was well loved. So much so it had birthed a confidence in her that enabled her to hug strangers, dance with abandon, and sing from a stage. She knew her role in this world—to love and be loved. "Lord, please don't let her lose that," I continued to pray. "Please don't let anyone steal that from her." As I prayed, I felt no assurance, no divine certainty that my prayer would be answered.

During my prayer, my angel finished her song and was lifted into her daddy's safe arms. As he continued to sing, her eyes grew so heavy they finally closed. A now sleeping angel, dancer, and star of the show rested her precious head on her daddy's shoulder, tired from just being her. More tears flowed down my cheeks. I cried for what would be lost in her future and for what had been lost in my past. "She is you and you were her," I thought. I was in a lonely silence when these words poured into my heart. I was not shocked by the revelation. In that moment there was no truer truth for me. God had spoken to my little girl heart.

It sounds strange to say it out loud, but right then I fell in love with me—the *me* I once was a long, long time ago. Another prayer erupted from my soul, but this one was all for me. "Lord,

I want her back. I want to be that me. It was once the most natural thing in the world to live like a well-loved child, hearing the sound of your voice and loving the sound of my own. But as I grew older, the whispers of 'Stranger, stranger, danger, danger" grew louder and caused me to hide my heart. Before I realized it, I stopped hugging strangers. I stopped dancing with abandon and I gave up the starring role of my own life. I stopped being me—on purpose. I exchanged that role for an understudy in other people's lives. I guess I hoped to share their applause, never believing I'd have any of my own. Oh, Lord, forgive me for believing that the audience of many could replace you as my Audience of One. Forgive me for loving cautiously instead of extravagantly. Forgive me for protecting my heart rather than sharing it. Forgive me for not being me, the *me* you created me to be." A holy stillness and quiet peace overcame my soul.

As I ended my prayer, the band ended their song and I was transported back into the real world. At the same time, my little angel opened her eyes and saw me across the room. As our eyes locked, I was infused with hope—hope for her and for me. She quickly left her daddy's arms and ran jumping into mine. "Can I go home with you?" she asked me very seriously. I laughed, hugging her tight. But before I answered her question, we danced around the room to the last of the music. I felt much younger than I had in a very long time. When it was time to leave, I promised Kayla with great conviction that I would take her with me wherever I went.

> *"Today I wish for you one perfect moment*
> *when you are utterly yourself,*
> *when you are convinced you are God's own child...*
> *when you realize that everything is within your grasp."*
> —Maya Angelou

Maya wishes it for you and I pray it for you, a moment...a perfect moment when you are utterly yourself. I love the sound of that. This is what our focus will be this week. Instead of one perfect moment, however, we are going to be asking God to show us multiple moments when we have had that experience—the experience of being ourselves. Your destiny may be doing what you have always done.

A Childhood Memory

Daily Discovery Process

Through my own personal journey of uncovering my identity and discovering my destiny, God used the lessons in this week's assignment to really clarify "who I am" and "what I am supposed to be doing." What I discovered was so simple. What I am supposed to be doing is exactly what I have been doing my entire life. I just needed my Creator to shine His lens of truth on my life. My encounter with little Kayla was such a lens.

Your life is writing a story—your story where you are the main character and the star! Like all good stories, there are times of intense struggle, glorious adventure, pitifully ordinary days, and seasons of pain. But when we view our lives through the lens of time, typically with the help of the Holy Spirit, we can begin to see a *common thread* that God, our Creator and Producer, has been weaving throughout the years of our life. With the busyness and distractions of life, however, that thread is very easy to miss. Your next exercise was developed to help you shine a light on the common threads of your life. For the next three days, you will be asked to write down very specific memories, one from childhood, one from your teen years, and one from your adult memory, when you were completely and utterly yourself. The purpose of this is to allow your Creator to bring out the very memories that reflect the true essence of you and find the common thread that unites them together. Let's begin.

My Memory
The childhood memory that God brought to my mind when I did this exercise made me smile, and again it was one I had not thought of in years. I performed in my first play when I was five. I loved every minute of being on stage. It didn't matter if I was a pilgrim or an Indian, a farmer or a cow, a tree or a flower—I played each part as if it were opening night on Broadway! No one had to encourage me to practice my lines. I would stand in front of a mirror for hours

perfecting my performance. When I was little, I loved to watch myself in a mirror. Mirrors and stages did not frighten me at that age. A few years into my young acting career, the annual productions were not frequent enough to fulfill my need to perform in front of an audience so I started writing and producing my own plays. Not only did I write the plays and produce them, I had the starring role. I found the costumes for the other actors, who usually included my brother, sister, and all the neighborhood children, I assigned them their parts, I advertised the event, I sold tickets for the event, and I knocked on doors inviting everyone I knew and anyone I didn't. My favorite part was seeing people come together in one place at one time for something I had a passion for. Sounds like a Courage Conference to me!

Your Story

Consult your Creator to bring out the very memory from childhood that reflects the true essence of you. What is one very specific memory when you were completely and utterly yourself? I am not asking for happy memories but instead for significant moments that can give you a glimpse of who you are and what you are supposed to be doing, despite your circumstances. This exercise is one that requires some time and prayer. Try to look back through the years as an observer instead of the participant in your own story. Don't be discouraged if nothing comes to you immediately—keep consulting your Creator. I would suggest you get out of your house or wherever it is that you normally complete this assessment and take a long walk with God. Let Him draw your mind to a very specific childhood memory when you were just being you and you loved it!

When you have remembered your moment, write a one-line summary of it, the details of how you went about doing it, and then describe what was most satisfying to you. This experience could have occurred in a ten-minute period, a day, a week, a summer, or even a year. This experience could have come from any part of your life—school, work, church, play-yard, neighborhood, home, extracurricular activities, volunteering experience, or travel—any segment of your life.

Here is an example to get you to thinking:

Describe the memory in one sentence. I led the crossing guard patrol in grade school.

Details of how you went about doing it. It was my responsibility to make sure the schedule was organized and that the kids had all of the stations around the school covered before and after school. I weeded out some of the more unreliable kids and replaced them with other kids I recruited to help. During our times on duty, I'd tour around and make sure everything was going well and help or direct kids when needed.

What was the most satisfying part of this activity, the thing you most looked forward to or were most proud of? We didn't have any accidents while I was on duty and the entire safety patrol worked better than it ever had before. I felt proud that I made this happen.

Here are a few other one-line examples to jog your memory:
- I befriended a Russian girl at school who spoke no English.
- My sister and I imitated all the movie stars and put on plays.
- I sang for hours alone in front of my mom's full-length mirror.
- I increased my paper route from 50 to 150 customers in three months.
- I helped build a three-story tree house.
- I cooked an entire meal for my family when I was eight years old with no help.
- I wrote my first poem and it was published in the school newspaper when I was ten.
- I stood up for someone at school when others were being mean to them.
- I made the winning shot at our 6th grade championship basketball game.

Childhood one-line memory:
_____

Details of how you went about doing it:
_____
_____
_____

What were you most proud of?
_____
_____
_____
_____
_____

My prayer for you as you end this day and this exercise is that you can recall a moment when you were completely and utterly yourself as a child. I pray that in this specific moment you can remember the ease and peace you had at just being you. I pray you will choose not to be discouraged if you can't remember yet. Continue consulting your Creator, asking Him what *He* wants you to know about you!

Your Youth

Daily Discovery Process

When I was in high school, I was leading a triple life. I had a church life, a home life, and my life as a teenager in high school. All three were very different identities. I was just trying to be who everyone wanted me to be. It was exhausting. Looking for relief, I decided to go on our summer youth trip with my church. The location was out in my beloved wide-open spaces. I can remember lots of trees and a huge lake. We'd walk down to the lake each morning for our time alone with God. I don't remember much else. I don't remember the activities. I don't remember the songs. I don't even remember the sermons. But I do remember I had a very real moment with God when I asked Him to forgive me. It was a physical experience. I literally felt a heavy weight lift off of my body when His grace was dispensed over me. I felt like a new person.

A day or two later, the youth pastor asked me to give my testimony. I wasn't sure what that was, but he assured me that it would be easy. I would just get up on stage (I had not been on a stage since I quit being me when I was eleven) and I would tell the hundreds of people from our church what had happened to me. I never hesitated. I wasn't the least bit scared. I just said yes. I don't remember writing out my testimony. I don't remember preparing in any way. But what I did do, what I felt compelled to do, was to call every single person in our church directory—close to a thousand people—and invite them to the service. I also called every one of my friends and invited them as well—friends who knew me as someone different than the church girl. I was about to take off my mask and unveil me. The urgency was overwhelming. I wanted to shout to the masses "God is real!" The God I had been taught about and believed in since birth was real. For the first time in my life I not only recognized His presence but I *felt* it. The night came and the room was filled. Everyone I invited seemed to have come. I took the stage. I spoke from my heart. I have no idea what I said but I remember seeing my parents' faces staring up at me. At the end of the service, I had friends who walked down the aisle and met Jesus for the first time.

This is my story. Now it is your turn. Your story doesn't have to be a religious experience. Just remember is must be a moment when you just felt like you. Alone or with people. Just doing what you love to do.

Here are a few more one-line memory examples to get you thinking:

- I designed clothes for my friends.
- I sang a solo in the church choir.
- I tried out for the school play and got the lead.
- I researched Mexican cuisine and cooked a four-course meal.
- I supported my family for a year while my mother was sick.
- I gave a speech at school and people told me I was a good speaker.
- I ran for student council and won.

Your Teen-age Story

Youth one-line memory:
_____

Details of how you went about doing it:
_____
_____
_____

What were you most proud of or what felt most satisfying to you?
_____
_____
_____
_____
_____
_____

All Grown Up

Daily Discovery Process

As I write my adult story, many come to mind. In my twenties, I was the person you called to find out which bar had been designated the "Happy Hour" location. My nickname was Social Director in the company I worked for. In my thirties, I planned fundraisers for my son's football team and introduced and organized southern supper clubs in our California neighborhood. In my forties, I trained for six months to climb Half Dome in Yosemite National Park. While I loved that experience, it just wasn't the same without everyone I knew coming with me. So the very next year after I had accomplished that feat for myself, I trained and took a group of thirty-five women back to climb that mountain with me. It was a powerful experience. I planned women's retreats for four years, as well as taking the stage and speaking at each one. I invited everyone I knew to join me. At this point in my life, I am coordinating Courage Conferences around the world as well as sharing my heart and my life from a stage. I am still passionately inviting everyone I know to join me, whether the conferences are in Tanzania, Africa or right down the street. I am now that missionary I longed to be as a little girl and I am still proclaiming as I did when I was fifteen years old, that "God is real!" In addition, I founded a non-profit organization that I now lead. We rescue young children from sex trafficking and build them homes. I finally got my daughters!

Now it is your turn. Can you pick just one? Remember to consult your Creator.

Here are a couple more one-line memories and examples to get your brain moving:
- I taught a young boy to swim and not be afraid of the water.
- I decorated my living room under budget and it looks beautiful.

Day Three

- I organized my children's building blocks by size and kind so they could access them better when they played.
- I won a long and difficult lawsuit.
- I designed and published a newsletter.
- I helped my daughter achieve all A's and B's in spite of her learning disorder.
- I planted more than one hundred tulip bulbs last spring.
- I encouraged a friend to stand up for herself at her job.
- I planned a fundraiser.

Your Adult Memory

Adult one-line memory:

_____

Details of how you went about doing it:

_____
_____
_____

What are you most proud of and which part brings you the most satisfaction?

_____
_____
_____
_____
_____

Consult Your Creator

"The Lord will fulfill his purposes for you."
— PSALM 138:8

This verse is such a great one for your 3x5 truth cards. You do *not* have to fulfill your own purposes. That is God's job! Doesn't that take the pressure off? Enjoy your daily walks and talks with your Creator. Enjoy this journey of "making a careful assessment of who you are and what you are to be doing." Your heavenly Daddy looks forward to talking and walking with you each day. He longs to hear your heart. Don't hold anything back. He can take it. God longs to resurrect your dreams, your desires, and memories, as well as plant new ones inside of you. He and all the saints, including my Mimi, are cheering you on! God certainly isn't in a hurry. It is your purpose, not your responsibility, to "bear fruit." But you won't bear any fruit until you are grafted into the vine. Abide in Him. When you are being you—the *you* God created—the world will see God!

Read John 15:7–17.

Ask God what He wants you to know through these words. Read it in the NIV and Message translations. Write your own paraphrase in the space provided below as if your heavenly Father is talking to you.

_____
_____
_____
_____
_____
_____
_____
_____
_____
_____

God planted a seed of desire in our spirits long before time began. It seems from the onset of our birth, the moment we arrive in this world, that our circumstances and others are trying to bury or kill off those dreams and desires. But God intends to fulfill them. He will fulfill His purpose for you! You just keep seeking Him with all your heart, with all your soul, and with all your strength. He longs to be found by you. He longs to bestow your identity upon you and reveal your wondrous destiny to you.

My prayer for you today is that you'll rest in the knowledge that God is working out His plans for you. You haven't messed them up. He hasn't given up on you. He is going to fulfill His plans for you. I pray you'll release your worries to Him. He loves you. He is so delighted that you are on this journey with Him. He daily waits for your time together. Do not leave Him out of the process. This assessment is of no value without Him.

Do What You Have Always Done

Daily Discovery Process

Now the fun really begins! Today we will ask God to help you locate the common thread(s) throughout all three stories. When I did this exercise, I almost fell out of my chair. What I could not articulate before now jumped off the page when I read back through my three stories. My spirit was stirred and jumping inside of me. *I bring people together for a purpose!* It was one of my biggest "Ah ha!" moments. I was doing this exercise in a hospital waiting room as my husband was having surgery and I almost jumped up and screamed it to all the weary family members waiting there with me, "I bring people together for a purpose!" Whatever I am doing, whatever I am passionate about (which has certainly changed throughout my life), whatever propels me into action—I want everyone I know, and a multitude of people I don't, to come do it with me! I don't like a party because there is no purpose. I don't like to just hang out unless there is a task. I couldn't see the contradiction before. I love people but I am task-oriented and driven. My heart and my passion are for people to come together for a common purpose and make a difference in this world. It is in every example and every story I write. I then came to realize I had not always been doing it for God's purposes. My Creator and I had a long talk about that. You can be who God created you to be but not doing what He created you to do! It was truly life changing for me to see that I was not random, that I was not an accident, but that I had been created on purpose for a purpose in such a tangible way! I was stirred up—body, soul, and spirit!

Your Story

Now it's your turn. Go back through all three of your stories. Consult your Creator. Ask God to help you locate the common thread(s) throughout all three stories. Is there something you are doing in all three stories? Circle any common words you used in the descriptions. Notice if when you are doing these activities that you are always with people or you are always alone. Note any commonalities in the stories and record them below.

_____
_____
_____
_____

Place a circle around the words from your three stories that show who you like to work with and write them in the space provided below. For example: groups, kids, parties, friends, women, yourself, everyone, homeless people, or teams.

_____
_____
_____
_____

Next, note if anything propels you into action. What gets you started and what keeps you going in your three stories? Write them below. For example: saw a need, had a deadline, discovered a problem, make them laugh, or broke my heart.

_____
_____
_____
_____

Go back and review any words, phrases, or sentences that describe your role and the relationship you played in your stories and write them in the space below. For example: supervisor, coordinator, leader, helper, planner, or follower.

_____
_____
_____
_____
_____

Highlight in a different color the themes you saw in each of the three stories. Is there a theme that played out in each of the stories or all they all different? Don't worry if you cannot see the themes. Your mighty warriors or righteous girlfriends will help you see them when you get together next. Think about what gave you the most satisfaction in each of the three stories. Was there a common thread in what you were most proud of? What common thread can you pull from your stories? For example, you made things better, made people laugh, led a team, planned an event, accomplished a task, solved a problem, helped someone, made a difference, or earned money.

Now connect the dots. Think of this exercise as a puzzle. Look at the pieces you have written above and attempt to write one sentence stating the reoccurring theme you see throughout the stories, throughout your life.

_____
_____
_____
_____

Do you see the common thread running throughout your stories? Do you see what you tend to do and what you tend to love? Remember to have a conversation with your Creator. If the blank page is looking oh-so-blank to you right now, pull out your Bible and re-read P<small>SALM</small> 139. Ask God to show you how He knit you together; how He created you on purpose for a purpose.

Here are a few examples to get you thinking:
- I organize people to solve a problem.
- I plan events to make people laugh.
- I sit alone writing stories to inspire others.
- I help others accomplish their dreams.

_____
_____
_____
_____
_____
_____
_____
_____

The Invisible Hand in Your Story

Daily Discovery Process

When we unite our purposes with God's purposes, the supernatural is engaged. When we quit trying to be who we want to be and do all we want to do, and instead let God guide that process, then miracles begin to happen. The power that God has deposited within us is ignited and the angels in heaven are dispatched to our aid. One of my favorite places this occurs in the Bible is in the book of Esther. Esther reads like a trashy novel! It starts off with a drunk, egotistical, controlling king and ends with an orphan girl reigning as queen. God's invisible hand weaves Esther's story together. He uniquely uses her in ways she "dared not to dream or imagine." God desires to do the same with us.

Grab your Bible and read Esther's story right now, even if you've read it before. I love the Message Translation. Try to imagine yourself as Esther. Your parents are dead. You are living with a loving relative when suddenly, against your will, you are dragged off to the king's palace in what I call the "virgin roundup." You are held hostage in the palace competing with other young virgins. You must wait your turn to have sex with the King —against your will. At first glance, you have no obvious choice. It seems there is no God in control. But read further. Read Esther's story carefully and see how her cousin Mordecai "directed her steps" and how God used Esther in a mighty way to fulfill His purposes for her and an entire nation. She did what she had always done. Obeyed.

Uniquely You — Day Five

As you read Esther's story, ask your Creator to show you the threads throughout your life—the good, the bad, and the ugly. In the space below journal how you have seen the invisible hand of God work in your life. It is often difficult to see His hand in the midst of our struggles but just as He was writing the plot to her story for His purposes, you can be assured He is doing the same for you.

My prayer for you this day is that you will see in a very tangible way that you were created on purpose for a purpose. I pray you will see that you and your life are not random, cosmic accidents but a carefully imagined and planned existence. I pray that you will consult your Creator when it seems you have no obvious choices. God is orchestrating your circumstances, just like He did Esther's. Remember, it is His responsibility to fulfill His purposes for you. I pray that you are beginning to realize that perhaps you were born "for such a time as this."

Righteous Girlfriend/ Mighty Warrior

Just Be You.

– Day 1 –

Share with your righteous girlfriends or mighty warriors your childhood statement. Don't share the common thread yet until after everyone has shared the childhood statements.

– Day 2 –

Share with your righteous girlfriends or mighty warriors your youth statement. Don't say anything yet, but do you see any common threads in your righteous girlfriends' or mighty warriors' stories?

– Day 3 –

Share with your righteous girlfriends or mighty warriors your adult statement. Are any light bulbs going off in the group?

– Day 4 –

Finally! Share the common thread you see in your own stories.

– Day 5 –

Ask your righteous girlfriends or mighty warriors to validate or confirm what they see in you from your stories. Remember, no advice giving, but know that God has used many, many people in my life to show me things I could not see for myself. If you have no idea what common thread there is in your stories, ask your righteous girlfriends or mighty warriors to seek God on your behalf. Stop and pray for revelation and wisdom.

> Pray for each other this week.
> Pray that God will give each of you the courage to be you
> – the *you* He created.

Your Mission is Impossible

*"Who am I? A water-walker.
What am I supposed to be doing? The impossible."*
— Jenny Williamson,
Do You Have the Courage to Be You?

You were created to do the impossible. That is why this entire journey requires courage. When your Creator reveals the details of your destiny to you, your first instinct will be to scream, *"That's impossible!"* You're right. Your destiny requires that you leave your comfort zones for the unknown. Alone, your destiny is impossible.

*"We must leave the human boundaries that define our lives
and step into a journey of total dependence on God's perspective
and commands; where He invades the impossible."*
—Bill Johnson, *Face to Face with God*

Your mission is not safe. Some would call it impossible.

All of the thought, all of the planning that went into creating you, was not so you could cruise through life sleeping on high-thread-count sheets and eating bonbons. You were created for great exploits. You were created to change the world.

My Story

Start an international organization to help people find their purpose. Copyright all the materials. You will travel the world. I will give you the financial resources equivalent to Starbucks. You will meet the needs of those in society that no one is meeting. You will build them homes. You will call them family. You will have daughters. You will start Courage Cafés. You will hire the best of the best and pay them marketplace salaries. You will be united as one. You will be of one heart, one mind, and one spirit. You will write a book. You will speak to stadiums full of people. Your children, the next generation, will take the organization to places you cannot dream of.

All of those words have been whispered to my spirit. Some have come true and others I am still believing for. When I first heard them, I was filled with a wonder and excitement that is difficult to articulate. I had spent so much time cementing my identity that when the words of my destiny were finally revealed, I was overwhelmed by my assignment. While my soul and my logical brain knew I could never attempt to fulfill these on my own, my spirit recognized that this was exactly what I was created to do. That for which I was chosen and prepared for humbled me. My entire life made sense as those words settled deep within my soul.

When I received my mission, I was reeling so much from a very intensive boot camp experience that (I did not realize at the time) was designed to solidify my identity and prepare me for this very destiny. All I knew was that boot camp felt a lot like war. On some days, I could not tell the difference. However, as soon as my mission was revealed, I realized my circumstances were ordained by my Maker to prepare me for my future. Through those difficult experiences, I gained a new level of trust in myself and in my Creator. How thankful I am for them all. I am still drawing encouragement from them today. Boot camp taught me to trust myself and my Creator at a whole new level—the level required for water walkers, giant slayers, and history makers. That is your destiny! You were created to do the impossible, not to play it safe. Jesus was pretty clear on this point and two of his disciples made certain we would know that by recording His words in their writings.

"I tell you the truth, if you have faith as small as a mustard seed, you can say to this mountain, 'Move from here to there' and it will move. Nothing will be impossible for you." — MATTHEW 17:18 (NIV)

"Risk your life and get more than you ever dreamed of. Play it safe and end up holding the bag." — LUKE 19:16 (MSG)

"The people who know their God shall prove themselves strong and shall stand firm and do exploits [for God]." — DANIEL 11:31–33

To do the impossible you must transition from the known to the unknown, from the possible to the impossible. Are you ready?

A Crazy, Divine Invitation

Daily Discovery Process

Have you ever tried to get out of a boat when it was sitting on water? If you have, then you know there is just no graceful way to do it. Picture it with me. You have one foot in the boat (a solid surface) and you are attempting to find another solid surface to put your other foot on (a dock). This exchange must take place before you can lift your body out of the boat. The feat is not easy because the boat will not be still. Your body and the boat are in constant motion because it is being pitched back and forth by the water. As you attempt to make the transition, your body is flailing about and you are somewhat suspended in mid-air. You feel unstable and less than confident in your own ability to make the transition at all, much less make it gracefully. This entire process, however, can be instantly redeemed, instantly changed when someone comes by and offers you their hand. Their hand provides stability and enables you to make the transition with grace.

My own transition from the boat of comfort and familiarity to the water of change and the unknown caused me to feel off balance, so unsure of the future. I felt less than confident of the unknown. That is, until I realized God offered His hand to steady me for the transition. As clear as the thoughts are in my head, I heard Him ask me to trust Him. He then asked me to take His hand and get out of my boat of comfort and come onto the water of the unknown with Him. Yes, of course I was scared—but you don't turn down a divine invitation from God himself to walk on the water!

 Uniquely You — Day One

This is how I began to learn the secrets of grace-filled transitions from the known to the unknown. A divine invitation from God himself is how it all begins. Determining whether the invitation to the unknown is divine is the tricky part, but well worth the time taken. On some days, the volume of God's voice fades to a mere whisper as my own thoughts, ideas, fears, and insecurities reach a fevered pitch. God knows that I am not getting out of any boat I'm in (a place of comfort and safety) unless I know that it is God himself calling me out of it! If the invitation is indeed divine, then I know that God will be in the place He is calling me to and He will equip me with all I need for the transition.

This knowledge came to me in two ways—the hard way (much life experience doing it the wrong way) and seeking out other successful water walkers (the preferred way). Peter (fisherman, literal water walker) knew that divine invitations are a must for grace-filled transitions. Take a minute to read MATTHEW 14. Before Peter made a move into the unknown, he cried out (in fear) from the bottom of the boat and in the midst of the storm, "Lord, *if it is you*, then command me to come out on the water." Peter wanted to walk on water, to do the impossible, but he knew without that divine invitation, without Jesus' presence, he would sink; he would fail. I've learned that, too—before I jump headfirst into the waves of the unknown (and I don't like getting wet unnecessarily), I am going to pause to ask for my own divine invitation. Only then do I dare get out of the boat! Once I have determined that God is indeed calling, I respond quickly. I am afraid that if I don't get moving, God just might blow a wave my way and tip over my little boat of comfort and throw me head first out into the water! Or worse, He could get tired of waiting on me to take courage, pass me by, and give my divine invitation to someone else. I don't want to live my life viewing other water walkers from the bottom of my well-decorated boat! I don't want to miss anything that God has designed for me to be, to see, or do! I want to walk on water.

Consult Your Creator

"As soon as the meal was finished, Jesus insisted that the disciples get in the boat and go on ahead to the other side while He dismissed the people. With the crowd dispersed, he climbed the mountain so he could be by himself and pray. He stayed there alone, late into the night. Meanwhile, the boat was far out to sea when the wind came up against them and they were battered by the waves. At about four o'clock in the morning, Jesus came toward them walking on the water. They were scared out of their wits. "A ghost!" they said, crying out in terror. But Jesus was quick to comfort them. "Courage, it's me. Don't be afraid." Peter, suddenly bold, said, "Master, if it's really you, call me to come to you on the water." He said, "Come ahead." Jumping out of the boat, Peter walked on the water to Jesus. But when he looked down at the waves churning beneath his feet, he lost his nerve and started to sink. He cried, "Master, save me!" Jesus didn't hesitate. He reached down and grabbed his

hand. Then he said, "Faint-heart, what got into you?" The two of them climbed into the boat, and the wind died down. The disciples in the boat, having watched the whole thing, worshiped Jesus, saying, "This is it! You are God's Son for sure!"
— MATTHEW 14:22–33 (MSG)

Your Story

Describe your "boat" or "comfort zone." Is it difficult for you to leave the known for the unknown? Do you like to try new things or do you like to feel protected and safe in the routine of what you know? Has God issued you any divine invitations that you turned down? Have you ever heard His still, small voice calling you out onto the water of the unknown? Did you say yes or no? Explain why or why not. Describe the experience. Do you want to walk on water, slay giants with a few stones, and fly on the wings of eagles? What holds you back?

_____
_____
_____
_____
_____
_____
_____
_____
_____
_____
_____
_____
_____
_____
_____
_____

My prayer for you as we end this day is that you will have the courage to say yes to Jesus' divine invitation to leave your boat of comfort, safety, security, and routine and get out on the water of the unknown—where you have no control, no assurances, no confidence in yourself but are utterly and completely dependent upon God. Yes, your heart will be racing, your palms will be sweating, and your knees will be knocking. But you will be fully alive doing what you were created to do!

A Good Fear

Daily Discovery Process

A healthy fear of God is another secret to experiencing grace-filled transitions, one where you transition from the comfort of the known, to the discomfort of the unknown where your destiny lies. When I was little and heard this phrase "fear of God" I thought I was supposed to be scared of God, but I never was. Previously in this assessment, we talked about how many of us confuse and co-mingle the relationships we have with our earthly fathers to our heavenly one. My earthly dad shaped my own vision of God. My dad loved me madly and I just assumed God did too. My dad was a strict and consistent disciplinarian but only when I deserved it (i.e., blatant disobedience). It seemed to my little girl's mind that God followed the same pattern as my dad—loving me madly but disciplining me when I deserved it. I tried very hard with both my dads to be a good girl. I was scared to death to get in trouble. I was not rebellious at all.

My dad loves to tell the story of my one and only spanking. I was five years old. My brother and I had talked during big church. The little girl I was had a difficult time sitting still and being quiet. Whispering is still difficult for me! My dad leaned over during the service and gave us "the look," the one he gave to let us know he was serious. We were promised a spanking when we got home. When we got home, we ate lunch and my dad started watching Sunday afternoon football. I knew he had forgotten about the spanking until halftime. We were called into the bathroom one at a time—that is where dad held his private conversations with his children. I volunteered to go first because I was the oldest. I started screaming and crying when the door closed. I remember my dad saying with amusement in his voice, "Sister, I haven't even said anything yet." I got the "It is going to hurt me more than it is going to hurt you" speech, but then my dad said something that has remained with me for most of my life. He said, "I want you to always depend upon my love, but I also want you to be able to depend upon my word. I told you that you would be punished—now I have to keep my word so you will always know you can depend on me."

I believe God wants us to know the same thing my daddy wanted me to know. This term *fear God* is one I now understand much better. I cling to it in times of transition from the known to the unknown. Depending upon God is the only way that transition can be a grace-filled one. My NIV Study Bible footnotes explain it better:

> *"To fear the Lord is to recognize God for who He is and who He says He is. Holy, almighty, righteous, pure, all-knowing, all-powerful, all wise, and in control of this crazy planet. When we regard God correctly, we regard ourselves correctly. When we recognize who God is then we recognize our place in his plans. We then fall at His feet in humble respect and only then will He show us the way—the way chosen for us."*

I love those words. My spirit quickens as I read them. That doesn't seem scary at all, does it? In fact, it feels quite freeing and exciting! The Bible says God will teach us to fear Him. Have you ever wondered just how He does that? After giving this much thought and by consulting my Creator, I have come to the conclusion that God likes to show off. Not like a little kid trying to get someone's attention by doing tricks on his bike, but more like a lover showing his beloved his strength—his ability to care for her. Or maybe like a parent who loves to show their children that Mommy or Daddy can dry their tears, kiss their boo boos, and provide the answers to all their questions. It seems so obvious to me that God is constantly trying to show who He is and what He can do. It seems to me that He tries in many different and unique ways to make it so clear to us that He is all we will ever need; that He is big enough to carry us through or around any of this life's plethora of storms. This is such good news for me personally, because I have found that in my life I need a very big God—especially in times of transition. I keep asking God for reminders of just how big and capable He is. My prayer usually goes something like this, "God, I need you to be big for me today!" He has never failed to answer that prayer. My favorite way he answers that prayer is with a visual picture. Sometimes I get them in my mind's eye and sometimes I get a literal picture.

Often when my circumstances seem big and scary, I go for a hike. I feel a need deep within my spirit to immerse myself in God's creation when my problems seem overwhelming or when what God is calling me to do seems impossible. I lived sixteen years of my married life near the Pacific Ocean. I had a favorite place to go during these times. It was high atop a cliff called Devil's Slide located on Highway 1. Highway 1 is a two-lane road that snakes around the mountain. One shoulder of the road is the Pacific Ocean and the other is the face of the mountain. It is a torturous drive. There is a vista point you can pull off and park your car with a trailhead that leads up to a higher point. I climbed that hill, watching the roads and the cars become smaller and smaller. As I walked up, I would begin to become aware of the smell and sound of the ocean. This part of the coast is wild, untamed, and vicious. The waves slam against the rock walls. I would stand with my feet on the edge, staring out into the vast face of the ocean. It seemed to go into infinity. I felt like the only human being on the planet. The roar of the waves pounded at my soul. The wind whipped at a frenzied pace. I stood as still as I could. I sensed the power of creation, the power of God. That's when it happened. I welcomed the feeling. As I began to feel small, my world, my struggles, and my problems did too, but my destiny seemed very, very big. Here in this place the impossible becomes possible. God shows off for me through His creation.

Another of my favorite places to feel small is atop Half Dome in Yosemite National Park. I've only had the courage to make it up the cables twice. That feat can only be obtained after a grueling all-day hike. But it is worth it. When you stand on the top at the edge of a gigantic cliff, the vast green valley below seems to get sucked under the mountain floor. When I focused my attention on the bottom, I saw movement. After a moment I realized they were cars moving on the valley floor. They looked like little toys on a manmade model of the world. The top of Half Dome is the size of a football field. I searched for a crevice where I could be alone. And it happened again—I began to feel small. As that change in my stature happens, everything else in my world gets smaller, too. It's when I begin to shrink that God gets bigger. I feel His majesty in the mountains. I feel His peace in the green pastures. I feel His presence in the vista. I welcome it all. I hear God better when I am small.

It also seems to me that God likes to reveal himself *before* we even know we need Him—prior to His planned transitions for our lives, prior to the divine invitation to walk on water. I take great comfort in that. I need it and apparently so did God's chosen people, the Israelites. God has the crystal ball. He knew their future and He knows ours. He knew His people were going to encounter scary things on their journey into their promised land— giants, large rivers, no food, and vast armies. God knew they were going to need a really big God to conquer their fears and get out of the boat. (Me, too, me too!) So God gave them the "fear of God"—He taught them to fear Him by putting Himself on display. He passed by and showed them His power, His strength, and His love. This made them feel small, and because of this, they received the confidence that they had a really big God on their side, who was big enough to handle anything that they encountered on this little planet. He gave them what they needed before they even knew they needed it, for one purpose, so they would trust Him, follow Him, and love Him. God prepares us for our transitions in subtle ways that we often miss. How do I know this? He says so in the Bible.

> *"See the former things have taken place, and new things I declare—before they spring into being I announce them to you."* — Isaiah 42:9 (NIV)

"Forget the former things; do not dwell on the past.
See, I am doing a new thing! Now it springs up; do you not perceive it?"
— Isaiah 43:18–19 (NIV)

"From now on I will tell you of new things,
hidden things unknown to you."
— Isaiah 48:6 (NIV)

Our destinies are in the future, not the past. God's divine invitation to walk on water begins now. This is one of the reasons I try hard to journal this walk with God. When I read back through my own words, I begin to clearly see God's invisible hand in my circumstances. That, too, makes me feel small. It quiets my heart and stills my soul knowing God is in control of my transitions—not only in control of them, not only allowing them, but He actually *orchestrates* them!

I have probably read Peter's water-walking adventure a hundred times in my forty-six years on this planet. But until recently, I had missed a tiny but hugely important detail of the story.

"Immediately, Jesus made the disciples get into the boat
and go ahead of him to the other side."
— Matthew 14:2

Did you see it? Jesus *made them* get into the boat. He put them in the boat on purpose and shoved them off into the night knowing they would encounter a storm! Seems a little premeditated to me. At first glance, it seems even a little cruel. But our God never does anything that is not for our good. He doesn't use scare tactics to teach us to fear Him in the traditional sense of the word "fear." So why in the world did He send them into that storm on purpose? Because He has the crystal ball! He knew what they needed before they knew it. He was preparing them to be who He created them to be! Long before they saw Him crucified, long before they could even grasp the enormity of the call upon their lives, Jesus knew this group of very ordinary men would need to be able recognize His voice (His divine invitation), and He knew they were going to need a really big God. So out on that body of water, in the darkest hour of the night, in the middle of a storm, He walked on water and instilled a bigger fear of God in them.

Oh, how they would come to appreciate that experience in the miraculous years to follow, especially during the times of transition. I, too, have learned that there is no graceful transition or any contemplated water walking until there is a fear of God. You can't. No matter how capable you think you are, the belief in ourselves alone is just not enough to get us through life's most difficult days or circumstances. It isn't enough to get us out of the boat! What God has called me to do and what God is calling you to do is impossible without him. Our knee-jerk reaction on most days is to hunker down in the bottom of the boat quaking in fear because of circumstances that feel so big. It is only by the fear of God that we even contemplate taking His hand to climb out of the known to walk into the unknown.

Consult Your Creator

Friends, get those 3x5 cards out right now. I've got some promises and truth for you today! Fearing God is required to walk on water, slay giants, and do the impossible.

Like a good daddy, God promises to teach us how to fear him and then give us success:

> *"He sought God during the days of Zechariah, who instructed him in the fear of God. As long as he sought the Lord, God gave him success."*
> — 2 Chronicles 26:5 (NIV)

Through our fear of God, He teaches us how to do what He has called us to do:

> *"Who, then, is the man that fears the Lord? He will instruct him in the way chosen for him."* — Psalm 25:12 (NIV)

If we fear God, He confides in us—isn't that mind-blowing?

> *"The Lord confides in those who fear Him;*
> *He makes His covenant known to them."*
> — Psalm 25:14 (NIV)

Fear of God and wisdom are linked:

> *"The fear of the Lord is the beginning of wisdom; all who follow His precepts have good understanding."* — Psalm 111:10 (NIV)

I don't know about you, but when I'm out there walking on water, it's good to know that the God of the Universe has His eyes on me:

> *"But the eyes of the Lord are on those that fear Him, on those whose hope is in His unfailing love."*
> — Psalm 33:18 (NIV)

Fear of the Lord leads to blessings for our children:

> *"Blessed is the man who fears the LORD, who finds great delight in his commands. His children will be mighty in the land; the generation of the upright will be blessed."*
> — Psalm 112:1–2 (NIV)

Fear in the Lord helps us avoid wickedness:

> *"Through love and faithfulness sin is atoned for, but through the fear of the Lord you will avoid evil."* — Proverbs 16:6 (NIV)

We get to feel God's delight when we fear Him:

> *"The Lord delights in those who fear Him and put their hope in his unfailing love."*
> — Psalm 147:11 (NIV)

Fearing God is something for everyone, and we should tell others about it:

> *"Therefore, since we know what it means to fear the Lord, we try to persuade people. If we are out of our minds it is for God, if we are in our right minds it is for you."* — 2 Corinthians 5:11, 13 (NIV)

God has an equation for His protection and provision:

> *"Fear the Lord your God, serve Him only...so that it may go well with you."* — Deuteronomy 6:13, 3 (NIV)

God knows what we need for our children's lives and for our lives to go well for us:

> *"Oh, that their hearts would be inclined to fear me and keep all my commands always, so that it might go well with them and their children forever!"* — Deuteronomy 5:29 (NIV)

Fear of God and obedience is the key to long life:

> *"Fear the Lord your God as long as you live by keeping all his decrees and commands that I give you, and so that you may enjoy long life."*
> — Deuteronomy 6:2 (NIV)

 Uniquely You — Day Two

Fear of God shines out to those around us, especially those we lead:

"When one rules over men in righteousness, when he rules in the fear of God, he is like the light of morning at sunrise on a cloudless morning, like the brightness after rain that brings the grass from the earth." — 2 SAMUEL 23:3

God inspires us to fear Him for our own good:

"They will be my people, and I will be their God. I will give them singleness of heart and action, so that they will always fear me for their own good and the good of their children after them. I will make an everlasting covenant with them: I will never stop doing good to them, and I will inspire them to fear me, so that they will never turn away from me. I will rejoice in doing them good and will assuredly plant them in this land with all my heart and soul."
— JEREMIAH 32:38–41 (NIV)

Read PROVERBS, Chapter 2. There are too many promises for me to write down here. Stop and look up this passage yourself. Write down the promises that God is speaking to you.

_____
_____
_____
_____
_____
_____
_____
_____

Your Story

Journal your thoughts and feelings on the concept of the "fear of God." Do you see the correlation between fearing God and fulfilling your destiny? Do you need a big God right now in your life? Is God calling you to walk on water? Do you only see the waves of the storm? Are you hiding in the bottom of the boat, clutching the sides?

_____
_____
_____

You will need these promises on the road to your destiny. You must choose to believe they are for you. They are your truth. My prayer for you as we end this day is for you to know the true meaning of fearing God. We aren't called to be afraid of Him, but to recognize and tremble at His power. That power is for our benefit. Your God, your heavenly daddy, is big enough for all that you are facing right now. He is extending His powerful right hand, offering you an invitation to walk on water and slay the giants that are standing in the way of your destiny. He wants you to participate in the impossible. Take His hand! He promises to do more than you dare, ask, or imagine.

 Uniquely You

Loosen Your Grip

Daily Discovery Process

Once you know you have, 1) received a divine invitation from God, and 2) possess a healthy fear of Him, it is time to take His hand, leave the safety of your boat, and head out onto the water of the unknown. But wait! Before you throw your leg over the side there is something very important that must happen first. A decision has to be made. You have to be prepared to let go. You have to loosen your grip on all that you think is yours, on all that you hold dear, on all that keeps you safe. You must do this before you are able to take hold of the hand He offers. The big secret here is that graceful transitions are impossible when you are holding on too tightly to the side of your boat. Or worse, you could be holding on to something or someone that will drag you under.

"Do not store up for yourselves treasures on earth, where moth and rust destroy, and where thieves break in and steal. But store up for yourselves treasures in heaven, where moth and rust do not destroy, and where thieves do not break in and steal. For where your treasure is, there your heart will be also."
MATTHEW 6:19–21 (NIV)

"But godliness with contentment is great gain. For we brought nothing into the world, and we can take nothing out of it."
1 TIMOTHY 6:6–7 (NIV)

Week Nine  Uniquely You

"Let us throw off everything that hinders and the sin that so easily entangles, and let us run with perseverance the race marked out for us."
— HEBREWS 12:1 (NIV)

It doesn't matter to what or to whom you are holding tightly. Anything you are grasping too tight is a certain recipe for disaster. On the day that God issues you a divine invitation, when He has begun to teach you to fear Him and extends His hand to steady you for the transition, if you do not let go of what you are holding on to, then I am afraid I can only offer two scenarios (both of which I have experienced and read about). He will let you sink while you continue trying to hold onto it, or He will pry (and I do mean pry) it from your hands. Trust me, neither way is fun, but they are for your own good.

Repeat after me.."Loosen your grip!"

I'll try and prove my passionate opinion on this topic. Recently, a friend asked me if I had ever had my heart broken. I said *no* and truly believed that I had answered her honestly. But the question stayed with me for a few days, tugging at my memories, haunting me. It shocked me when I realized that I had lied. My heart had been broken twice and by the same man—my oldest son. It wasn't his fault, it wasn't intentional, and at the time it happened he wasn't even a man. What I realized was that the only reason he had the power to break my heart was because the hold I had on him could only be described as a "death grip." Oh, God pried my hands off of him all right. The first time it happened, I didn't learn my lesson very well and I just re-gripped him and held on even tighter. The second time I had to let go was no easier than the first. I can still feel the pain. It was emotional and physical. But I learned a truth that startled me even more than the pain did. God loved my son more than I did. I had repeated those words a million times while I was raising him, but I didn't really believe them. I believed that no one could love him more than me. God taught me that my love was strangling him, that he wasn't mine to hold on to. He was never mine to keep. The day my heart broke was the day God set my son free.

But He also set me free. By letting go, I learned that God was in control and had a unique plan for my son's life that was bigger and grander than anything I had ever imagined. His actions and his choices were his own. I got the pure pleasure of just loving him. By letting him go, he was free to become the man God created him to be. I learned that by holding on to him so tightly, I had stopped him from becoming that man. Therefore, I urge you to have a loose grip—especially on those you love.

God also taught me this truth with things, specifically with my home and my money. When we bought a house in the San Francisco Bay area, a friend of mine at church asked me if we tithed. Though it was over eleven years ago, I remember my exact, quick response, *"You cannot tithe and own a home in California."* Her response silenced me, *"Then we won't own a home."* I have never forgotten her words. That was the day I chose to loosen my grip on my stuff. It was the day I gave my house to the Lord and told Him that the desire of my heart was to tithe, even though I had no money to. Not only did I give my house to God but I asked Him to make it holy, set apart for His work, and for His glory. I had to practice this every day to get it right—to get it from my head to my heart. I'd go for a walk and when I returned to my driveway I'd give Him my house all over again. I'd thank Him for the privilege of its use, but I'd remind Him and myself that it was His to do with as He pleased. So that summer, when He said, "Give it back to me," it was easy to let it go. Of course I was sad (I'm not superhuman), but I wasn't devastated. I knew if God asked me to let go of something, He very often had something else amazing to place in my hand.

It was easier because I had already been practicing how to loosen my grip. I've actually become quite good at it; practice does make (almost) perfect. One year it was our 401(k)—every penny of it was gone to reduce business losses. I remember crying, "Lord, that is our savings; our family's security for the future!" And God told me, "I will be your security. Do you trust in my unfailing love? Do you put your hope and trust in me or your savings account?" That one stopped me dead in my tracks. But because of the divine invitation to the unknown, a healthy fear of the Lord, and the loose-grip lessons He had previously taught me, I could honestly say, "You Lord, you Lord!"

Consult Your Creator

"If you cling to your life, you will lose it; but if you give up your life for me, you will find it." — MATTHEW 10:39 (NLT)

"As he looked up, Jesus saw the rich putting their gifts into the temple treasury. He also saw a poor widow put in two very small copper coins. 'I tell you the truth,' he said, 'this poor widow has put in more than all the others. All these people gave their gifts out of their wealth; but she out of her poverty put in all she had to live on.'"
— LUKE 21:1–4 (NIV)

"Anyone who intends to come with me has to let me lead. You're not in the driver's seat; I am. Don't run from suffering; embrace it. Follow me and I'll show you how. Self-help is no help at all. Self-sacrifice is the way, my way, to finding yourself, your true self. What kind of deal is it to get everything you want but lose yourself?"
— MATTHEW 16:24–28 (MSG)

Do you know why we tithe, why we practice stewardship? It is this loose-grip concept! It is God's way of reminding us that He has given us all we have. We first do it out of obedience, but before we know it, we give because we get it. The head knowledge seeps deep within our hearts and then we begin to practice it. The more we give, the more we receive, and I am not just talking about money. When we begin to loosen our grip, like the old hymn says, *"The things of this world will become strangely dim in the light of His glory and grace."* [1]

Your Story

What are you holding on to? Do you have a death grip on something? Is God asking you to give Him back a gift, a dream, a desire, or a person you thought He had given or promised to you? It could be a standard of living, a career, a hobby, a possession, or someone you dearly love. In my opinion and in my experience, letting go is one of the most difficult things God asks us to do. When God asks you to let go, He asks for tangible evidence, not just a verbal pronouncement. Sell it, move it, quit it, sign it—these actions are meant to pry our hands off of whatever is keeping us in the boat. In my own life, though scary and painful at times, I have learned that God's desire for me to successfully walk on water is greater than my own. He knows I am quick to make a little god out of anything—even my destiny. God values our relationship, our intimacy with Him more than anything you will ever do. Your destiny, dreams, and desires are designed for God alone to fulfill. Your destiny is what God wants to do through you for others. You are to be a facet of His face, character, and grace. When God asks for something back it is because we are holding on too tightly, or we have settled for less than what He created us for. Ladies and gentlemen, loosen your grip. You can't walk on water holding on to the sides of the boat! Journal your thoughts and feelings for today, asking your Creator to reveal what you are clutching that is keeping you from walking on water.

_____

_____

_____

_____

_____

_____

_____

_____

_____

_____

_____

My prayer for you as we end day three of this week is that you will open you hands and let go of all that you are holding on to. I pray that you will trust God's love and plans for you. George Mueller, who was a father of thousands of orphans during the nineteenth century, said, "Our heavenly Father never takes anything from His children unless He means to give them something better." I can testify to this truth. Friends, have courage and let go!

1 Turn Your Eyes Upon Jesus, by Helen Howarth Lemmel.

Uniquely You — Day Four

Perseverance
(I Hate That Word!)

Daily Discovery Process

Just because I've shared a few secrets with you, I don't want you to get the wrong idea. I'd be lying to you if I told you that transitioning from the boat of the known to the water of the unknown is easy. It is not. But most of us are old enough to vouch for the truth our moms told us when we were little that "anything worth having takes hard work." No one promised life would be easy. Even Jesus told us not to worry about tomorrow—it will have troubles of its own. If this destiny thing were easy, everyone would be doing it! Hard work is involved but it also requires a fierce determination to not quit in the face of difficulty. As I type these words, I realize it is even more than that. To transition from the known to the unknown, you are going to need some teeth-gritting, divinely bestowed perseverance. We'll call our next secret for graceful transitions a "divine perseverance coupled with an awareness of a purpose that is greater than your immediate circumstances." That is a mouthful! For this lesson today, I believe we need to consult our Creator immediately!

Consult Your Creator

"Let us throw off everything that hinders and the sin that so easily entangles, and let us run with perseverance the race marked out for us. Let us fix our eyes on Jesus, the author and perfecter of our faith ... so that you will not grow weary and lose heart." — HEBREWS 12:1, 3 (NIV)

Do you get that verse? I didn't for years! Think about the implications as you reread the words. Jesus persevered. He endured the pain and humiliation of the cross because of the joy of the big picture, not for the sake of suffering. If we do not see that there is a purpose—something bigger than us in the midst of our difficult circumstances, insurmountable obstacles, and painful experiences—then we will quit. We will grow weary and lose heart. Your destiny is just on the other side of a big battle. Don't quit!

The words of JAMES 5:11 never seemed to encourage me when my life seemed scary and out of control: *"We are considered blessed when we persevere."* I need more than "blessed" to keep me from going to bed and pulling the covers over my head! I need to know that there is a purpose; that there is something bigger going on than random pain and suffering. I prefer the angel's words spoken to Daniel. In the book of DANIEL, CHAPTER 9, I find reason to persevere. We learn that Daniel was a slave, held in captivity by a king in a city that was not his own. Still, Daniel persevered in prayer. Daniel begged God for mercy—mercy for the people of Israel and for Jerusalem, his home. He knew the desecration of both would last seventy years because he had read the prophecy of Jeremiah. Daniel pleaded and fasted before God. Daniel told God he prayed as an imperfect man counting on God's mercy and love. In the midst of crying out to God, an angel named Gabriel appeared and said he had come to give Daniel insight and understanding. He told Daniel that as soon as he had begun to pray, an answer had been sent. But the answer had been delayed twenty-one days because he had to engage in a battle with the powers of evil and darkness. Then he told Daniel he was highly esteemed and loved.

I don't know about you, but Daniel's story gives me great strength to persevere. I can keep on fighting, keep on walking toward my destiny if I know I am loved. Sometimes when I don't receive an answer right away from God, I am quick to think He doesn't care about me. I need to be reminded that everything isn't about me and that there is a lot going on that I can't see!

> *"Let us not become weary in doing good, for at the proper time we will reap a harvest if we do not give up."* — GALATIANS 6:9

These are words I can sink my teeth into when I'm not seeing results or when my circumstances aren't changing as fast as I think they should. I receive this verse as a personal promise from God that my efforts, my prayers, and my suffering are not done in vain. I see purpose in my efforts even when I don't see results from them. Work hard and don't give up; in time you'll see something happen.

Jesus talked a lot about farming. The soil has to be prepared, the seed planted, the ground watered, the plot fertilized, and then the waiting begins. This is perseverance—a lot of hard work for the purpose of a harvest. It is a lot of hard work before results are ever seen, but we are confident they will come to fruition. The farmer perseveres for a purpose—the harvest. His hard work matters; it isn't for nothing. If he didn't do the hard work, there would be no harvest. Ponder that a moment. My effort matters. Your efforts matter. In God's plan, our hard work and our ability to persevere matters. Don't quit! Never give up. Results are coming, God promises! More than that, God wants us to experience and to participate in His process, in His plan, in His purposes for this world. He wants us to share in something bigger than ourselves. This is often God's intention and design when He calls us into the unknown. He wants us to experience more than just our own efforts for the sake of ourselves!

There is another story in the Bible that highlights this concept of "perseverance with an awareness of a purpose bigger than your immediate circumstances." In the Old Testament, we learn about a man named Joshua. He was the leader chosen by God to succeed Moses. His job was to lead the Israelites into the Promised Land.

Read Joshua, Chapter 6.

We learn that Joshua has just crossed the Jordan River, which was no easy feat—a miracle was involved, and he has now come upon the town of Jericho. Jericho had the strongest military in that region of the world, and with that distinction came the implication of immense power. The town's walls were fortified more than most. They stood twenty-five feet tall and twenty feet thick and were considered impenetrable. Joshua knew he must attack this city in order to proceed with God's plan of leading the Israelites to the Promised Land.

Before Joshua even contemplates a battle plan, an angel appears before him and says (paraphrased from verses 2–5), "Don't worry, you will win. I am giving you the victory in advance. You will take this city." Of course, walking around a city until the walls fall down wasn't exactly a typical battle plan. Notice something very interesting, something that is very much a God-thing. Even though Joshua had been guaranteed the victory by the divine hand of God, he was instructed to persevere until the "walls fall down." He had some hard work ahead in the next seven days. Not the type of work you'd expect in a battle, but he didn't get to sit around doing nothing while waiting for God to perform a miracle. No, in God's plan, we get to and are expected to participate in the divine process. Where in the world do we get the belief that this life is supposed to be easy? God takes us (if we will allow Him) out of our mundane existence and allows us to participate in His plans for this planet. It just blows my mind! It makes me try a little harder, push a little more, persevere when I can't see any results, and most importantly, keeps me from quitting! I want to be a part of something bigger than my life—I long for it. This story helps me see the benefits of persevering in my own life. God often asks us to work hard, but He asks us to do what we are capable of doing and turns it into the divine. To conquer this city, God just asked the people to *walk*. That doesn't seem very glamorous. It was scary, because they didn't understand it. It was probably pretty boring and tiring. But it was something they could do if they just chose to do it. My goodness, they should have been pretty good at it since they had been walking around in circles for forty years in the desert! Now God asks them to walk for just seven more days.

It was a lot of hard work before results were ever seen, but they got to participate in the process of the divine. That had to make all that walking worthwhile. You know they felt like they were walking on water when they saw those so-called impenetrable walls come tumbling down because of their effort, because of their perseverance. I am dancing and cheering with them—I bet no one felt tired; I bet they felt alive!

I'm going to show you another story as an example of perseverance. This is where most people start sinking, where most people quit and run back to the comfort of the bottom of the boat. If you are like me, you have heard this one a million times, and probably told it once or twice if you have kids. It's the loaves and fishes story.

Read Matthew 14:13–21

Open your mind up with me and think outside of what you know about this story. Don't you think that Jesus could have fed all those people on that hillside with one nod to the heavens and served lunch with celestial beings acting as waitresses if he wanted? Then why didn't he? Could it be that instead of just performing the miracle, he wanted the disciples to experience involvement in the miracle? He had them participate in the process. That's hard work and perseverance. Think about it with me. How long would it have taken twelve people to serve an estimated ten thousand people *by hand* and then pick up and put away all the leftovers, just as Jesus directed? Hours? Most of the afternoon? I bet they worked long and hard before they saw any results. I bet they had to sweat. But because they worked hard and persevered, they were a part of a miracle firsthand. Oh, how I want you and I to experience that!

Why is perseverance God's preferred method of blessing? Let's be honest. Perseverance doesn't feel fun or divine. But ponder this question. Which will a teenage appreciate more? A car given to him or one that he had to work years to save enough money for? Which will he appreciate more, take care of more, be more responsible with? I can feel the light bulbs going off! Say it with me: "The one he had to work for." We all know it is true. It is just human nature. I wish it wasn't so, but I am exactly the same way and God knows it. I'd venture to guess that we all hate the word *perseverance* because the implication is that it isn't going be easy—and we like easy! It doesn't feel good or natural, but then again, neither is walking on water or transitioning into the unknown. But because our God knows us, knows what we value, what we hold onto, He has designed situations and circumstances that require us to persevere often with no tangible results for the privilege to participate in His divine purposes and plans. And this isn't just for our own lives but for an eternal harvest. Don't quit. Keep walking around those proverbial walls until you see them come tumbling down. God has already announced your victory if you persevere.

Day Four

Your Story

Where are you right now in your life, in your journey of uncovering your identity and destiny? Are you getting tired? This has been a long journey so far. Are you thinking of quitting or giving up? Do you sense a spiritual battle in the heavens over your identity or destiny? Ladies and gentlemen, I just want to encourage you. I have been on this journey for fifteen years and I do not have it all figured out. God keeps revealing new things to me about Himself and about me. I am still persevering. I still battle to hold on to my identity and destiny. I still have to depend on God daily for His presence and His power. Alone I can do nothing. I know there is more than I see, and I choose to believe what cannot be seen. I choose not to quit. I pray you won't either! Pour your heart out to God.

Move Forward!

Daily Discovery Process

Another key to successful water walking is taking courage. I am going to tell you up front, you will be scared. You just can't get around it. And it is just plain hard to persevere when you are quaking in your boots. God knows you are going to need a big dose of courage. Courage is not a scary word. Courage simply means *action in the face of fear*. Easier said than done, right? *"Do not be afraid. Do not be afraid. Do not be afraid."*

Do you know how many times God tells us to fear not in the Bible? Three hundred and sixty six times. One for each day of the year plus an extra one, just in case it's a leap year. Because He said it so many times, you have to believe that God knew we were going to get scared transitioning from the known into the unknown, persevering and participating in His purposes and plans for our lives. But if He can get us to move, to have courage, to act in the very face of that fear, *then* we get to walk on water. The title of John Ortberg's highly recommended book says it simply: *If You Want to Walk on Water, You've Got to Get Out of the Boat*. My pastor gave this book to me at the beginning of my own journey and I remember thinking, I hate this book! He is encouraging me to do what scares me. Many years later, I now know Mr. Ortberg is exactly right.

God wants us to participate in the process, to participate in the miraculous. But fear, especially of the unknown, tends to paralyze us. Moving into the unknown feels more than scary—it actually feels impossible. How many times have you said, "I can't," when what you really mean is "I'm scared"? At this point, we come face-to-face with a crucial, life-altering choice—*proceed into the invisible wall of fear or turn tail and run*. Here is an excerpt about this very decision from one of my favorite books The Dream Giver by Bruce Wilkinson.

With every step back toward the middle of Familiar, Ordinary grew more comfortable. But he quickly noticed he was also growing sad again. And he knew why: with each step he took, he was leaving his Big Dream farther behind. Then he heard the Dream Giver again.

"Why are you going back?" he asked.

Ordinary stopped. "Because I'm afraid! Leaving Familiar feels too scary and too risky."

"Yes, it does."

"But if I was supposed to do this Big Dream," Ordinary exclaimed, "then I'm sure I wouldn't feel so afraid!"

"Yes, you would," said the Dream Giver. "Every Nobody does."

Ordinary hung his head. He thought for a moment. "But you could take away the fear. Please take the fear away!" he begged. "If you don't, I can't go on!"

"Yes, you can," the Dream Giver said. "Take courage, Ordinary."

And then he was gone. Ordinary saw his choice clearly now. He could either keep his comfort or his Dream. But how do you "take courage" when you don't have any?

Ordinary decided. If his fear wasn't going to leave, he would have to go forward in spite of it. Still trembling, he picked up his suitcase, turned his back on Familiar, and walked to the sign. And even though his fear kept growing, Ordinary shut his eyes and took a big step forward—right into the invisible Wall of Fear. And there he made a surprising discovery. On the other side of that single step—the exact one Ordinary didn't think he could take—he found that he had broken through his Comfort Zone. Now the Wall of Fear was behind him. He was free and his Dream was ahead. [2]

Wow. I cry every time I read that little book because it describes how I feel on most days—very ordinary and very afraid. I confess my longing for comfort to God every day because I know my destiny lies outside my comfort zone within the great unknown. I know I must courageously walk through the invisible wall of fear.

Here is an important concept to remember for graceful transitions—the people we call courageous simply took action in the face of their fear. Author Beth Moore emphasizes this by using an acronym to remind us: F.E.A.R. = False Evidence Appearing Real! Fear is designed by Satan to keep us from ever becoming who God created us to be. Fear keeps us in the boat where we feel comfortable, where we begin to contemplate settling for less than we were created for.

I believe that there is an epidemic in our culture. It is called low self-esteem. If you conduct an Internet search of "poor self-esteem," you will pull up thousands and thousands of articles. Let

2 Bruce Wilkinson, *"Dream Giver."* (Colorado Springs: Multnomah, 2003).

me save you some reading time. Do you know what the experts say is the cure for low self-esteem? Just *do* something! Remember the verse we started this assessment with: "Make a careful assessment of who you are, what you are to be doing, and then just do it." We are getting to the "just do it" part!

Set a goal. Speak your dream out loud. Move! Tell someone you are going to make a God-inspired change in your life and then set about doing whatever it takes to just do it, in spite of your circumstances and in spite of your fear! That is the simple cure for poor self-esteem—doing something you didn't think you could do. Courage is simply action in the face of our fear. It is getting out of the boat and walking on water. Courage is a choice. It is a choice to move and sometimes it is a choice to speak your dream out loud.

When I embarked on my own journey of purpose, I realized I had one huge obstacle to overcome—sharing all I had experienced with my husband. The thought of doing that scared me to death. I did not want my husband to think I was crazy, or worse—*religious*. I didn't want our relationship to change. I was comfortable in my marriage and was madly in love with my husband. However, I had a divine invitation to get out of the boat, and my longing to change the world was greater than my fear of embarrassment. It would take an enormous amount of courage for me to tell my husband the extent of the dreams God had put on my heart.

With courage, I concocted a plan. I took my husband out for dinner, ordered a fabulous bottle of wine, and shared the dreams I secretly carried. Nervously, I began to speak, pouring out my heart and all the dreams that had been locked away for so long—an international non-profit organization, speaking engagements around the world, a book, homes called Courage Houses, and income generators that included an exclusive merchandise line and Courage Cafés. I was talking ninety miles an hour. Through it all, my husband did not say a word. I never gave him a chance! His face never once betrayed his thoughts. As I laid out my dreams, I began to *feel* foolish.

In light of our financial circumstances, these dreams made no sense. As I spoke them aloud for the first time, they sounded crazy, even to me. However, I believed them all. When I finished, I took a deep breath and poured another glass of wine, waiting for my husband to speak. When he did, I almost fell off my chair.

> *"The only thing stopping you is the anchor you have placed around your own neck."*

I caught my breath as I grasped the fact that my husband believed in me more than I believed in myself. Revelation dawned. My fear had been self-imposed. My feelings were not truth! What if I had listened to the voices of doubt and kept silent? Without courage, I would have never heard his words or experienced the elation I felt at that moment.

I had walked through the invisible wall of fear. Confidence surged within me. My husband's belief fueled the dreams in my heart and gave me courage to take steps toward making them a reality. Yes, I was still scared. My dreams were huge and seemed impossible. I felt paralyzed by the sheer weight of them, but I declared fear would never rob me of anything ever again—especially my destiny. That night, while talking with my husband, I realized that courage simply meant moving forward one step at a time, even when I felt afraid. Courage was a choice, not a feeling. This was an eye-opening, life-changing discovery for me.

Do you have the courage to be you; the *you* God created?

There's one other thing you're going to need. I don't know about you, but I have determined that I am just a bit more courageous and a tad bit braver if someone is standing shoulder-to-shoulder, shield-to-shield with me. Sometimes my fear just gets the best of me and God knows I can't do it alone! I need His presence and the tangible presence of another righteous warrior. Sometimes that comes in the form of a swift kick in the butt, a hand to hold, or a shoulder to cry on. That, too, is God's design. During creation, way back in the beginning, God said only one thing in the garden was "not good." He said, "It is not good for man to be alone." He created us to need each other. I love that! I have found that grace-filled transitions require intimate, authentic relationships with other water walkers.

When I hear God's divine invitation to the unknown, the ONLY people I want to talk to, the only people I want praying for me, and giving me advice are other experienced water walkers. Earlier in this assessment we called them battle buddies. I have a truth I'd like to reveal to you .. the other people that are surrounding you in your boat of comfort are NOT water walkers. I'll tell you another thing I've learned in transitions from the known to the unknown: when you get ready to walk on water, all the non-water walkers in your life are going to try and hang onto your leg! Once you rock the boat by trying to get out, you are going to start stirring things up for other people—they don't want to be alone in their mediocrity! My advice? Just shake 'em off and keep on going.

So, my dear righteous girlfriends and mighty warriors, that's all you need—a divine invitation; a healthy fear of God; and a loosening of your grip on all you hold dear. You'll need perseverance through difficult circumstances and confidence in God's big picture and your identity as a child of God. Take courage in the face of fear and find fellow water walkers to cheer you on and pray for you.

One last thought—it is never boring transitioning from the known to the unknown and walking on the water with Jesus! It is your destiny.

Your Story
Are you ready to walk on water? Is there anything that is holding you back? Do you recognize God's divine invitation? What are you afraid of? What invisible walls of fear do you need to

walk through right now? Do you have a dream that you need to share with another? Do you have other water walkers you can lean on? Journal your thoughts.

My prayer for you is that you are filled with a restlessness to be and do all you were created for and that you will begin taking courageous, water-walking steps to discover and fulfill your world changing destiny.

Righteous Girlfriend/ Mighty Warrior

Your Mission is Impossible

– Day 1 –

Describe to your RGG or MWG the boat or comfort zone you know you need to leave in order to walk on water. Has God issued you a divine invitation into the unknown? Have you accepted, refused, or delayed it?

– Day 2 –

Share with your RGG or MWG your understanding of and why you need "the fear of God" to fulfill your destiny. Did your relationship or the lack of relationship with your earthly father correctly or incorrectly influence your "fear of God"?

– Day 3 –

Share with your RGG or MWG what you are holding on to that is prohibiting you from "getting out of the boat."

– Day 4 –

Describe to your RGG or MWG ways in which you need to persevere. It could be in the form of holding on to your identity or through circumstances that are designed to prevent you from seeking God and discovering your destiny. Can you see God's big picture in the perseverance? Can you detect God's purposes or are you just choosing to trust Him day by day until He sheds light on your life?

– Day 5 –

Share with your RGG or MWG any invisible walls of fear you have stepped through this week, or walls that are currently in your way. Ask other water walkers for their encouragement to help you step through.

Allow time this week to individually pray for each and every RGG or MWG out loud.
As you pray, hold the person's hands, touch his or her shoulder—let that person feel your tangible presence as he or she senses God.

Clues! Passion, Fears, Anger & Broken Hearts

"The Lord will lead us in the path he has chosen for us."
— Psalm 25:12

I pray that God is unveiling and unfolding your world-changing destiny to you. It's easy to get frustrated when we don't have our answers quick enough but the Psalm above assures us that He will lead us in the path He has chosen for us. He wants us to experience and succeed at all He has planned for us more than we do. He holds our hand as we take baby steps of faith, leaving bread crumbs and clues along the way, all the while increasing our faith and trust in Him. Secret, childhood dreams He planted in us long ago are remembered as we consult Him. He plants within us passions and desires that drive us forward, and He introduces us to issues in the world that break His heart. He's given us friends and family that have gone before us, who have led by their example for us to emulate and follow. He gives us the courage to conquer our fears so we can be and do all He created us for. He alone directs our path to our destiny. Take a deep breath. It is not up to us.

I moved from Mississippi to the San Francisco Bay Area in 1992. I was completely and totally unprepared for the differences in the two geographical areas. Culture shock was not a term I was familiar with. I had never given much thought about California or specifically the Bay

Area. It seemed like a far, far away land. At that particular moment in my story, all I cared about was getting married. Because of that impending union, I would be leaving my home of thirty-two years and the beautiful, hospitable state I was raised in. I wasn't contemplating my identity or giving much thought to my destiny. I was just dreaming dreams of happily ever after with my handsome new husband, Michael, and my then eleven-year-old beloved only son at the time, Austin.

On the much-anticipated day of our departure, I was gleefully saying my goodbyes (and I do mean gleefully) at the airport. Mother, father, brothers, sisters, and the in-laws were all there struggling to let us go gracefully. My mom was the last in line. She hugged me longer than she usually did. As I attempted to untangle myself from her embrace, she only let me break away slightly so that she could look into my eyes. I wondered if my mom had ever held my gaze for that long. Her eyes were saying something to me that she had difficulty expressing with words. She clung to me again, silently crying tears of loss for her oldest baby. I broke her grip and gaze. I was so anxious to begin my new life that I was unsympathetic to her mother's pain. I picked up my suitcase and grabbed Austin's hand, ready to follow the tarmac to my destiny. Before I could escape, my mom found the words for the truth in her eyes. She touched my shoulder one last time. "California will be your mission field." She blurted out uncharacteristically of her quiet nature. I turned and looked over my shoulder wondering who she was talking to. Me? Did I mention I was a single mom about to get married? Mission field? What was she talking about?

I didn't realize until many years later, but on that day, at that moment, and with that declaration, God was "guiding me on the path He had chosen for me." I smile now as I think back on my mom's words. She was remembering something I had long forgotten—my promise to travel to faraway places, telling the people there about God. One thing is certain—neither God, nor your mom ever forget the commitments you make to Him, even as a child. My mother remembered my desire to be a missionary and a mom.

When I was a child, those were the only two things I wanted to be when I grew up. One carried no more weight in my heart than the other. I was a little over ten months old when my brother, Chad, was born. Yes, we are less than a year apart in age. He was more like my twin. I mothered him and every other child I came in contact with when I was young. Soon after Chad, came my baby sister, Charline, another sibling to mother and boss around. To my utter delight, when I was fifteen years old, my mom and dad had an "oops" baby and provided me yet with another baby to mother and carry on my hip, my baby brother, Corry. (Whom everyone thought was my child since we were rarely apart the first two years of his life.)

I loved babies and baby dolls. I loved mothering my siblings. I loved babysitting. I dreamed of being a mom at a very early age. I wanted ten daughters. (In my young mind, I thought boys all got married and left home but daughters stayed home forever, or so I thought.)

The missionary desire also came about at a very young age. Every year in my home church, the missionaries we supported around the world came to give their annual report complete with a slide show. Click. Click. Click. I sat riveted to my seat as they showed photos and told of people in faraway places that had never heard of a God who loved them. My spirit would jump and my soul would ache as I listened. When the end came and the pastor would ask, "Who will go?" I would jump out of my seat and literally run down the aisle, hand raised declaring, "Send me! I will go!" I gave this same response year after year, always promising to go.

I wanted to be a very specific kind of missionary, a foreign missionary in a land far, far away from home. This desire was so real and so compelling that I told everyone of my plan if given an opportunity. I was never surer of anything in my life. I knew this was God's plan for my life, my destiny. In my little girl mind, I would combine my two great desires into one by marrying the man of my dreams and taking him, along with all my sons and daughters, to a far away, exotic land, like Africa or South America, to tell the natives there about God's love for them. I was going to major in home economics so that I could teach them to cook and take care of their families. That was my little girl dream.

Fast-forward twenty years to the day when I stood at that airplane departure gate, stunned by my mother's prophecy. Her parting declaration seemed ludicrous to me. I had no memory of those childhood desires. I was divorced. I was a single mom. I had failed at my first marriage and now I had a second chance. I was taking my only child and leaving my home for the first time at the ripe old age of thirty-two to start a new life with a man I loved madly. I had never left the country or traveled to faraway places. Though I still went to church on Sundays, I didn't share my faith with anyone.

My life had not quite turned out like I had dreamed. In fact, I had stopped dreaming long ago. I dismissed my Mom and her prophecy and quickly boarded the plane to California and my new life. The plane's destination held more promise for me than my mom's words. I was delighted with my new life, my new home, and the new friends I met in California. Everyone loved my southern accent and my southern cooking. When they learned I went to church on Sunday and believed in God, they thought that was equally as *cute*. That was a phenomenon no one prepared me for—people who didn't believe in God here in the United States. Talk about a culture shock! In my thirty-two years on this planet, I had never met anyone who did not believe in God and His son Jesus Christ.

I had never met a self-proclaimed atheist. To my surprise, they looked just like everyone else and they were really nice. My husband often says I am very naïve but for the first time I realized that there is such a place called the *"Bible Belt."* Not only was there such a place, but I grew up on the buckle of the belt. Until my move to the San Francisco Bay Area, I had no idea that right here in the United States of America there were people who openly stated (and didn't get hit by lightning) that they didn't believe in God. To say I was shocked would be putting it ever so mildly. I had a box in my mind for "those" people, however the very nice people in my new life would not fit there. They were just like me except I went to church on Sunday and said grace before we ate dinner. They loved their children and their husbands as much as I loved mine. We had more in common than not. They were honest and hard working. They were caring and compassionate. They were so nice that I actually let my children spend the night at their homes, which in the south I would have never considered. (What happens in the Bay Area stays in the Bay Area!) Seriously, in my new life, my friends—my very best friends—didn't believe in God.

I was slap dab in the middle of a famine—a famine of Christians. Though we had much in common, they didn't speak my language, which we Christians call "Christian-ease." I remained committed to the Sunday-church-going ritual I had participated in since birth. I put on my make-up, my panty hose, and my best dress each week searching for a church that resembled the ones I had left in the south. I loved huge churches, with thousands of people in the audience and hundreds of people wearing long satin robes in the choir, a serene nursery for the babies, and my favorite part—a pipe organ and stained glass windows! I found a few in the Bay Area but everyone attending there was over seventy-five-years old. By now I had birthed two more baby boys so I craved a church where my boys would learn of the God I loved. I shopped around for seven years, longing for a church that looked like home. On this journey to find a church, I swear I heard God saying to me the same thing the Wizard told Dorothy in the *Wizard of Oz*, "You are not in Kansas anymore child." How true. I was no longer in Mississippi. The San Francisco Bay Area and Mississippi do not have much in common, even in churches.

One Sunday in November 1999, just after my thirty-ninth birthday, my parents came for a visit. It was Thanksgiving and it was raining cats and dogs. Dragging a three- and four-year-old, along with a seventeen-year-old, to continue my search for a church in the pouring rain did not sound like much fun. My mom noticed a church had started up in the community center across the street from my house. She suggested we leave the kids at home with the dads and just she and I go. I looked at her as if she were half crazy. A church in a community center? You have got to be kidding. She was born and raised in the South; I was shocked that she was suggesting such a thing. She showed me the brochure she found under my very southern welcome mat at the front door. Fully Alive Community Church it was called. Had the woman gone mad? With that name, I just knew this start-up church was code for some type of California cult. We had heard about those things in Mississippi. Despite what my husband said, I wasn't completely naïve. In the midst of my self-righteous hissy fit, I noticed the photo of the pastor on the flyer. I remembering thinking he was cute. Who has a cute pastor, much less a young one? What the heck? By that time I had already given up on stained glass windows, pipe organs, and choir robes. I had nothing to lose.

I will never forget that day, that very ordinary, rainy, post-Thanksgiving Day. God was truly leading me in the path He had chosen for me. A cosmic explosion resembling the Big Bang happened inside of me that Sunday morning. I walked into that Community Center, where no one had on panty hose except me, and I saw something I had never seen before. I saw people worshiping God..without choir robes! This was so different than people singing hymns, which is what I was accustomed to. I was mesmerized as I watched them. Their eyes were closed, hands raised, and faces upturned toward the ceiling. I could easily imagine they were staring into the throne room of God. It was very obvious to me they saw something I didn't see. I longed to be where they were.

The worship concluded and I was unaware of the tears flowing down my cheeks. I had not cried in church in a long time. My spirit recognized the beauty of the moment, though my mind and my soul had no idea what was going on. Later in the service, the young pastor—who wore blue jeans—concluded his sermon with prayer. The first words out of his mouth almost knocked me off my folding chair. *"God, I love you so much."* It was not said in a religious, formal, stuffy, or trite way. It was intimate. My spirit recognized that the one who uttered these words truly meant them. My heart felt like it stopped beating. I felt as if I were alone in the room. In my heart, I heard the words to an old song I grew up singing,

> *"Jesus loves me, this I know.*
> *For the Bible tells me so.*
> *Yes, Jesus loves me.*
> *Yes, Jesus loves me."*

I had known *that* truth my whole life. Jesus loves *me*. But me loving God? That was an entirely new concept to me. I knew I had stumbled upon a group of people who had something I did not. *They were fully alive.* I wanted what they had. God used that hunger and desire to propel me into the year 2000, the year of my fortieth birthday, the year I intentionally chose to begin seeking God with all my heart for my identity and my destiny. That little church played such a role in my journey. God directed my path to them and let me assure you, He is directing your path to your water-walking, giant-slaying, and history-making destiny. Trust His direction. Seek Him daily.

In the process of seeking God, not only will you find Him, but you will also find *you*! He leaves us clues to our destiny like breadcrumbs along the way. I pray today that you will begin to trust that He is guiding you on the path that He has chosen for you.

Secret Desires

Daily Discovery Process

I want to encourage you to find a life-giving, Bible-teaching church that gives you the freedom to be you as God leads you on this journey of uncovering your identity and discovering your destiny; one that allows the Holy Spirit to "complete in you what He started" (PHIL. 1:6). I truly do not know who I would be if it were not for the people at Fully Alive Community Church. They continuously pointed me to God and they loved on me along the way. I thank Him for arranging my path and my life to intersect with that amazing group of people who daily desired to be the church described in ACTS 2:42.

My Story
Every day during my journey of discovery, I would walk the levee with my dog, Jake. As I continued to seek God, the Lord began to do something new inside of me. I was gaining confidence in my new identity as the "precious, beloved daughter of the King." I was suddenly feeling slightly courageous enough to say, "Yes, I have the courage to be me," while I practiced each week on my new righteous girlfriends. My church provided me with a new, much-needed safe place to belong and gave me tangible evidence I was a part of something bigger than myself. But God started messing with me. He began "stirring up my spirit," as the Bible says. I called it a "holy restlessness." I was suddenly and completely dissatisfied with my life. This was very strange because my life was good! I loved my life. My husband was making more money than he ever had. My teenage son, Austin, was preparing to leave for college. My two little boys, Michael-Dean and Ben, were healthy and happy. We had just moved into my dream home in an amazing neighborhood right across the street from the elementary school and the church. I was only working part-time, so I could volunteer at my kids' school and my new church. However, I still was restless, for what I had no idea.

Uniquely You

Day One

People I normally loved being with were now bugging me. Activities I had once looked forward to now bored me. Everything that had brought me happiness, everything that I had found pleasing and satisfying, now were not. I had no idea what was going on. The only way I can explain it was that I felt like I was supposed to be doing something. I just wasn't sure what in the world that something was.

I didn't realize it at the time but God desired to take me to a new place, spiritually speaking. I had uncovered my identity, and now He was beginning to lead me into my destiny. God used two very profound methods to lead me on that new path—the secret, long-buried desires of my heart and the stories written by others on their own water-walking, giant-slaying, history-making journeys. He resurrected and breathed life into my long, dead desires and introduced me to dozens of ordinary individuals that He used to do extraordinary things through.

In the midst of my restlessness, I began to journal my long forgotten dreams as God began to bring them to my mind, and I began reading every Christian book I could get my hands on. Faced with just reading the Bible was a little bit daunting to me at the beginning of my journey, so I decided to sacrifice my dearly loved novels and committed to reading Christian books as a part of my attempt to intentionally seek God. I loved it! I hit the Stairmaster every morning devouring every book Brennan Manning, Max Lucado, Dutch Sheets, John Eldridge, C.S. Lewis, Henri Nouwen, John Ortberg, and Phillip Yancey wrote. All this reading had an added bonus in that I exercised longer. My mom, who was my ever-present cheerleader on my journey toward God and myself, found out of my new love affair with Christian books and began sending me more. One book was deceptively ordinary and thin. The title gave away nothing of its treasures. It was called, *Spiritual Mothering* by Susan Hunt. Something caused me to choose that book first out of all the ones she had sent. As promised, God was leading me on the path He had chosen for me.

I remember settling into my favorite chair with this tiny book. I didn't recognize the author or the title. I had no great expectation of its contents but I was divinely drawn to it. So I read. A few pages into the first chapter, the simple, unadorned words began to confirm a truth in my soul that God must have deposited in my spirit long before time began. The words leapt off the page into my heart and announced to me, *"You will have daughters."* I immediately noticed the plural! I wept. It was as if God had the angels announce this proclamation from heaven just to me, just for me. In that moment, I heard God. His voice and His vehicle on that very ordinary day was a very little, ordinary book my mom had sent me in the mail with the most ordinary of notes: "I thought you might enjoy this. Love, Mom." On that day, in a way I never would have expected, God resurrected my little girl dreams and desire for daughters. I had buried that dream in a place deep within my heart and marked it *"Not meant to be."*

I learned something very important about God and dreams that day. Our little girl or little boy dreams are very often a roadmap to our destiny, a destiny God intends to fulfill. God does not put dreams and desires in our heart just to mess with us. He doesn't say, "Bummer. You really wanted that but you can't have it!" God instructs us to think of ourselves as parents. When our children ask us for something such as bread or a fish, do we hand them a snake? (MATTHEW 7:9, paraphrase) No! God used that parallel so we could see the ridiculousness of that thought. God intends to fulfill the desires He deposited within us before time began.

Don't get me wrong. Everything you desire is not of God. The Bible attributes an inordinate number of words explaining the difference between desires of our spirit and desires of our flesh (our body and soul). That is why I often ask people to look to their childhood dreams and desires for clues to their identity and destiny because very often they are in their purest form, placed there by God.

When God resurrected my dreams and desires, I was a married for the second time, forty-two-years old with three sons and my tubes tied. I had no natural means to produce daughters on my own. But God could. In an indescribable moment, I knew my dreams for daughters weren't dead. I knew God was speaking to me. I recognized His voice. My spirit knew what my soul stopped believing. I did not know how, but I knew I would have daughters. I was perfectly content just knowing my little girl dreams and desires were not dead. This allowed me to open myself up to the possibility of the impossible.

Let's consult our Creator. Look up the following verses and fill in the blanks.

"Delight in God and he will give you the _____ and secret petitions of your heart of your heart. Commit your way to the Lord; trust in him and he will do this." — PSALM 37:4,5 (AMP)

"God who redeems your life from the pit and crowns you with love and compassion, who satisfies your _____ with good things so that your youth is renewed like the eagles." — PSALM 103:4, 5 (NIV)

"You open your hand and satisfy the _____ of every living thing." — PSALM 145:16 (NIV)

"He fulfills the _____ of those who reverently and worshipfully fear him; he hears their cry and saves them." — PSALM 145:19 (AMP)

"The _____ of good people lead straight to the best, but wicked ambition ends in angry frustration." — PROVERBS 11:23 (MSG)

Desire. The Bible is clear. Your Creator minces no words here in these verses. He *will* give you the desires and secret petitions of your heart *if* (and it's a big "if" here) you delight in Him, worship Him, and revere or fear Him. He will open His hand and satisfy your desires with good things. There are more truth verses in the Bible that talk about our desires.

Theses verses are worthy of our 3x5 cards.

I feel I should issue a caveat here before we move forward. If you are not spending time alone with your Creator, letting Him bestow your identity upon you and reveal your destiny to you, then you will attempt to fulfill your own desires in ways that are not of God. In fact, you may begin to chase after desires that God did not deposit in your spirit before time began. There is a holy "but" in this desire-fulfilling business of God. God wants to give you the desires of your heart, *but* you must go to Him for that fulfillment. If left to our own devices, our own wants and our own needs can get us into some big trouble. We can become obsessive and selfish, demanding that anyone and everyone meet our desires. This cannot happen, however, when you draw near to God. He purifies and refines your desires so only He can fulfill them. He wants to fulfill them for His purposes. Trust Him in this process.

> *"All my longings and desires lie open before you O Lord—even my sighing is not hidden from you."* — PSALM 38:9 (NIV)

Your Story

Are you experiencing any "holy restlessness" with things, people, jobs, or routines that in the past had satisfied you? If so, list them below.

_____
_____
_____
_____
_____
_____
_____
_____
_____
_____
_____
_____

When I first started this journey of uncovering my identity and discovering my destiny, I did not remember my dreams of wanting daughters. I just felt a kind of sadness as each year passed and the realization crystallized that I would not have more children. I ignored the powerful longing in my heart when I held girl babies or kissed my nieces. I just laughed off the longing and said something trite like "I'm waiting on granddaughters," burying the desire deeper and deeper. I also had forgotten the other part of my desire—the one to be a missionary in a foreign country. I passed it off as an irrational childhood fantasy. But in reality, I was settling for less than God planned for me.

Friends, be encouraged! God never forgets the childhood dreams and desires of your heart. He intends to fulfill them. Like me, you may have to let go of your preconceived ideas of *how* that will happen. *God* is the how! Ask God to resurrect and bring to your memory the dreams and desires He placed in you and those He intends to fulfill. What were your little girl, or little boy, dreams and desires—the ones that you may have forgotten, or the ones that just won't go away? Ask God about them. Ask Him to help you sort out which of those dreams and desires He planted in you "before time began," and which ones He wants you to let go of because He has something better planned for you.

"I know the plans I have for you says the Lord, plans to give you a hope and a future. Then you will seek me with all your heart." — JEREMIAH 29:11, 13 (NIV)

_____
_____
_____
_____
_____
_____
_____
_____
_____

Now that you have listed them, write a letter to your Creator laying your heart, your desires, and longings bare before Him. Don't withhold your sighs or your tears. Tell Him of your buried desires. The ones you don't ever see happening because of your age, your financial situation, your marital status, or whatever obstacle or circumstance you find yourself in. Dare to write down the seemingly impossible desires of your heart. You can trust God with them. Ask Him to resurrect any desires you have buried and forgotten. Ask Him to purify the ones you have.

Day One

Take courage! Be completely honest and open with God and yourself.

___

My prayer for you as we end this day is that you are beginning to see what a "good" heavenly father you have. Not only does He delight in bestowing your true identity upon you, but also in fulfilling the dreams and desires of your heart. I pray you will begin to recognize the truth about yourself and about God that can only be found in His Word and confirmed in your spirit. Trust that still, small voice in the manner He chooses to speak. I pray you will open your mind and heart to the possibility of the impossible. He loves you, dear one. He has good plans for you—plans to give you hope and a future.

Your Passions Play a Part

Daily Discovery Process

Are you restless to know why you are on this planet? What purpose you play? Are you ready to do something? There may also be clues to your destiny in what you are passionate about.

My Story

I can't even keep a straight face as I write this word—*passion*! Oh, how I remember this part of my journey. After God had resurrected my long-buried dream for daughters, the restlessness I described yesterday still continued. Not only did it continue, it increased! My intentional daily discipline to consult my heavenly Daddy for my identity was now a lovely habit I looked forward to, but my spirit was being stirred beyond anything I had ever experienced. I was even more restless! I was ready for some action! I needed to be doing something! I contacted my pastor at this momentous time in my life, describing to him what was happening inside of me. He said he had something I could do—stuff envelopes at the church office. That was not exactly what my spirit was yearning for.

Instead, I signed up for a class at church that promised if I attended, I would discover my spiritual gifts. I was excited about this class. I had never been told I had spiritual gifts before! I was even more thrilled with this new concept because I believed that I was not born with any natural talents, and I did not consider myself gifted at anything. How could you excel at talking, being loud and bossy? I had become convinced I had nothing to offer to "wow" the world. This class, and the promise of a spiritual gift, had my name written all over it. I tried to explain the concept of the class to my husband and came up with a Christian personality profile. He was all for it and gave me the grace to be away from home every Thursday night for six weeks, even though that meant he was alone with a three and five year old. I was confident in what the advertisement promised—if I faithfully attended each week, I would have a spiritual gift by the end of the class. I didn't dare hope for more.

I almost quit on the very first night. We each introduced ourselves stating why we have enrolled in the class, and then watched a video. Both of those were painless. Then our first thought provoking question of the evening was posed: "What are you passionate about?" The instructions were to write down your reflections on that question and to share your thoughts with the group. I tried to remain calm. My pulse raced. I stared at the blank piece of paper. I felt like I needed to breathe in a paper bag. I picked up my pen. I doodled stars, dots, and squares on the paper that waited for my life's passion. I looked around the room. Everyone else was writing but me. Maybe I could copy someone's answers. I felt like I was back in Sophomore High School Latin class. My brain replayed the question over and over again. "What am I passionate about?" Nothing! Nothing! I could not think of anything I was passionate about.

The week before my husband and I had a similar discussion. I had told him that I envied his passion for golf. He would go out in the cold and pouring down rain just to hit a bucket of balls, just to be better. He played at least once a week, more if his schedule allowed.

Nothing I could think of would get me out in the cold and rain. Nothing. My passion? The question loomed and time was running out.

My anxiety mounted as the group began putting their pens down, each person's paper full of their passions. My paper was blank and wet from my sweaty palms. I was dreading my turn. I had no idea what I would say. For some reason, it felt hideously wrong to say I did not have a passion. It began and around the table we went. I started getting that icky feeling in the pit of my stomach as it got closer and closer to my time. I recognized that feeling. It was my old friend embarrassment. Finally my name was called. "Jenny? What are you passionate about?" The facilitator must have recognized my anguish because she embellished the question a bit more by saying, "What could you sit and do for hours and hours?"

First of all, this was so the wrong question for me—I don't sit for hours and hours and "do" anything! Sitting still is not one of my spiritual gifts. My mind was filled with random thoughts like these while I stalled for time. Then a new phenomenon occurred. I was struck mute! Rarely have I been rendered speechless. Tears welled up in my eyes threatening to spill over onto my already wet, perspiration-soaked paper. I felt like I was in the second grade. Everyone was staring at me. It was a long three seconds.

Suddenly from somewhere deep inside of me, without any rehearsed thought, my mouth opened and out burst the cry of my heart. *"I am passionate about everything and anything. I have a passionate opinion about everything. I am so passionate I wear myself out on a daily basis!"* The facilitator smiled a knowing smile. I wondered if she knew something I did not. As the words left my mouth and the sound traveled up to my ears, I knew in my spirit it was truth. My problem was not a lack of passion; it was an overwhelming abundance of it. As soon as I had this revelation class was over. I left feeling more restless than ever. What was I to do with this new self-awareness? The facilitator had an answer: do my homework. Our assignment was to ask someone who knew us well for help in defining, or, in my case narrowing, our passions. I was fighting my old demons of embarrassment and humiliation; I was confident they would make an appearance now that I was asked to involve another in my journey.

When I got home, I found the answer I was longing for in the least likely place—my bed, with the least likely person—my husband. He was in bed watching television when I burst into the room in tears, interrupting his favorite passion—golf. If the man can't play golf, he watches it on T.V. I flung myself on his chest explaining my lack of a specific passion. "Passionate about everything isn't an answer!" I blubbered. He was surprisingly patient with me though self-awareness is so not his thing. I told him I had to have someone help me narrowly define my passions and it had to be someone who knew me and loved me.

Though he qualified as that person, I never once entertained the notion that he might volunteer his services. Calm, confident man that he is, he took my now soggy homework paper that I was clutching in my hand, skimmed over the hundreds of questions, threw it on the floor, and with great wisdom said, "I know what you are passionate about." Time stood still. I hopped expectantly up to my knees. Could it be this easy? The man who loves and knows me better than anyone in the entire world—could he have my answer? I must have looked like a love-starved puppy. I desperately wanted to know my personal passion, my purpose in this world. My husband delivered his answer with no fanfare, "Your girlfriends." Because of the perplexed look on my face, he expounded. "Your girlfriends are always calling you, asking for your advice, asking for your help—children, husbands, marriage, jobs, arguments. You are the 'Dear Abby' of Redwood Shores. Honey," he lovingly concluded, "you are their encourager, you are a cheerleader of the masses—and to me."

Be still my heart. I did have a passion and my husband had uncovered it for me. I am an encourager, a cheerleader of the greatest kind. I see people's potential. I have a passion to see people become and do all they were created for, not more, but absolutely refusing to settle for anything less. I deeply desire all those who cross my path to uncover their identity and discover their destiny.

This profound discovery of my passion, coupled with my resurrected dream to have daughters, led me to action. With my knees knocking and all the courage I could muster, I opened my home weekly to a small group of women for conversation with each other and our Creator. We laughed, we cried, and we loved as we sought God and built authentic relationships with each other. I thought I had died and gone to heaven. I was doing something! My restlessness subsided. This group of women became the first righteous girlfriend group (RGG). I was so passionate about having them in my home every week. We shared our hearts, our lives, and our journeys to God. Many of these women became my spiritual daughters, just as God had promised.

As I considered this week of writing, I did a word search on *passion* since is seemed so difficult for me to define in my own life. I wanted to give you a clearer understanding of its importance in discovering and fulfilling our destinies. Webster defines passion as "any powerful or compelling emotion or feeling, such as love or hate." Compelling. Power. That begs the question, "To find your passion, consider what do you love, hate, or totally get emotional about—so much so that it moves you to action?" (You'll answer that in a bit.) However for those like me who are emotional and strongly opinionated about a hundred things, this definition may also provoke a struggle.

I grabbed my Bible to consult my Creator only to find the word *passion* three times. This word in which we use often did not seem to merit much weight biblically. Was I focusing on something that did not hold clues to my destiny? I was compelled to continue. When I looked up the word *passion* in the Greek and Hebrew, I saw a familiar word, our word from yesterday. *Desire*. Wow! That word is used frequently in the Bible. I consulted the Hebrew, the Greek, and my friend Webster to help me truly understand this word *desire*. It seemed an important clue. All three sources agreed: *desire* means "an acute, emotional longing!" God's word for passion is desire and as we learned yesterday, He intends to fill the desires of our heart if we delight in Him. Realization came crashing in. The passion I felt as a woman could be traced back to my little girl dreams and desires. These desires, these acute emotional longings, were a roadmap to my destiny.

Consult Your Creator

*"When I heard these things, I sat down and wept.
For days I mourned and fasted and prayed before God.
Then I went before the King to ask for what I needed. I was so afraid."*
— Nehemiah 1:4, when he heard about the ruin of the wall in Jerusalem.

*"I am a woman who is deeply troubled. I have been pouring out my soul to the Lord.
I have been praying here out of my great anguish and grief."*
— 1 Samuel 1:15, Hannah, who couldn't get pregnant.

"One day after Moses had grown up he went out to where his own people were and watched them at their hard labor. He saw one of his own people being beat by an Egyptian and he killed him."
— EXODUS 2:11–13, Moses, after he sees the bondage of his people.

"When David ran to greet his brothers and was talking with them, Goliath, the Philistine champion, stepped out from his lines and shouted his usual defiance and David heard it. When the Israelites saw the man, they all ran from him in great fear. David went to Saul and said, 'let no one lose heart on account of this Philistine, your servant will go and fight him.' So David ran quickly toward the battle line to meet him and killed him."
— 1 SAMUEL 17, David, when Goliath was mocking his God, his family, and his people.

"So Mordecai showed a copy of the text to Esther and explained to her that she must go into the king's presence to beg for mercy and plead with him for her people, for if you remain silent, relief and deliverance for the Jews will come but who knows but that you have been born and reached this royal position for such a time as this.' Esther fasted and prayed for three days and then she said, 'I will do as you ask, I will go before the king whether I live or die.'"
— ESTHER 4, Mordecai and Esther, as they face the total destruction of the Jewish people.

"Jesus landed, saw the large crowd, and he had compassion on them and he healed their sick."
— MATTHEW 14:14, Jesus, trying to mourn the death of his cousin John in solitude.

Each of these stories from the Bible highlights a person's unique passion and how it propelled them to action. For some, it was righteous anger over an injustice. For others, despair over a loss. Some felt a strong desire to build something tangible. Jesus was passionate about people. *"He had compassion on them"* is a statement used over and over by Jesus' friends and followers, Matthew, Mark, Luke, and John in their books about his life.

Compassion and passion. I couldn't help noticing our word *passion* within the word *compassion*. I felt another word search coming on. Dictionary.com confirmed my suspicions. "Compassion is *a feeling of deep sympathy and sorrow for another who is stricken by misfortune,* **accompanied by** *a strong desire to alleviate the suffering."* Or as I paraphrase it, "an overwhelming desire to just do something"!

I'm so excited I could just jump out of my skin right now. Wait till you see the Greek definition for compassion. The Greek word is *splagchnizomai*. I have *no* idea how to pronounce it, but I love the meaning! *"A movement or impulse that wells up from within one's body."* This is a deeply physical and emotional word, a gut reaction some would say.

Are you as excited as I am? Can you see the implications? If not, hang in there. Soon you will.

I wondered about the meaning of the first syllable of compassion. Was it important? What did *com-* mean? You guessed it! I looked it up in the Greek and I almost fell off my chair. Com- in the Greek means "an intensive force." Now watch this. When you break down the word *compassion*, you first have *com-*, which is "an intensive force," and *passion*, which is "an intense desire." Friends! Your compassion and passions are a force to be reckoned with. They are what get you out of the bed in the morning and propel you through your day. Your compassion and passions are greater than your fear or your lack. In the verses above, each of them had to overcome fear, despair, and impossible circumstances. They took courage by allowing their passion and compassion to lead them. Pay attention to what you are compassionate and passionate about. They are clues to your destiny, the very reason you are on this planet. Let them move you! When you do, you are fulfilling God's destiny for you because He placed them within you to bring about His plans for this world. Every single time the word *compassion* is used in conjunction with Jesus' name in the Bible, there is always **an action that followed the emotion.** "He felt compassion for the people *so he healed them."* "He felt compassion for the hungry so he fed them." "He felt compassion for a woman who lost her son *so he raised him from the dead."* Like Jesus, our compassion is to lead us to action. I can hear Nike and the apostle Paul encouraging us to "Just do it!" Can you?

Compassion and courage. Both are action words. Let your passions lead you to action.

Your Story

Now it's your turn. I have provided you with some open-ended statements to help you attempt to find your passions. Articulate your answers as best you can. Ask God to unveil your passions. Pay close attention to the things that break your heart and/or make you angry. Reflect back on yesterday's journaling when you wrote down your little girl or little boy dreams and desires. See if there is a correlation between your passion(s) as an adult and the desires of your little girl or boy heart.

I have always had a passion for:

_____

_____

I have always loved to:

I hate to:

I'd be happy if I never had to do the following again:

When I was young I could spend hours:

Who do I feel compassion for?

My prayer for you as we end this day is that God will reveal to you the specific passion He deposited in you long before time began. I pray that you will have a new divine awareness of the people and situations that move you to compassion. I pray that, like Jesus, compassion will lead you straight to action in spite of your fears and in spite of your circumstances. I pray you will consult your Creator daily to be reminded who you are and the inheritance you hold. You were created on purpose for a purpose and your passions hold a clue!

Clues from the Past

Daily Discovery Process

I am just so excited in my spirit. The Lord has me totally stirred up! How I long to look deep into your eyes and tell you that your life matters. I long for you to know that. God created you on purpose for a purpose. You, your life, and your destiny lead to being a history maker, life changer, water walker, and giant slayer! Whether you realize it or not, whether you are intentional about it or not, you are impacting lives and situations daily. Good and bad, positive and negative. Does that stop you in your tracks? It does for me. It actually boggles my mind when I take the time to ponder and contemplate the hugeness of that concept. My little life, my decisions, and my choices are greatly affecting the people around me. I can wrap my brain around believing I may have some impact on my family or friends, but complete strangers or people who have not been born yet? Those I had not given much thought to until recently. Now I see it as a part of God's plan.

My Story

I got "the call" at 6:00 a.m. on March 13, 2005. I had been waiting on this call for years ever since the day I moved to California. When you leave home from all those you call family and friends, you *know* that one day you will get "the call" that comes in the middle of the night and drives you to your knees. The one that tells you someone you have loved is gone, his or her life has come to an end. Knowing it and expecting it does not lessen the pain when you answer it. It doesn't even lessen when the end is welcomed because suffering has ceased. The Bible says we were created for eternity. Our spirits certainly know that truth. When death steals a loved one from us we, too, feel a piece of us has died.

My call was about Elizabeth, my Mimi. Her spirit left her worn out body, although her mind had been gone awhile. She was ninety-two years old. As her obituary chronicled, she was survived by two daughters, seven grandchildren, twelve great-grandchildren, and one great-great grandchild. Funny how they sum up a life in the newspaper that way—survived by, gone before her, born, lived, died. It struck me as funny when I first read it; then I was sad. My Mimi's life was so much more than a paragraph in the back of a newspaper. Her life and her choices had impacted so many people. I was determined she was going to have a grander send off than that. Much to my surprise, my compassion led me straight to action. I was going to give her eulogy. It did not matter that I had never done a eulogy before. I just knew in my spirit it was what I had to do.

Originally, I had planned to visit my Mimi when I made my annual pilgrimage home to Mississippi. I had asked God to clear her mind, just for a moment, so I could look into her eyes, hold her hand, and tell her how much her life, her choices, her decisions, and her obedience to God meant to me. How her love for Him had affected my life. I wanted to thank her. I wanted to tell her that all the hardships she endured, all the rejection and pain, all the battles she fought were not in vain—they were for me, for us, and for the generations that followed. I doubt she ever pondered me, her unborn granddaughter, as she went through the daily routines of her life. I am quite sure she never contemplated her choices in light of how they would affect those that would come after her. But they did and I wanted her to know that. But she left this world before I ever had the opportunity. It seemed God had other plans. Instead of talking to her face to face, I was to give her eulogy telling the audience at her funeral all that I had longed to tell her. I just could not leave that task to the young pastor, who had only known her as an old woman that had lost her mind, didn't know her children, and cried for her Mommy. When he met her, she had not been my Mimi for a long time.

I am laughing and crying as I remember her. Even without her mind, she was a force until the day she died. My mom and aunt went to choose her casket before she died at the prompting of the doctor since she "didn't have much time left." But he didn't know my Mimi. No one told her what to do or when to do it—especially when to exit this world! After selecting her casket and planning her funeral, she lingered for another seven days. She was a fighter and a giant slayer until the very end. Five-feet tall, one hundred and ten pounds soaking wet, and full of spit and vinegar was a common description of my Mimi. Still, she was scared to death to fly in an airplane—she never did—and to the day she died hated being left alone or in the dark. She was such a contradiction. My aunt told me that once as a young girl she ditched school, put on her roller skates, and hooked a rope to a car so she could skate around town. Fearless one moment and frightened the next. She was little, but strong. Humble, yet willful.

She wasn't going anywhere until she was good and ready. I told everyone at the funeral she probably lingered on this earth, waiting for someone in heaven to go get "my Daddy-Jay" (her husband) off the lawn mower somewhere in the back forty of heaven to be waiting to welcome her home as she made her quiet entrance into heaven. My Daddy-Jay. He'd been gone for almost twenty-three years and my Mimi missed him every one of those days. The two of them could make you believe in true love, fairy tales, and soul mates. Even their love for each other impacted my life and many others. I sought my Creator asking Him how in the world I would ever find words to honor her life.

Funny, the first people to hear her eulogy were a group of third and fourth grade children. The day I received that phone call was a Sunday morning, and I was scheduled to teach the children's class at church. The story I was to teach was about David and Goliath. The focus word for the kids was *courage*. I was an emotional mess. Everything that morning reminded me of my Mimi—especially this particular story and word. As I stood before my audience of nine and ten year olds, I began to weave the story of David facing the giant. I did not have to embellish the story to hold their attention. Kids love hearing how a shepherd boy defeated a nine-foot giant armed only with a little slingshot, some common river rocks, and an enormous belief in his God. Their little faces were shocked when I told them that David actually went looking for a fight, running into battle. I told them the reason David could do this is that God have given him supernatural powers to kill a lion and a bear with just his hands. David had a history with God. He knew first-hand that God could do what He says He can do.

As I finished telling the story, I promised these children God would never ask them to fight a nine-foot giant with a slingshot. I did promise them, however, that at some time in their life—and probably more than once—God would ask them to do something that was very difficult, very scary, and could only be accomplished with an enormous belief in God. Every adult in the room nodded their agreement. I told my very attentive students that I knew all of this because God had been doing it for generations. He even asked my little grandmother to fight a giant, but the giant wasn't a nine-foot tall Philistine. The giant God asked my Mimi to fight was a mean one—prejudice and racism in the Deep South during the early 1940s and 50s. She was the slingshot.

My Mimi's heart broke and her spirit screamed at the injustices being levied against black people in her community. Her compassion drove her straight to action. She ran across well-defined racial lines and railroad tracks to teach vacation Bible school to the little black children in her community. Because of her courage and obedience to God, she was thrown out of her own church (the one her daddy started) and received death threats by the well-meaning Christians in her town—her friends and neighbors. Like David, she chose to ignore the taunts of the giant and those souls that tried to stop her. She said, "God did not mean for me to remain silent." So she wasn't. She became what we would call an activist today. She just called it "the right thing to do." Her passion forced her into the arms of her Creator because she knew alone she could never defeat this giant of prejudice and racism. So she just loved kids one at a time and told them about her friend Jesus. Her compassion for them caused her to open her home and take in children, orphans abandoned by life, circumstances, or their parents. The rescued became the rescuer.

Jesus said, "To much is given, much is expected." My Mimi always felt she had been given much.

Her efforts on this planet never earned her much in the way of recognition or awards, and that was fine with her. She just loved people and her God. She performed for His pleasure and His alone. With the love and protection of my grandfather and the strength and power of God, she impacted her world in a mighty way, including complete strangers and unborn children. Undeterred by her fears and inadequacies, she was propelled into action by her compassion.

Where did she get that kind of courage? How could she run into battle? The answer is one we have talked about on and off in this assessment. She knew her Creator. She had a history with her God. She knew Him as her personal giant slayer and rescuer. Though left in an orphanage, she grew up beloved, belonging, and believing that she was the princess, daughter of Eleanor, Benjamin, and God. Her name declared her heritage. Because she had personally experienced God's divine protection and provision as a young child, a little thing like racism, prejudice, death threats, and rejection were nothing compared to her God's power. When God called my Mimi into battle, just like David, she ran toward it. She knew He would provide the stones; all she had to do was show up with an enormous belief in God's ability to do what He says He can do. Her life continues to impact others. At my grandfather's funeral years ago, an old black gentleman shuffled into the funeral parlor to stand in front of me. I'll never forget his words: "If it wasn't for Miss Liz and Mr. J.D., I would have never known the Lord Jesus as my Savior—'cause they had come to teach the children."

What a eulogy, what a testimony.

In the Bible it says, "Those who love the Lord and follow his ways will be blessed and their children for generations to come." That's me! My life bears witness to that truth. That is what I wanted to tell my Mimi before she died. Her life impacted mine. By the time I was born, my Mimi's giant slaying days were over. I only knew her as my grandmother. That is, until recently. As God began uncovering my identity and revealing my destiny, He pressed upon my heart that those who had gone before me fought battles so I would never have to fight the same ones. Their victories were my inheritance. I have received blessings in my life that are a direct correlation to my Mimi's love of Jesus and the actions of her compassion. The ceiling of her life became the floor on which I stand gazing into my destiny. Oh, how I pray my children can say the same of me.

Generation after generation stands in awe of your work; each one tells stories of your mighty acts. — Psalm 145:4

Your Story

Seeing God's hand on our family in the past can give us glimpses into our future destiny. Consider your family's past and those that have gone before you. What did they do for a living? Where did they live? What were their personalities? What type of impact did they have in their community, their family, or the world? Could their ceiling of accomplishment be your floor to start on? If so, in what ways? Do you see a parallel in their passions and yours? Can you look through the lens of time and see where pieces of their past may intersect with God's plan for your future? Is there a thread of destiny running from those who came before you? If you do not know, ask some family members. I did not learn about my family history until I was over forty and started asking questions. I do feel I need to add a word of caution here. Do not get hung up on the mistakes of the generation before you. We all have them. Remember, you are mining the past for nuggets God may have placed there to help you discover and fulfill your water-walking, giant-slaying, history-making destiny.

My prayer for you as you end this very long day of reading, writing, and remembering is that you will begin to consider your passions, your secret desires, and which will propel you to action. Ignore the "what ifs" and "how will I ever" taunts of the giant. God will provide you with all the slingshots and rocks you will ever need. He has been in the giant slaying business for a long time. HEBREWS 11 highlights the lives of ordinary people filled with great faith that did crazy exploits for God. HEBREWS 12 says those heroes of the faith surround us and I believe they cheer us on. My Mimi has now joined them and I bet they are having a grand time trading stories. I promise you, she is encouraging us to "Just do it!" Blessings, dear one!

Face Your Fears

Daily Discovery Process

I hate that I have lived most of my life afraid. Afraid of what others would think, afraid of losing my job, afraid of losing my home, afraid of losing my kids, afraid of losing my breasts, afraid of losing my husband, afraid of being embarrassed, afraid of speaking, afraid of writing, afraid of being used, afraid of going bankrupt, afraid of failing, afraid of everything, afraid of nothing.

I once heard that human beings are the only species that can scare themselves. That's me.

Afraid, afraid, afraid...

That is why for so long I hated the word *courage*. It implied you were going to have to do something you were afraid of. I had avoided that most of my life. I believed courage was a personality trait. Either you had it or you did not. And I did not have it, nor did I want it.
The further I have walked on this journey of purpose, the more I have come to love the word for I learned it simply meant *action*. Action I love; it is fear I try to avoid.

Former First Lady Eleanor Roosevelt disagrees with me. She suggested a person should, "Do one thing every day that scares you." My mind screams, *why?* However, even as I ask the question, I know the answer. Doing something that scares me, something I fear, requires me to choose courage; it requires action on my part. Fear paralyzes me, but courage moves me through its invisible wall. When I break through that wall, a sense of accomplishment and confidence embraces me. After a while you become accustomed to doing things scared. With experience, you soon realize your fears, like your feelings, are not true indicators of truth. With enough practice, you will find that you do not even require courage anymore because at some point in time when you were not even aware, you have become bold. That is when you become dangerous—when you are a full-fledged member of the water-walking, giant-slaying, history-making club.

I have found that fears can even be helpful in identifying your unique world-changing destiny. The very thing that at one time scared me the most was exactly what I was created to do. My dog, Jake, taught me that lesson.

As I mentioned before, Jake is a Labrador Retriever. Labs were created on purpose for a purpose—swimming and hunting. They love to get wet and they love to fetch. They are literally made for it. Labs have thick tails called otter tails that are designed to propel them through the water at great speed to fetch the ducks their owners shot out of the sky. Their hair is much like a duck's feathers; it repels water. Getting a Lab soaking wet is a difficult feat. All Labs love water—except Jake. He did not swim or fetch. He was scared to death of the very thing he was created for.

It all started when we gave him a bath as a puppy. Bathing a dog is an unnatural act, but because Jake was being groomed to be a housedog and not a hunter, he needed to smell good if he was to be granted access to our home. On this particular day, Michael, my husband, and my two young sons, Michael-Dean and Ben, were lathering up Jake with rosemary-scented dog soap. Ben was holding Jake while my husband held the water hose. Michael-Dean's job was to turn the water on and off when his dad yelled, "Turn it on!" and "Turn it off!" The directive was shouted and Michael-Dean turned on the water. When he did, the force of the water whipped the hose out of my husband's soapy hands, hit Jake in the head, and sprayed water all over his poor face. In the process, Ben got soaked, too. He screamed, causing Jake to run out of the backyard with the entire family in pursuit. When we finally caught him, he was hiding in the neighbor's hedge. We dragged him out by his front legs. The emotional trauma that poor dog endured was severe and long lasting. Thank heaven my husband and boys were unscathed. Jake never recovered. From that day forward, Jake refused to go near *any* body of water. He would cross to the other side of the street if he saw a puddle or a sprinkler. Swimming? No way. He shook like a leaf if near any type of water.

We tried everything, even throwing him in. (In hindsight, I do not advise this course of action; it only made things worse.) Jake had become afraid of the very thing in which he was created to thrive. Now, do not feel too sorry for Jake. Though he was not being and doing all he was created to be and do, he lived a very good, comfortable life. Though he did not swim, he loved riding in the car and was allowed to go most places we went. He loved tennis balls but never got the whole fetch thing. He was terribly afraid of rain, so we let him inside the garage because his big otter tail knocked over everything in the house. Gradually we let him come inside only if he could courageously endure a quick, fragrant bath, complete with a blow dry. (He hated blow dryers as much as water.) He liked barking at the dogs on the television. We did not let him on

the couch but got him his own feather bed—which he chewed to pieces if left alone. He seemed happy with his domestication. When he was outside for any length of time, he managed to escape because he did not like to be alone. I think I rescued him seven times from the pound or from one of the neighbors who would graciously take him inside. He was always glad to see me but seemed content to stay where he was as long as other people were around. He liked people better than other dogs, thus he was never enthusiastic about doggy parks. However, he loved our walks on the levee, yet he always remained far from the water. That is, until one day when he was about eight years old—about sixty-two in dog years.

We were on our regular daily purpose walk. I had taken Jake to our church, which backs up to the San Francisco Bay, so he could sniff and be off the leash. That day, I was not attuned to Jake's wanderings as I was contemplating my own identity and destiny. Suddenly, I saw a quick movement out of the corner of my eye. To my utter amazement, Jake was running. I mean really *running*—like a dog—straight in the direction of a large body of water that had two ducks sitting on it. It is difficult to explain what happened in those few minutes, but I can only describe it as that which Jake was created for became more powerful than his fear. I saw him gracefully fly through the air and belly flop on the water. It was a thing of pure beauty. Then he started swimming toward the ducks. They started to fly and he chased them. I do not know who was shocked more: Jake, me, or the ducks! I watched in stunned silence. (This was in the days before cell phone cameras.) Jake was swimming.

On this particular day, Jake took courage. He did it scared.

Jake finished his swim and ran to my side. I swear he was smiling and that big ole fat tail was wagging at a crazy speed. Soaking wet, he shook his entire body, spraying me with water. I sank to the grass and hugged my wet dog. Laughing all alone on the wet grass, I contemplated the divine gift I had just received. It was the gift of watching my dog overcome fear and do the very thing he was created to do—the very thing that his fear had stolen. It was as if time stood still.

A tear slipped down my cheek as I hugged my very courageous dog, and I sensed these words:

You are no different from Jake. You too have become domesticated. Your fears are unfounded. The very thing you are afraid to do is the very thing I have created you for.

Now I wept. I knew it was true.

My fears seemed pitiful and small. I feared regret, failure, criticism, and laughter. I realized I only did the things I felt comfortable with and was good at. I was afraid to try anything new because my old enemy—embarrassment—just might come for a visit. I was a forty-something-year-old woman and the bottom line was that I was afraid to be me. I remembered that bold, passionate little girl and knew that fear was keeping me from fulfilling my destiny. I vowed to walk through my invisible walls of fear so that I could be and do all I was created for. Jake was my inspiration. However, Jake had a natural instinct kick in when he saw the water and ducks; you and I must daily make the intentional choice of courage, of taking action in spite of our fear.

I began to do things that scared me—things that deep inside I longed to do and things that I had done as a child. I volunteered to lead a small group. I publicly shared my testimony. I trained for a sixteen-mile hike to the top of a mountain. I led a group of women to the top of Half Dome in Yosemite National Park. I led a ministry. I spoke on a stage. I taught a class. I organized conferences. I shared my faith. I spoke up. I started a non-profit organization. I began to write a book.

I practiced being me. And I did it scared. I was determined to have the courage to be me.

Your Story

What about you? What are your greatest fears? Could they be keeping you from your destiny? Do your fears actually provide a clue to your destiny? Like my old dog, Jake, have you been domesticated? Is comfort keeping you from doing what you were created for? Consult your Creator and ask Him to give you the courage to step through any invisible walls of fear that have paralyzed you and are keeping you from your destiny. Journal your thoughts here.

You were chosen. You were picked before Day One of creation. You have been lavished with all the wisdom, understanding, and knowledge you need to know your Creator. He desires to unveil the mystery of His will to you. It brings Him great pleasure. You are His beautiful creation. He has pronounced you "good," and through the power of Jesus, He has prepared good works and a unique destiny for you and you alone.

Let God lavish His love on you just say *no* to the negative voices and old erroneous beliefs that are trying to tell you something different. Drown out their voices by speaking truth out loud. Say to the heavens—"I am the daughter/son of the King. I have a purpose!"

"He chose us before the creation of the world to be holy and blameless in his sight. In love he predestined us to be adopted as his children. He lavished on us all wisdom and understanding so that we may know him better. He has made known to us the mystery of his will according to his good pleasure. For we are God's workmanship, created in Jesus to do good works which God prepared in advance for us to do." —Excerpts from EPHESIANS 1 & 2 (NIV)

"Our father wants to take us to the high places of blessing in him. Long before he laid down earth's foundations, he had us in mind, had settled on us as the focus of his love. Long, long ago he decided to adopt us into his family. What pleasure he took in planning this. He wanted us to enter into the celebration of his lavish gift-giving hand of his beloved son. We are a free people. Not just barely free, abundantly free! It is in Jesus that we find out who we are and what we are to be living for. Before we heard of him, he had his eye on us, had designs for our glorious living. It is part of his plan. Now God has us just where he wants us; with all the time in the world and the next to shower grace and kindness upon us. Saving is his idea. All we have to do is trust him enough to let him do it. It is God's gift from start to finish."
—Excerpts from EPHESIANS 1 (MSG)

My prayer for you as we end this day is that you will take God at His word and receive His promises of blessing, freedom, grace, family, kindness, and purpose. My prayer is that you will take action in the face of your fear.

My prayer is that you will begin trusting your Creator and His plans for your life. Do the one thing today that scares you to death. Do the thing that you want to do but are scared to do. You may find it is exactly what you were created to do.

What Breaks Your Heart?

Daily Discovery Process

Your desires, passions, family history, and fears may all provide clues to your destiny. They certainly did for me. However, seven years after I began this journey of purpose I ran into an evil that broke my heart while at the same time clarified my purpose.

It's a Home

It's a home. It's a home. It's a home. Those words were whispered to my heart one Sunday morning as I sat in church, as I had most every Sunday morning of my entire life. Being raised in Mississippi, the Bible belt, this habit was established early in my life, but in all those years of church attendance, never once did I walk through those doors expecting my life to change. However, on Sunday, July 22, 2007, my life did just that.

I sat in the huge auditorium, waiting for the service to begin, engulfed by three thousand people. I did not know a single one of them aside from my two teenage sons who sat beside me. My husband was playing golf. I was feeling lonely and melancholy that particular day. We had been in Sacramento for a year, fighting to survive. We had lost our home, and we missed our friends and the comfortable life we had built in the Bay Area. Hanging on to my identity and destiny during this time was extremely difficult. However, I took courage and chose to believe—daily, in spite of my feelings and circumstances. The whispered words of my Creator kept me going.

"Don't reduce the size of your dreams and desires to accommodate your present circumstances. They won't fit."

Daily, I vowed to try. Thank God I did. Because on this day, everything suddenly changed, everything suddenly made sense, and I suddenly knew what I was supposed to do.

It's a home.

There was a guest speaker at church that Sunday morning, Don Brewster. Although a preacher, he did not preach. Instead, he told of how his own heart was broken and then recalibrated by God over an issue I had never heard about: sex trafficking.

With his words, he painted a picture I did not want to see. Children being sold for sex in the world I live in.

He told of children in Cambodia as young as five years old, who were systematically sold to men for sex. Sold as if they were a commodity with no value, no feelings, and no purpose. My body was literally racked with sobs, much to my sons' embarrassment. At one point, I looked around the room to see if I was the only one pierced by the images created in my mind's eye. Everyone looked so normal. I felt I was the only one of the thousands attending that day who could hear these children's cries, feel the trauma they endured, and see the pain in their eyes.

I could feel my heart breaking, violently ripping inside of me. I doubted I would ever be the same.

It's a home. I continued to hear this whispered to my spirit as Don began to tell how his own life had changed when he learned of the plight of these Cambodian children. When he and his wife, Bridget, learned of this hideous crime against children from a T.V. show they watched, they knew they had to do something. So they did what any of us would do with the same knowledge (*not*, as my teenagers would say). They quit their jobs, sold everything they owned, and moved to Cambodia to start a home for children rescued from the sex slave trade—all with absolutely no idea just how to do that. He made it sound so simple.

It's a home. At this point in the service, the atmosphere dramatically changed. Instead of horror being recounted over and over, there was hope being delivered in large doses. Don began to tell stories of what a difference a home and a family make in the lives of these vulnerable, yet invisible children. He read stories of children who had the privilege of living there; children who had names, who had beautiful faces, and who I knew had a unique destiny.

It's a home. I wrote those words over and over on my church bulletin. The stories Don told of tangible restoration. The stories of hope and of transformation were ones I believed God was writing, and they caused a seismic shift inside of me. I wanted to be a part of that restoration story. I wanted to bring people together for that purpose. I wanted to shout it out loud that these children were created on purpose for a purpose. I could hardly remain silent. The stories Don told reminded me of the ones I had heard as a small child going to church on Sunday. It was the story of God doing extraordinary things through ordinary people. Don said he was one. I wanted to be another. I realized it was a story our Creator wanted to write on each of our lives .. including the lives of these vulnerable children.

It's a home. For days after that church service I prayed, "Cambodia? You want me to go to Cambodia?" I really did not think my husband, in our current financial and emotional situation, was going to agree to move our family to Cambodia. In fact, I was certain of it. So instead, I wrote the biggest donation check that would clear our bank account to the Brewster's non-profit organization, thinking that would satisfy the ache in my heart and maybe even the prompting of my Creator. It did not work. I still cried for weeks. I literally cried for all the children around the world being sold to strangers by the parents who were supposed to love and protect them. I cried as if they were my own daughters. When I confided to a friend that I thought I was going crazy with grief for children I had never met, who felt like my own, she told me that she believed God was letting me feel His heart for these precious little ones. "It's unbearable," I sobbed.

Eventually, I had a fight with my Creator over this hideous issue of selling children for sex. "You could make this stop. You could take it off the table. Make this issue, the issue of selling children, cease!" I angrily demanded.

I felt a whispered response to my heart: *What age would that be? Five years old? Ten? Is it okay for a fifteen-year-old to be tortured, raped, and sold for sex? A twenty-five-year-old?* I could see this arguing with my Maker was going nowhere, so I shouted from the depths of my soul, "JUST DO SOMETHING!" And before I had time to take a breath, He said to me, *Why don't you?*

That was a holy moment.

Time stood still.

It's a home.

"I'm *just* a mom," I whined.

Good, because that is just what they need—a mom, a family. These are your daughters, the daughters you have longed for. Find them, build them a home, call them family.

I gasped. These were my daughters. Everything became clear. My dreams were about to be fulfilled. Courage House, it's a home for children rescued from sex trafficking and I was to build it. I quickly needed to become an expert in what broke my heart.

Do Something

As the weeks and months of 2007 came and went, I continued to be brokenhearted for children I had never met but who felt like my own. Though I daily battled through our family's difficult financial situation, the desire to *do something* for these kids did not diminish but accelerated in my spirit. During the beginning of 2008, I sought direction, answers, and wisdom from the place all God-fearing people go ... Google. I began researching the words "sex trafficking" and "human trafficking," expecting to see details of this horrific crime in faraway countries I had never visited. I was shocked to the core of my being when this word appeared on my screen: Sacramento.

Sacramento? My home? My city? Through my research, I learned children were being sold for sex right in my own backyard—in my city, my state, and my country. While the reality of children being sold in Cambodia broke my heart, the news that they were being sold in my own backyard outraged me and propelled me into action. This time I did not have to take courage: I was angry and bold.

Anger was my fuel and energy.

I remembered the Enneagram assessment I had taken back in the early years of my identity boot camp, and anger had been identified as a facet of my personality. I remembered being confused because I really did not get angry with much. However, as I made a careful assessment of who I was, I learned my Maker had deposited anger inside me when I encountered injustices that required change. Up until that point of my life, I just had not encountered much that you would call injustice.

Now I got it. At that moment, I believed with everything I was that I had been created on purpose *for this purpose*, because I was totally confident in my identity and I knew rescuing these children, my daughters, was my destiny.

Everything made sense. My life was at the pivotal point of convergence—when everything in your life lines up—when every experience, every job, every conversation, every assessment, and even every struggle makes sense. I knew what I had to do. But even more exciting, I knew what I was created to do. I had been divinely equipped for it my entire life. My journey of purpose during the last seven years served to show me how. I am a mom—a nurturer. I am a cheerleader—an encourager. I am a conduit—a leader to gather people for a passionate purpose. I am a communicator—a loud voice angry at injustice. I am an activist—I have to do something. Though still extremely ordinary, I am a water walker, giant slayer, and history maker.

These invisible children were my long-awaited daughters, and my purpose at this point in my life was to build them a home and call them family. My life and my journey had led me to this moment. I felt like I was standing on the ledge of an airplane and someone was screaming, *"JUMP!"*

Week Ten  Uniquely You

So I did.

What broke my heart gave me a compassion for children who were sold for sex that propelled me into doing things that scared me to death. My mom had been right. California was to be my mission field, but it was also the place I would remember who I was and have the courage to be and do all I was created for. It was the place where my dreams and destiny were launched and some fulfilled.

Your Story

What breaks your heart? List them all. After listing them, circle the one that makes you the saddest—that hurts your heart the most.

_____
_____
_____

Finish this statement. "I get so mad when I see or hear about:"

_____
_____
_____
_____

And this one. "If I didn't have to earn a salary, work at my job, clean the house, wash clothes, etc., I would spend my time:

_____
_____
_____
_____

Consider all you have learned about yourself in this assessment. What gifts, talents, and experiences do you have that could affect the thing that makes you the most angry or broken hearted? What could you do now about this issue? Consult your Creator on this one.

_____
_____
_____
_____
_____

Consult Your Creator

We will start the way we began.

"Make a careful assessment of who you are, what you are to be doing, then just do it."

You have done this for the past ten weeks. You have made a careful assessment of who you are. You may now have some ideas and/or clues about what you should be doing. With the knowledge and revelation you have received during our time together, write down your first action steps towards fulfilling your water-walking, giant-slaying, and history-making destiny.

_____
_____
_____
_____
_____
_____
_____
_____
_____
_____
_____
_____
_____
_____
_____
_____
_____
_____
_____
_____

My prayer for you today is that you will take one courageous step toward being you.

Righteous Girlfriend/ Mighty Warrior

Clues! Passion, Fears, Anger & Broken Hearts

– Day 1 –

Share with your righteous girlfriends or mighty warriors any little girl or little boy dreams you have remembered this week. Did you know *what* you wanted to be when you grew up? Allow your righteous friends to help you see behind the role or job you wanted to discover *who* you wanted to be. (For example, my friend wanted to be a lawyer because she was always arguing. God helped her to see that she was always arguing about injustice, about what was wrong in this world. She is now a rescuer and advocate for the oppressed instead of a lawyer.) Are you experiencing any "holy restlessness" with things, people, jobs, or routines that in the past had satisfied you?

– Day 2 –

Can you define your passion(s) to your righteous girlfriends or mighty warriors? Was there a correlation between your passion as an adult and the desires of your little girl or little boy heart?

– Day 3 –

Share with your righteous girlfriends or mighty warriors anyone (even from generations before) that has greatly impacted your life. Could their ceiling be your floor? This could be a family member, friend, teacher, or even a person from the Bible.

– Day 4 –

What is one thing that scares you to death? Did you take the challenge to do the thing that you want to do but are scared to do? Share with your group.

– Day 5 –

Share what breaks your heart and propels you into action. Share your first action steps with the group.

This is your last group. Do you now have a better understanding of who you are and what you're supposed to be doing? Do you have the courage to be you? If time allows, share the answers to those questions. Discuss with your RGG or MWG the likelihood of continuing to meet weekly after the Uniqueness Assessment is completed.

Righteous Girlfriend Group and Mighty Warrior Group meetings are a dream God put on my heart as I facilitated a group of my own for seven years. I believe there will be RGG/MWGs around the world. I cannot imagine being me without my own RGG. I thank God for all of them!

Go! Change the World!

c2bu.com/vid9

I was walking off a stage at Green Valley Church in Placerville, California, after giving an emotional talk on the reality of child sex slavery in our country. When I concluded, Pastor Ken was to follow me to wrap up the evening and ask the church for an offering. However, when he got to the stage he could not speak. Silently he stood very still on the stage. I could feel his emotions and watched as he struggled to control them. Silence enveloped the room, and you could hear people crying just imagining the reality of children being sold for sex while slept safe in our homes.

Finally the pastor looked up and passionately declared,

"The church needs to go straight to hell!"

There was a pregnant pause before he continued.

"Because that is where these children are—in hell."

He was right. These children, my daughters, are living in hell. These children are not going to come knocking on our doors asking for help. Someone is going to have to rescue them. Someone is going to have to fight for them, figuratively and literally. I learned that my destiny would require me to be one of those *somebodies*. It was going to require me to take bold action.

Your destiny is going to require you to do the same. Someone is waiting for you to have the courage to be you. Someone is waiting for you to do something. Someone is waiting on you to have the courage to be you—but you may have to go to hell and back.

Don't let our time together be wasted. You have made a careful assessment of who you are, you have discovered your true identity as the child of the King, you now know you were created on purpose for a purpose, you have chosen to believe truth and not your emotions or circumstances. You have been given clues to what you are to do .. now it is time for action. Yes, you will be scared—but you are called courageous. I have a secret to share with you. You will not always be scared. There will come a time when you no longer need to take courage. Something changes in you as you step out courageously into your destiny. Eventually, you become fearless and then you become bold.

My last word search for you. The dictionary defines *bold* as,*"to trust, to be confident, secure, sure, to be frank in speech, confident in demeanor, outspoken, blunt, assured, to be bold, to be free, open and plain, commanding, break the silence, courageous, daring in all things and in all matters, in speaking and acting."*

I love this. The word *bold* paints a picture of living out your destiny.

Boldness comes from making courageous choices over and over again. Listening to your Creator, feeling a bit crazy, facing impossible situations, or feeling ordinary but doing the extraordinary. You have been given the honor of participating in the process. You will never feel so alive. You now have something you can live for, but you also have something you would die for. You are now dangerous to your enemy. There will be a battle to be you, however God prepared you in boot camp to be victorious.

I end this book as I began it—telling you that you were created on purpose for a purpose. You have an important part to play on this planet. There is something for you to do that only you can do and if you do not do it, it will never get done. Your unique destiny and contribution matters to so many. *It matters if you quit.*

Your destiny may be tied to loving and believing in someone when they cannot love or believe in themselves. *It matters if you quit!* Your destiny may involve consistent and persistent parenting of a child who struggles to learn. *It matters if you quit.* Your destiny may require you to build, write, or create something tangible to share with this world. *It matters if you quit.* Your destiny may be a discovery that literally saves lives, or it may involve giving a hug or writing a note that makes another feel that life is worth living. *It matters if you quit.* Your destiny may be one of persevering in prayer for someone's safety, salvation, or healing. It matters if you quit.

"I would literally be dead if you had quit or said no. Thank you for having the courage to be you."

I was shocked when the first girl at Courage House said this to me. When God first asked me *"Do you have the courage to be you?"* in the year 2000, I had no idea the implications of my answer and the impact it would have upon another. I had no idea these children were praying a prayer waiting on God and He was waiting on me.

That is why you cannot quit. Someone is praying a prayer and waiting on God, and **He is waiting on you.**

Do you have the courage to be you?

Journal your closing thoughts to this question.

_____
_____
_____
_____
_____
_____
_____
_____
_____
_____
_____
_____
_____
_____

My prayer for you as we conclude this assessment is that you know you are the beloved, child of the King and that you were created on purpose for a specific purpose. You have a place to belong. You were meant for a water-walking, giant-slaying, history-making purpose, and you are the answer to a prayer someone is praying.

I pray you will do great exploits for God. I pray you take courage and be and do all you were created for—absolutely refusing to settle for anything less—then encourage everyone in your life to do the same! Blessings, dear one. I have enjoyed being your coach.

Bibliography

Chapman, Gary. *The Five Love Languages: The Secret to Love that Lasts.* Chicago: Northfield Publishing, 2015.

Laird, Rebecca, and Nouwen, Henri. *Parting Words: A Conversation with Henri Nouwen. Sacred Journey: The Journal of Fellowship in Prayer 47,* December 1996.

Rath, Tom. *Strengthsfinder 2.0.* New York: Gallup Press, 2007.

Rohr, Richard, and Ebert, Andreas. *The Enneagram: A Christian Perspective.* New York: Crossroad Publishing, 2014.

Williamson, Jenny. *Do You Have the Courage to Be You?* Las Vegas: Next Century Publishing, 2015.

Report of the Dietary Guidelines Advisory Committee on the *Dietary Guidelines for Americans,* 1995, pp. 23–24.

About Jenny

Jenny Williamson is a published author, keynote speaker, successful business leader, modern day abolitionist, and social entrepreneur. On an individual, personal level, she helps people answer the very personal questions **Who am I?** and **Why am I here?** by examining their stories, personalities, and experiences to unearth their unique purpose, while inviting them to follow her on a water-walking, giant-slaying, history-making journey. Jenny's own journey led her to a population of children being sold for sex; she wonders where yours will lead you.

At a corporate and professional level, Jenny promotes cultures of courage and unity, exhibits fearless leadership, singleness of purpose and enormous vision for the future. She is a maximizer and activator with a high level of passion, commitment, and integrity. Jenny expounds a message of corporate responsibility to the community encouraging co-branding with non-profits for the purpose of changing the world one individual at a time. She is the Founder and CEO of Courage Worldwide, an international, non-profit organization that is building homes for children rescued out of sex trafficking. Through personal passion and professional leadership, she works tirelessly to inform communities about child sex trafficking and involve individuals and businesses in building Courage Houses – homes where more children can be rescued and restored. Jenny is a voice for the voiceless, promotes social justice and entrepreneurship to meet the needs of the marginalized in our society by helping them find their unique purpose so they too can make a difference in this world.

As an author and speaker, Jenny is known for her energetic and encouraging messages. Her workshops and conferences are engaging and powerful, and her call to action is challenging and inspiring. Jenny is driven by a desire to see all people equipped, encouraged, and empowered to live out the purpose for their lives despite their circumstances. Her candid, humor-filled approach is relevant and life-changing. Jenny believes that discovering and fulfilling one's unique, God-given purpose is the adventure of a lifetime.

For her impact and efforts in the community, Jenny was awarded the FBI Director's Community Leadership Award. She is a L'Oréal of Paris Woman of Worth Honoree. She was also awarded the Community Spirit Award by Sacramento's District Attorney. In addition, William Jessup University awarded Jenny their prestigious Community Impact Award, and Soroptomist International's Ruby Award.

Because of her leadership and knowledge with the issue of child sex trafficking, Jenny has been invited to be part of the California Attorney General's Working Group on human trafficking as well as Shared Hope International's Practitioners Working Group for their National Colloquium meeting in Washington, D.C. She speaks locally, nationally and globally as an expert in long-term residential care for victims of child sex trafficking. Jenny was also honored to receive the George H. W. Bush Presidential Points of Light Award.

She and her family live in Northern California, where she also acts as chief financial officer of their family business. To book Jenny to speak at your next event, complete the speaker request form at jennytwilliamson.com. You can also follow Jenny on Facebook, Twitter, or Instagram.

For more information on the organization Jenny founded, or to be one of the million somebodies who are going to build one thousand homes in one hundred countries in ten years so hundreds of thousands of children can be rescued from the evil of sex trafficking, go to www.courageworldwide.org.

Other Books by Jenny Williamson

Do You Have the Courage to Be You?

Do you have the courage to be you? was the provocative question that changed the entire trajectory of one woman's ordinary life and became the impetus used to propel her on a journey of purpose. Before time began, you were imagined, planned, and created for a specific and unique destiny—one that involves water-walking, giant slaying, and history making; that is, if you have the courage to be YOU!

Jenny Williamson's book tells of her journey of discovery as she realized that there is something she was created to do and if she didn't do it, it would never be done. Her passion and storytelling promote a sense of urgency for us all to find the courage to be and do all we were created for. Someone is waiting for you to be YOU.

Jenny's journey led her to a group of vulnerable children being sold for sex, who needed a home and a family, inspiring her to found Courage Worldwide, a non-profit focused on building homes for children rescued out of sex slavery.

Where will your journey lead you?

Fifty percent of proceeds from the sale of this book will be donated to Courage Worldwide.

To find out more, visit www.courageworldwide.org.

Transitions—Navigating Change with Grace

You were created to walk on water, slay giants with pebbles, and change the course of history. But you won't get there by being comfortable or by playing it safe. Water-walking, giant-slaying, history-making destinies are found squarely in the midst of the unknown. There is rarely a strategic plan or well-marked road map. Sadly, few have dared to venture there. The journey is by faith, the destination is unfamiliar, and the voyage is extremely uncomfortable—especially in the beginning.

"I'll be the first to admit I like my comfort zones—I worked hard for them. I wrestle with the idea of the unknown. No one likes being tossed to and fro by waves of uncertainty. I want to feel confident, like I know what I am doing. When things are good, I want them to stay that way forever. Of course, this has not been my life experience.

Over time, we all learn that nothing stays the same.

Change is inevitable. And it is also necessary. Why?

Change transitions us from our comfort zones to the unknown and is often the very impetus God uses to move us from where we are to where He wants us to be." (Excerpt from *Transitions* by Jenny Williamson, available on Snippet at www.thesnippetapp.com.)

About Principles To Live By

Principles To Live By is a 501 c (3) organization that seeks to be a clear voice for God's principles of life. Our mission is to declare, apply, and demonstrate God's unchanging principles through a variety of resources, such as books, podcasts, seminars, conferences, small group studies, classes, and coaching. We train and disciple individuals, families, churches, and communities to fulfill their unique purpose so they can fully express the good works that God has designed for them.

PTLB Publishing partners with authors and discipleship thought leaders to propel their messages of wisdom, insight, and instruction out to the world. As a full-service, royalty publisher, we work side-by-side with each author through the entire publishing process, from writing and editing assistance, to book formatting, cover design, book printing and distribution in digital and print formats, and marketing/promotion assistance.

For more information, visit us at www.ptlb.com.

Principles To Live By Resources

Available in print or E-book formats at www.ptlb.com, or Amazon.com.

BOOKS

Becoming a Godly Husband

Becoming Courageous

Breakfast with Solomon, Volumes 1 - 3

Breaking Satanic Bondage

Deep Happiness: The Eight Secrets

Delighting in God

Delighting in Jesus

Developing a Christian Worldview

Foundations: Building a Solid Christian Life

God's Radical Plan for Wives

Going Deep In Prayer: Forty Days of In-Depth Prayer

Keeping Visitors

Leading a Thriving Ministry

Marital Intelligence

Mission Possible: Winning the Battle over Temptation

Proverbs: A Devotional Commentary, Volumes 1 - 2

Satan and The Origin of Evil

Secrets of God's Armor

Spiritual Disciplines of a C.H.R.I.S.T.I.A.N

The Gift of Seeing Angels and Demons

The Schemes of Satan

They Laughed When I Wrote Another Book about Prayer, Then They Read It

Touching the Face of God: Forty Days of Adoring God

Weapons of Righteousness Study Guides

Why There Has to Be a Hell

PODCASTS

Becoming a Godly Parent

Biblical Meditation: The Keys of Transformation

Deep Happiness: The Eight Secrets

Everyday Spiritual Warfare Series

God's Guide to Handling Money

Marital Intelligence: There are Only Five Problems in Marriage

Intensive Spiritual Warfare Series

Spiritual War Surrounding Money

The Four Keys to a Great Family

The Ten Commandments

Thrive Conference:

    Marital Intelligence: There are Only Five Problems in Marriage

    Raising Your Leadership Level: Double Your Impact

    Spiritual Warfare: Using the Weapons of God to Win Spiritual Battles

Weapons of Righteousness Series

If you would be interested in having one of our consultants teach or speak to your group or consult with your staff or church, you can contact us at

www.ptlb.com.

www.ingramcontent.com/pod-product-compliance
Lightning Source LLC
Chambersburg PA
CBHW080330170426
43194CB00014B/2514